Air War East Africa
1940-41

Air War East Africa
1940-41

The RAF Versus The Italian Air Force

Jon Sutherland
& Diane Canwell

Pen & Sword
AVIATION

First published in Great Britain in 2009 by
Pen & Sword Aviation
an imprint of
Pen & Sword Books Ltd
47 Church Street
Barnsley
South Yorkshire   S70 2AS

ISBN 978 1 84415 816 4

Typeset in Ehrhardt
by S L Menzies-Earl

Printed in the UK by the MPG Books Group

Pen & Sword Books Ltd incorporates the imprints of
Pen & Sword Aviation, Pen & Sword Maritime, Pen & Sword Military,
Wharncliffe Local History, Pen & Sword Select,
Pen & Sword Military Classics and Leo Cooper.

For a complete list of Pen & Sword titles please contact
PEN & SWORD BOOKS LIMITED
47 Church Street, Barnsley, South Yorkshire, S70 2AS, England
E-mail: enquiries@pen-and-sword.co.uk
Website: www.pen-and-sword.co.uk

Contents

Introduction

It was to be an impossible campaign, a crazy campaign, one fought by handfuls of British and Commonwealth troops in an arena of 700,000 square miles and defended by over a quarter of a million enemy troops.

Quite rightly, the focus of the Second World War in Africa has been on the events in the Western Desert. Yet the odds facing the British and Commonwealth troops in East Africa were even longer than in North Africa. To oppose the Italians and their colonial troops were just 10,000 men, spread out across Kenya, the Sudan and Somaliland. Within a year of the Italians declaring war in July 1940, five British and Commonwealth divisions, supported by local units and a mixed bag of obsolete aircraft, were driving the Italians out of the region on four different fronts.

The architect of the victory was Field Marshal Sir Archibald Wavell, yet the builders of the victory were the British soldiers, Indians, South Africans, Sudanese, Kenyans, West Africans, Australians and Abyssinians.

It was a dark time for the nations opposing the Germans and Italians in Europe, for continental Western Europe had fallen, and the sudden collapse of France in May 1940 had made Mussolini, the Italian Dictator, bold. He threw his not inconsiderable strength behind offensive operations in North Africa. But there still remained the vast army led by the Duke of Aosta in Italian East Africa. The Duke fully appreciated the unpreparedness of his troops to defend the vast territories so recently won. He determined to deliver a knockout blow against the British before reinforcements could be sent to the region. His offensive plans were at first rejected by the Italian Chief of Staff, Badoglio. Badoglio was adamant that the Duke of Aosta's army should adopt only a defensive stance.

The Italians could strike at Port Sudan in the Sudan, against Mombasa, Kenya, in the south, or against British or French Somaliland in the east. The Italians became firmly of the opinion that Britain was on the verge of collapse and that a German invasion of the British Isles was imminent. At that point they gave the Duke of Aosta free rein to mount an offensive. The Italians would aim to seize British Somaliland, the easiest of the three options.

Strategically, Italian East Africa, encompassing Abyssinia, Eritrea and Italian Somaliland, bounded Kenya, Anglo-Egyptian Sudan and British and French Somaliland. Given the fact that the Italians were firmly in control of Libya, the possible link-up between these two vast Italian-held territories would have had severe repercussions for Britain's war effort. Italian East Africa threatened Red Sea shipping and Aden, vital gateways for transporting material and troops from the British Empire and supplies from the United States. Yet the campaigns in the early months of the war, after Italian involvement, were 2,000 miles away from the Italian East African theatre.

It was no mean feat for Wavell, responsible for maintaining operations and defence on both fronts. He would have to carefully husband his military resources. From Cairo he would mount his operations against Cyrenaica in Italian Libya. From Khartoum he would need to protect the Sudan from Eritrea and the northern border of Abyssinia. From Nairobi in Kenya he would have to protect both Kenya and Uganda from Italian Somaliland and the southern border of Abyssinia.

Italian East Africa had only been conquered in the late 1930s. It was still a volatile region, and any hint of weakness on the part of the Italian army would swell rebel forces and threaten the civilian population. As a consequence, the Italians and their colonial forces could muster at least 300,000 men, supported by at least 400 artillery pieces and in excess of 200 aircraft. Eritrean airfields lay within striking distance of key British targets. Upwards of 100,000 Italian troops were available along the Sudan border. Facing them were just three British battalions. The entire Sudan Defence Force mustered some 4,500 men, protecting a frontier of 1,200 miles. In all, to support the 7,000 Allied troops, there were just seven obsolete aircraft: all this to defend an area as large as Germany.

Outnumbered at least ten to one, the defenders of the Sudan would be sorely pressed by July 1940. To the east the Italians would launch a powerful, full-scale invasion of British Somaliland on 4 August. The capital, Berbera, would fall, with the last Allied troops evacuating at 1300 on 16 August. Seven months later, to a day, the British would return.

The capture of British Somaliland would effectively be Italy's only victory. On paper, the Duke of Aosta had sufficient troops to not only overrun British Somaliland, but to take the whole of the Sudan. Churchill certainly appreciated the importance of the Sudan, and realised that its capture would mean that Egypt was severely threatened. As a result he began to reinforce from August 1940. As the Italians would discover, at Agordat, Keren, Massawa and Amba Alagi, the same outnumbered men would defeat them time after time. Admittedly Italian tactics showed little imagination. Time after time Allied nerve brought spectacular victories. The Italians did fight well, but always on the defensive. Their morale was brought down not only by the Allied advances from February 1941 in Eritrea and Somaliland, but also by the dreadful news of massive defeats in the Western Desert and in Greece. The defence of Keren in Eritrea was conducted with great verve. But when it fell it was a shattering blow for the Italians, and they never really recovered. By March 1941 the Italians were fighting a series of rearguard actions. Their great victories had all gone so terribly wrong. The illusion that Italy was a first-class military power was shattered.

Throughout the conflict, limited numbers of Allied troops were supported by impossibly small numbers of aircraft, yet despite being outnumbered, ground and air fought as a team throughout – something that would be replicated when Montgomery went on the offensive in the Western Desert.

Undoubtedly the campaigns in Italian East Africa were some of the strangest and most improvised, and truly fought on a shoestring. Although the Duke of Aosta would formally surrender in May 1941, upwards of 7,000 Italian troops would remain at large, some even continuing to fight beyond the date when Italy abruptly changed sides and joined the Allies in 1943.

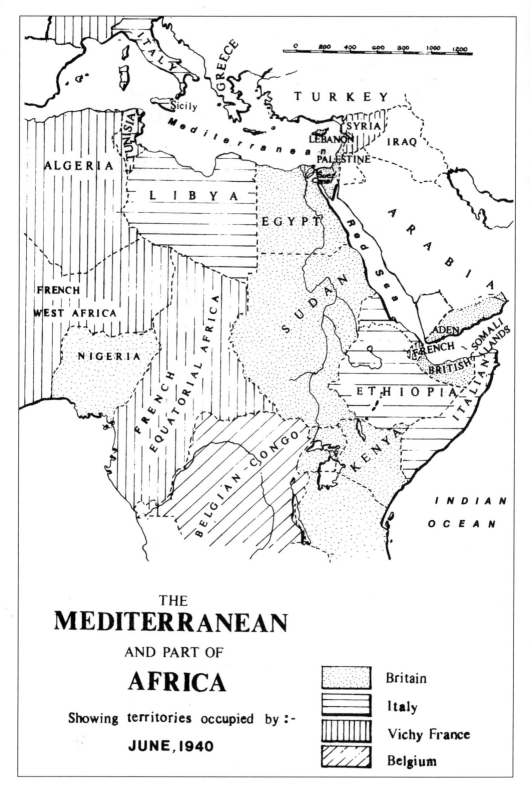

THE
MEDITERRANEAN
AND PART OF
AFRICA

Showing territories occupied by :-

JUNE, 1940

	Britain
	Italy
	Vichy France
	Belgium

Territories occupied in the Mediterranean and Africa 1940.

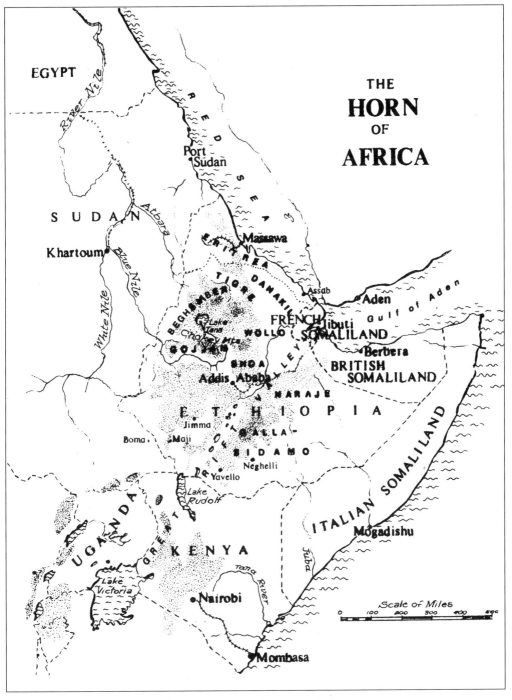

Map showing the Horn of Africa.

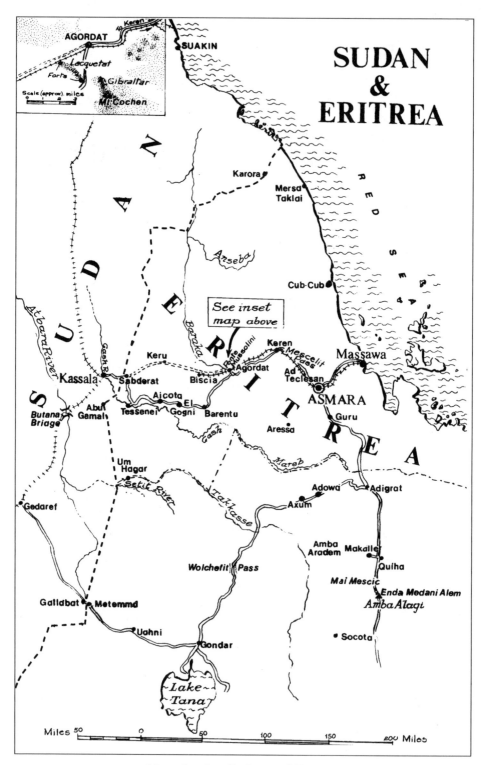

Map showing Sudan and Eritrea.

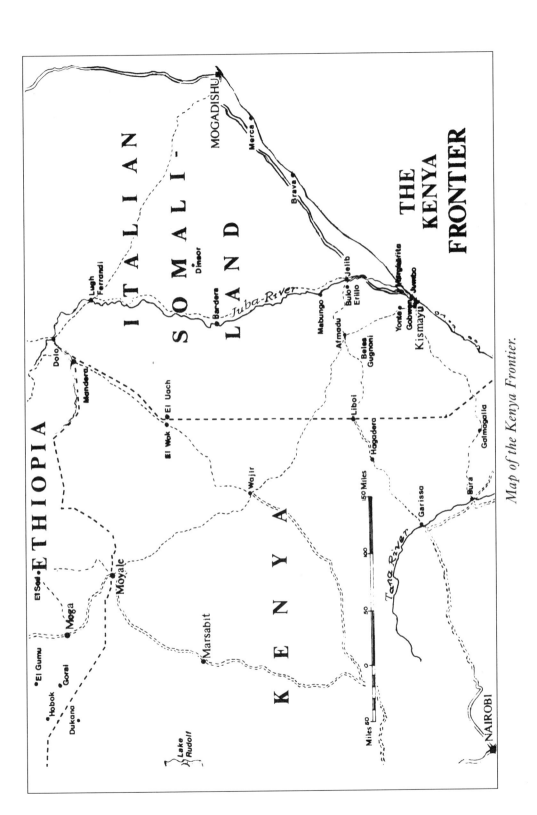

Map of the Kenya Frontier.

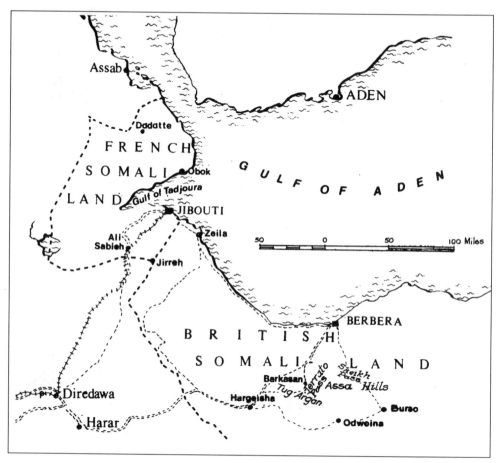

Map of French and British Somaliland.

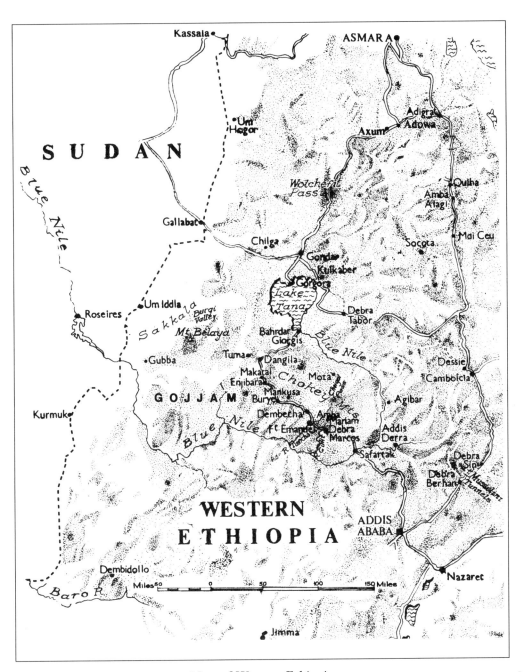

Map of Western Ethiopia.

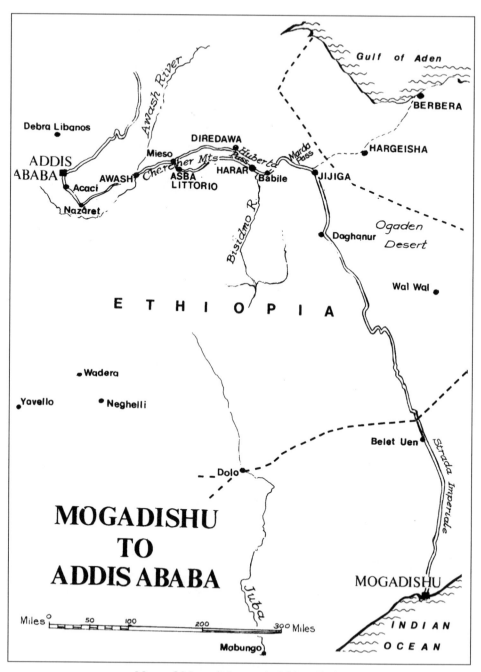

Map of Mogadishu and Addis Ababa.

CHAPTER ONE

Uneven, Uneventful and Inglorious

The first war between Italy and Abyssinia took place in 1895. It was to herald a victory for Abyssinia, the only African nation that was to successfully resist European intervention. In 1889 Menelik II conquered Tigray and Amhara with the support of the Italians, and declared himself Emperor of Abyssinia. In May 1889 he signed a treaty with the Italians, which effectively ceded them Eritrea on the Red Sea coast.

The problem with the Treaty of Wuchale was that in the two languages in which it was written, Italian and Amharic, the intent was entirely different. Menelik II believed that he was signing a treaty that allowed him access to negotiations with foreign powers via the Italians. In the Italian version he had signed to agree to an Italian protectorate over Abyssinia.

By 1893 Menelik II was sufficiently in control of Abyssinia to repudiate the treaty. The Italians crossed into Tigray in December 1894, determined to enforce their version of the treaty. Unbeknown to the Italians, Menelik II had been building up stores of modern weapons and ammunition. The Italians, however, soon occupied Adwa, the capital of Tigray.

On 7 December 1895 Italian troops in positions at Amba Alagi were overrun by the Abyssinians. A small Italian garrison remained at Meqele, but the bulk of the Italians were concentrating around Adigrat. The Abyssinians closed in on Meqele, surrounding it on 18 December. Menelik II, at the head of a large Abyssinian force, tried to storm the position, but failed. However, by the end of January the Italians had surrendered and withdrawn.

Menelik II still hoped that there would be a peaceful resolution. But the Italian commander, *Generale* Oreste Baratieri, was certain that if he held his nerve the Abyssinian army would fade away, as it would be impossible to keep such a large force in the field.

On 1 March 1896, with around four brigades of infantry and fifty-six guns, Baratieri launched an attack against the Abyssinians in mountainous terrain to the north of Adwa (Adowa). The Italians launched their attack with around 14,500 men, the rest being used to guard the supply lines. Facing them was Menelik II's army of at least 80,000, and possibly 150,000. A large proportion of the Abyssinian army was armed with rifles. The Italians had hoped to catch the Abyssinians still sleeping, as the attack went in at 0600. The Abyssinians were, in fact, already awake and at prayer, and quickly responded to the Italian attack. Initially the Italians beat the Abyssinians back, but sheer weight of numbers and the releasing of 25,000 reserves turned the tide.

The first Italian brigade, cut off, was slaughtered. The remaining two brigades were destroyed near Mount Belah. By 1200 what remained of the Italian army was in retreat towards Eritrea. The Italians were said to have lost at least 7,000 killed and 1,500 wounded, and a further 3,000 were taken prisoner. The Abyssinians lost upwards of 5,000 killed and 8,000 wounded. Most of the Italians would later be released, after the signing of the Treaty of Addis Ababa. The Askaris, regarded as traitors by the Abyssinians, had their left feet and right hands amputated.

Italy had been forced to recognise Abyssinia's independence, and the Italians would have to wait for nearly forty years before exacting their revenge.

The second Italo–Abyssinian war broke out in October 1935. It was a short and vicious conflict that would end in May 1936. The war became infamous as a result of the Italian use of mustard gas and phosgene, a chlorine-based colourless gas. Italy and Abyssinia had clashed on the border of Somaliland in 1935 at Welwel. Both countries had approached the League of Nations to arbitrate. The League of Nations responded very slowly, and this gave Mussolini the opportunity to redress the indignities that the Italians had suffered in the first war against Abyssinia.

The Emperor of Abyssinia was Haile Selassie. The Emperor, wary of Italian intentions, had mobilised his country. He had managed to recruit some 500,000 men, but most of them were poorly armed, with weapons that would have been more common a hundred years before than in the twentieth century. Some, admittedly, did have modern weapons, but most of these were outdated models from the turn of the century. The Abyssinians could muster in all upwards of 760,000 men, around half having rifles of some description. The army also had 200 old artillery pieces, fifty anti-aircraft guns, some armoured cars and Italian tanks of World War One vintage.

The mighty Imperial Ethiopian Air Force consisted of three biplanes. The Italians were not, however, taking any chances. In Abyssinia there were mountain, Blackshirt and regular divisions, amounting to some 480,000 troops. This was in addition to the colonial troops that amounted to some 200,000. They could now deploy 6,000 machine-guns, 2,000 artillery pieces, nearly 600 tanks and 150 aircraft. Ammunition and supplies had been built up and there would be no shortages.

Led by *Generale* Emilio de Bono, the Italian army crossed into Abyssinia at 0500 on 3 October 1935. Under his command were nine divisions. To the south, emerging from Italian Somaliland, were two divisions and supporting units commanded by *Generale* Rodolfo Graziani. The Abyssinians pulled back in the face of the overwhelming invasion. The Italians took Adwa and Adigrat. De Bono continued to advance slowly, taking Makale on 8 November. He was replaced at the end of the month by *Maresciallo d'Italia* Pietro Badoglio.

The Abyssinians now launched a counter-offensive, and in fact the new Abyssinian plan was to drive the Italians out of Eritrea. On 26 December Graziani requested permission to use mustard gas. It was to be used by both the artillery and the Italian Air Force. Quickly it began to have a drastic effect on the outcome of the campaign.

By 20 January 1936 the Italians were able to resume their offensive. In the first battle of Tembien they made indiscriminate use of mustard gas and phosgene. At the battle of Enderta, fought between 10 and 19 February, once again poison gas was used, and in fact forty tons of mustard gas alone was dropped on the Abyssinian army. By March the Abyssinian forces were reeling under the enormous pressure and the use of the poison gases. Still, however, they fought on.

The Italian Air Force, dropping poison gas, was a key factor in destroying an Abyssinian attempt to invade Italian Somaliland. By February the Italians had cut deep into Abyssinia. They bombed Harar and Jijiga on 22 March, reducing both of the cities to ruins. At the end of the month the Italians won the battle of Maychew after a failed counter-attack by the Abyssinians. Thousands of Abyssinians were killed in the retreat after the battle.

The Italian offensive towards Addis Ababa began on 26 April. By now Abyssinian resistance had been broken. Haile Selassie arrived at Djibouti in French Somaliland on 2 May. From there he fled to England and to exile. The Italians marched into Addis Ababa on 5 May 1936, and although there was never a formal surrender, Abyssinia, Eritrea and Somaliland now became known as Italian East Africa.

There was still scattered resistance in Abyssinia, and the Italians continued to use mustard gas to deal with rebels. However, the colony of Italian East Africa was to be short lived, and on 18 January 1941 Emperor Haile Selassie would cross the border into Abyssinia and raise his flag and march at the head of his irregular army into Addis Ababa on 5 May.

The second Italo-Abyssinian war was devastating for Abyssinia. Over three-quarters of a million people were killed, half a million houses were destroyed, along with six million cattle, seven million sheep and goats, a million horses and mules and two thousand churches.

By June 1940 the balance of power, as we shall see, was entirely in favour of the Italians. The bulk of British strength was concentrated to defend the Suez Canal, and so was in Egypt. There were small forces of both British and French troops in their respective Somaliland territories.

With France falling in May 1940, the Mediterranean, the Middle East and East Africa were all vulnerable. It was very much a question of what Mussolini would choose to do, as it seemed that the initiative was very much with him. It would have been relatively easy for the Italians to seize almost anything for very little cost.

There was an enormous danger with Italy joining the war for the Mediterranean to become untenable for the Allies. If Italy were to press its claim for control of the Mediterranean, then British forces bound for the Middle East would have to be brought all around

Africa and come into the Middle East via the Red Sea. This, then, made East Africa all the more important. A strong and determined Italy, in control of the entrance to the Red Sea, could place Britain's tenuous control of the Suez Canal, Egypt and vital oil assets in jeopardy.

Some attempts had been made to strengthen the Royal Air Force in the Sudan, British Somaliland, Kenya and Aden. Any such move, however, would only seek to weaken the already stretched forces in Egypt. There could be no hope of launching any offensive action in this theatre either on the ground or in the air. What assets could be spared in East Africa were little more than police forces and patrol units.

Although Italian East Africa was vast, it was not an ideal theatre of war with its enormous highlands, deserts and rainy seasons. Across the region there were areas that were virtually deserts, while others were sub-tropical. There were few good roads, and in the rainy season they became almost impassable. There were just two railway lines: one ran from the Eritrean port of Massawa to Asmara and Tessenei, and the other ran from Addis Ababa to Djibouti in French Somaliland.

Although Italian East Africa was some 600 per cent larger than Italy itself, it was effectively cut off. To send troops, supplies or ammunition meant that the vessels would have to pass Gibraltar and then proceed down the west coast of Africa, around the Horn and up the east coast towards Italian Somaliland. In any case, both the Italian army and the air force were designed primarily as a colonial force. There was only a single, regular, Italian division – the Savoy Grenadiers. There were also territorial units, or Blackshirt battalions. These were men predominantly middle aged, with little in the way of training or equipment, who had somehow been persuaded to avoid the humiliation of unemployment at home for the uncertain virtues of life in East Africa.

The bulk of the army was, however, native units. They were recruited on a tribal basis. They were not designed to fight conventional wars; they lacked mobility, were terrified of artillery fire and were led by aloof Italian officers on horseback. There were also native scouts and skirmishers, again led by Italian officers. Added to this there were also irregular troops, who tended to be used for police duties. To support the ground forces there were a handful of tanks and armoured cars, mostly old and poorly maintained. The artillery was also outdated, and even anti-aircraft defences were poor. In all, the ground forces could muster some sixteen battalions, a pair of armoured car companies, two squadrons of tanks, ten artillery units, 123 native battalions, eight units of cavalry, some light artillery carried by mules and some irregulars. In total the Italians could muster upwards of 280,000 men. This was increased to 330,000 in June 1940. Reservists had been called up, although most of these men were either too old or too poorly trained to be of any use. There was a shortage of rifles, and many native units had been deployed as road builders.

Considering the enormous distances involved and the poor infrastructure, added to which the troops available were not suitable for large-scale offensive actions, it was understandable that Italian commanders in East Africa were unwilling to consider much more than defence.

Facing the northern borders with the Sudan were some 100,000 troops. These were primarily concentrated from the Red Sea coast to the border facing Khartoum. Some 83,000 men were on the borders of French and British Somaliland, 20,000 men formed the Army of the Juba, 40,000 were in central Abyssinia and just a scattering of forces covered the rest of the Sudanese border and the border with Kenya.

Ground forces were supported by a small Italian navy based in the Eritrean ports of Massawa and Assab. They had two squadrons of destroyers and eight largely unserviceable submarines.

The Italian Air Force, or *Regia Aeronautica*, was of a reasonable size. The bulk of the aircraft were Caproni Ca 133s. They were perfectly designed for their original purpose. The aircraft were monoplanes with three engines, and could be used for bombing, troop carrying or cargo carrying. But they were only any good if the enemy did not have their own aircraft or anti-aircraft defences; simply they were too slow and too poorly armed.

Another common aircraft was the Savoia S.81. This was a three-engined monoplane with fixed undercarriage. It would turn out to be so poor that it would only be used at night. Another aircraft deployed by the Italian Air Force in June 1940 was the Savoia S.79. It was a three-engined monoplane with a retractable undercarriage. Two of its five machine-guns were 12.7 mm, and it was without doubt the best aircraft to be deployed by any force in the region. The third engine, in the nose, limited its effectiveness, particularly when it was used on bombing missions. Added to this, there were very few spare parts for the aircraft.

Two of the fighter squadrons were flying the Fiat CR.32. It was a biplane, and, as the Italians would discover, it was far too slow to catch their bombers. Three other fighter squadrons were equipped with Fiat CR.42s. It was to be one of the more successful Italian aircraft in the theatre. The Italian pilots would discover that it was more manoeuvrable than the Hurricane and faster than the Gladiator. The three squadrons of CR.42s – 412th, 413th and 414th Squadrons – would have mixed fortunes. The best squadron was the 412th.

Another fighter squadron, the 110th, was flying Meridionali Ro.37bis, twin-seat biplanes. They were originally designed for reconnaissance, observation and army co-operation. They were to prove particularly useless when ordered to intercept enemy aircraft.

The most powerful striking force of the Italian Air Force in East Africa was, of course, the three main bomber groups. The fighters were scattered all around East Africa. *Generale* Pietro Pinna was the air commander in East Africa. His instructions on the outbreak of war were to hit any British airfields or ports within striking distance. The availability of bombs was to be a considerable problem. He would reserve his 250 kg bombs for stationary ships in port. Ships at sea would be attacked with 50 kg bombs.

In all, across Italian East Africa, there were nine Italian aircraft groups. Each of the groups could have from two to eight *squadriglie*. Broadly speaking, the strength of one of these was similar to an RAF flight. However, the Italian fighters were usually in the larger *squadriglie*, and these could be as large as an RAF squadron.

The Italian Air Force was organised into three distinct areas. *Comando Settore Aeronautico Nord* (Air Sector Headquarters North) was based in Asmara in Eritrea. The 26th Group could muster twelve Caproni Ca 133s (11th and 13th *Squadriglie*). These were based at Gondar and Bahar Dar. The 27th Group had the 18th and 52nd *Squadriglie*, also with a dozen Ca 133s at Assab. The 118th

Squadriglia, also part of 27th Group, with half a dozen Savoia S.81s, was also based at Assab. At Zula was 28th Group with the 10th and 19th *Squadriglie*, and they had twelve S.81s. The 62nd and 63rd *Squadriglie* of 29th Group were based at Assab with a dozen S.81s. The rest of the group was scattered, apart from 413th *Squadriglia*, with its nine CR.42s at Assab. The 412th *Squadriglia* had four CR.42s at Massawa and five at Gura. Also at Gura was the 29th Group's final *squadriglia*, the 414th, with six more CR.42s. At Agordat there was Gasbarrini Group, with twelve Caproni Ca 133s (41st *Squadriglia* and *Squadriglia Dello Stato Maggiore Del Settore Nord*).

On the western side of Italian East Africa, based at Addis Ababa, was the *Comando Settore Aeronautico Ovest*. The 4th and 44th *Gruppi* were based at Diredawa. The 4th *Gruppo*, consisting of the 14th and 15th *Squadriglie*, mustered some twelve Savoia S.81s. The 44th *Gruppo*, consisting of the 6th and 7th *Squadriglie*, had twelve Savoia S.79s. The 49th *Gruppo*, based at Jimma, was made up of the 61st and 64th *Squadriglie* with some twelve Caproni Ca 133s. Both the 110th and 410th *Squadriglie* were also at Diredawa; the 110th had nine Ro.37bis and the 410th had nine CR.32s. Based at Addis Ababa was the 411th *Squadriglia*, also with nine CR.32s, and *Squadriglia Dello Stato Maggiore Del Settore Centrale* with six Ca 133s. The 65th *Squadriglia* had six Ca 133s and was based at Neghelli, and the 66th *Squadriglia* was at Yavello with three Ca 133s.

Based around Mogadishu was *Comando Settore Aeronautico Sud*. This consisted of the 25th *Gruppo*, which had the 8th and 9th *Squadriglie* with twelve Ca 133s. Half of these were based at Gobwen, and the other half at Lugh Ferrandi. Finally, at Mogadishu were the seven Ca 133s of the *Squadriglia Dello Stato Maggiore Del Settore*.

The Italians also had a considerable number of transport aircraft. There were nine Savoia S.73s and a similar number of Ca 133s. There was one Fokker FVII and six Ca 148s. The reserve forces consisted of thirty-five Ca 133s, six CR.42s, five CR.32s, four S.79s and two Ro.37bis. In addition to this were aircraft that were currently under repair, and these included forty-eight Ca 133s, sixteen S.81s, eleven CR.32s and two of each of S.79s, CR.42s and Ro.37bis.

Although the numbers of aircraft presented an impressive total, one of the key problems was the position and the state of the airfields. The bulk of the airfields were at the edges of the Italian territories and therefore potentially vulnerable. Many of the airfields had also been designed primarily for use by Ca 133s, and as a consequence the runways were too short for S.79s and CR.42s. The crews were not, by and large, the most adept of pilots; few had decent navigation skills; maps were at a premium; few of the aircraft had radios, and this meant that it was difficult not only to communicate between ground and air but to co-ordinate the flights themselves.

Allied forces in the region were neither that impressive nor necessarily well positioned. In the Sudan, based at Erkowit, was the impressively named Advanced Striking Force of the RAF. It comprised 254 Wing, which had three squadrons, all of which had been supplied with the Vickers Wellesley. This was a single-engined bomber, and in every other theatre barring the Sudan it had already been phased out. No. 47 Squadron, commanded by Wg Cdr J.G. Elton, was actually based at Erkowit. At Port Sudan was Sqn Ldr A.D. Selway's 14 Squadron, and at Summit was 223 Squadron, commanded by Sqn Ldr J.C. Larking.

Attached to 47 Squadron was D Flight of the Sudan Defence Force, commanded by Gp Capt Macdonald. They had been supplied with seven Vickers Vincent biplanes. On 3 June 1940 they were reinforced by nine Gloster Gladiators of 112 Squadron. They would be based at Summit and would be responsible for protecting Port Sudan and other bases in the Sudan. By August 1940 Air Cdre L.H. Slatter would be in position to take command of all forces in the Sudan, as part of 203 Group.

AVM G.R.M. Reid commanded both the ground forces and air assets in the Aden Protectorate. Reid's responsibility was not only to deal with tribesmen in Aden, but also to protect vessels passing through the Red Sea. Based at Khormaksar was 8 Squadron, commanded by Sqn Ldr D.S. Radford. No. 8 Squadron had a flight of Vincents and a flight of Bristol Blenheims. No. 94 Squadron, based at Sheik Othman and commanded by Sqn Ldr W.T.F. Wightman, had a single flight of Gladiators. Working alongside 8 Squadron at Khormaksar was 203 Squadron. Wg Cdr J.R.S. Streatfield had Blenheim IVs, which had been converted to operate as long-range fighters. In June 1940 Blenheim Is of 39 Squadron were en route from India to Sheik Othman, and more Blenheim Is were coming from Singapore, as part of 11 Squadron. They were also due to set up at Sheik Othman.

To the south of Italian East Africa, in Kenya, there were no RAF units available at the start of 1940. In April, 1 Squadron of the Southern Rhodesian Air Force arrived at Nairobi and became part of 237 Squadron. They were equipped with Army Co-operation biplanes, mainly Hawker Harts, Hardies and Audaxes.

Additional air assets would be provided by the South African Air Force. In September 1939 the South Africans could muster sixty-three Hawker Hartebeests (these were converted Hawker Harts), eighteen Junkers Ju86s (these were former South African Airways airliners that had been converted into bombers and reconnaissance aircraft), six Hawker Fury Is, four Hawker Hurricane Is and a single Blenheim IF.

Britain had provided South Africa with several additional aircraft by May 1940, including Avro Ansons (maritime reconnaissance) and some Vickers Valentia Transports. A further ten Ju52/3M aircraft, belonging to South African Airways, had been requisitioned as military transports. The South Africans had also been able to create three squadrons of Hawker Hurricanes and Furies. The flights, commanded by Capt S. Van Schalkwyk, Lt B.J.L. Boyle and Lt S. van Breda Theron, became operational by the middle of 1940. The unit was commanded by Maj N.G. Neblock-Stuart.

On 13 May 1940 the pilots of the first two flights were transported to Egypt to be converted to use Gloster Gladiators. They were trained on Gloster Gauntlets. Once the training period was over, they would ferry their own aircraft south to Nairobi. Six days later, on 19 May, Maj R. Preller's 11 Bomber Squadron, with twenty-four Hartebeests and a Fairey Battle, headed for Nairobi.

There was more reshuffling; 12 Bomber Squadron had their Ansons replaced by Ju86s, and along with 1 Squadron's Hurricanes they too headed for Nairobi, arriving there on 25 May. The Ju86s were commanded by Maj C. Martin, and the Hurricanes were led by Lt Theron. Once 12 Squadron had arrived at Nairobi, together with 11 Squadron, they became 1 Bomber Brigade under Lt Col S.A. Melville. No. 1 Squadron's Furies were disassembled on 26 May and ferried to Kenya on board the SS *Takliwa*, arriving in Kenya on 1

June. Two of 11 Squadron's flights shifted to Mombasa.

By the second week of June there were forty-six South African aircraft, a single Rhodesian squadron and additional aircraft for liaison duties available in Kenya. No. 12 Squadron's Ju86s were dispersed, with A Flight, commanded by Capt Raubenheimer, at Dar-Es-Salaam, B Flight at Mombasa under Capt D. Meaker, and Capt D. Du Toit's C Flight remaining at Nairobi.

Completing the Allied air forces available was a tiny force in French Somaliland. This was the *Armée de l'Air*. It had eleven Potez 25 Army Co-operation biplanes, four Potez 631 reconnaissance bombers, three Morane 406 fighters and a pair of Potez 29 transport and liaison biplanes.

Italy declared war on Britain and France at midnight on 10 June. For many it was not to be unexpected; only a week before, what remained of the British Expeditionary Force had been evacuated from the beaches of Dunkirk. The British had been able to evacuate over 200,000 men, but had had to leave at least 50,000 behind to remain as captives for as long as five years. Britain was truly at a low ebb. All that many of the men had been able to bring back with them were the clothes on their backs and perhaps a rifle. Vital tanks, transports and field guns had all been abandoned in France. For all Britain knew, the Germans were preparing a cross-Channel invasion, and understandably the priority would be to cobble together some defences to prevent this.

By this stage it was clear that Britain was pretty much alone, with the exception of the loyal Commonwealth. Churchill even believed that not only was France out of the war, but that she could also prove to be ultimately hostile. The Mediterranean was clearly under threat, not only from the German navy, but now from the hundred or more submarines. Transports and merchantmen would be at threat as a result of the enormous losses of escort vessels during the Dunkirk evacuation.

Britain now faced a war on four fronts. She would face the Italians in the Western Desert, which could very easily turn to disaster if the Italians managed to cross the Suez Canal. The oil in the Middle East would be under threat. As we have seen, Wavell, commander-in-chief of the Middle East, had 36,000 men in Egypt and a further 27,500 in Palestine. In Libya there were 250,000 Italians and an air force that outnumbered the RAF by at least two to one. For Britain the only immediate source of reinforcements was Australians and New Zealanders and anything that could be spared from India.

The Air Officer Commanding Middle East, ACM Longmore, had twenty-nine squadrons to cover an area of 4.5 million square miles. Most of his aircraft were obsolete, most were out of production and spares were almost impossible to come by.

It was not just the RAF that faced insuperable odds; the Royal Navy often had to engage the enemy with limited ammunition, and Wavell's only armoured division was under strength, lacking two full regiments of tanks. Most of Wavell's artillery was either obsolete or in short supply. Increasingly it seemed that the Horn of Africa and the Red Sea held the key, not only to holding on to Egypt and the Middle East, but also to Britain's only chance of remaining in the war. It seemed perfectly possible that if the Italians launched a comprehensive offensive they could take the Red Sea coast and the Horn of Africa in a matter of weeks. If their aircraft could be arrayed to prevent transport using the Red Sea, then Britain would be reduced to an impossibly long supply route to sustain her forces in Egypt.

We have seen that the Italians had on paper an enormously large force in Italian East Africa, and we have also noted its shortcomings. Equally we have seen the large Italian Air Force, but once again its own particular difficulties. But what was certainly true of Italian East Africa was the fact that it was so isolated. As far as Churchill was concerned, he believed that as long as the Italians did not launch offensive actions, Allied forces could slowly blockade Italian East Africa into submission.

The Italians' relative inaction has much to do with their very poor intelligence system. They believed, for example, that Wavell's army in Egypt was at least 100,000 strong. They believed that there were 7,000 British in British Somaliland and at least 10,000 French dug in around Djibouti. In fact, in British Somaliland there were 500 of all ranks of the Somali Camel Corps and a battalion of the Northern Rhodesia Regiment – fewer than 1,500 men in all. The Italians were also firmly of the opinion that the British could rapidly reinforce British Somaliland with elements from their 10,000-man garrison in Aden. In fact Aden had just two Indian battalions.

Mussolini's initial territorial plans were limited. He intended to take both British and French Somaliland, though this would not have appreciably improved his position in the theatre. Had he chosen to strike at Port Sudan and Khartoum while also striking from Libya into Egypt, the British would have had little hope. Again the Italians were misinformed as to the exact strength of British forces in the Sudan. They believed that there were upwards of 31,000, mostly concentrated around Gallabat. In fact there were just three British battalions and 4,500 members of the Sudan Defence Force, in all fewer than 9,000. The British in the Sudan had no tanks, the Sudan Defence Force had a handful of armoured cars, there was no artillery apart from a pair of guns used for ceremonial purposes at Government House (admittedly the Sudan Horse was under training to man a battery of 3.7 in. howitzers).

To the southern flank was of course Kenya. Italian East Africa shared a 300-mile frontier with the British possession. The Italians believed that there were 39,000 British troops in Kenya; again this was hugely overestimated. There was a pair of brigades of the King's African Rifles, two light howitzer batteries and another battery from India and a newly raised one from East Africa. There were no more than 8,500 men. By the end of June, however, two more brigades of West Africans began landing at Mombasa, and additional reinforcements were coming up from South Africa. The South African Tank Corps consisted of a dozen obsolete Mark V light tanks that had been rejected for use in Egypt. By mid-July a South African field battery had arrived, along with an infantry brigade.

On the four fronts facing the British in the Middle East none looked particularly promising. In June 1939, before the French were knocked out of the war, Wavell had consulted French military commanders. They discussed the prospect of having to wage war in East Africa. It was decided that if the Italians became a belligerent force then the only viable route of attack into Italian East Africa was from Djibouti itself. An offensive would strike towards Hara and Jijiga. The French and the British also agreed that they should do everything in their power to support and encourage rebels within Italian East Africa. This was despite a gentleman's agreement that had been made between the British and the Italians in January 1937. Britain had agreed not to send agents into Italian East Africa. Much of the information and support for the rebels had actually come from the French. They had worked in secrecy with the British along the Sudan border.

Emperor Haile Selassie had been orchestrating actions against the Italians since their occupation of his country. The four main groups in Abyssinia – the Amhara, the Tigreans, the Shons and the Galla – were all resisting the Italians to varying degrees. The revolt kept going throughout 1938 and 1939. But by June 1940, after several months of world war and the fall of France, the rebellion was beginning to falter. Haile Selassie arrived in Khartoum on 3 July 1940. Maj Cheeseman, an intelligence officer, was keen to offer British support for the Patriot Movement.

For the British, if it came to either offensive action by the Italians or the prospect of launching an offensive themselves, it would be vital for the rebels to tie down as many Italian battalions as possible. It would also be vital for the rebels to infiltrate Abyssinian levy units under Italian command and encourage them to desert. The policy would indeed work extremely well: during the height of the fighting the equivalent of fifty-six battalions of Italians were forced to remain in the Amhara and Walkait areas to hold down the rebellion just when they were needed elsewhere. Thousands of Abyssinian levies would also desert at the first opportunity.

By June 1940 any prospect of launching offensive action by the British was a dream. Defence would have to be the primary goal for some time. War was coming to East Africa. The first blow would be struck by the RAF on the first morning after the Italian declaration of war. A few days later British troops would cross into Eritrea. But these actions were simple posturing by the British, and a true offensive would soon be launched by the Italians themselves.

CHAPTER TWO

Drive on Berbera

This was the first phase of the war in East Africa. Initially it saw air action until the beginning of July 1940, when Italian troops advanced from Eritrea into the Sudan. The high point of this first phase of the war culminated in the Italian push into British Somaliland at the beginning of August 1940. Understandably, although British forces put up a stiff fight, the outcome was a foregone conclusion, and Berbera, the capital of British Somaliland, fell to the Italians by mid-August.

At dawn on 11 June 1940, eight single-engined Wellesleys of 47 Squadron, based in the Sudan, took off to strike at Italian airfields at Asmara, Gura and Massawa. They managed to blow up 780 gallons of petrol, but Plt Off B.K.C. Fuge's Wellesley was hit by Italian anti-aircraft fire. The aircraft was seen belching smoke, and it subsequently crashed and the crew were captured.

In the south, four Junkers Ju86s, led by Maj De Toit, lifted off from Eastleigh and flew to Bura for refuelling. They took off again at 1000 hours and struck an Italian camp at Moyale with 250 lb of bombs. Interestingly this was actually some six hours before South Africa officially declared war on Italy.

Elements of 237 Squadron in their Hawker biplanes launched reconnaissance sorties over the North Kenyan border. Meanwhile, a Blenheim of 203 Squadron from Aden took photographic reconnaissance shots of Italian positions, while six Blenheim IVFs bombed Assab and Diredawa.

The only Italian response was from a pair of Savoia S.81s. One of them attacked Port Sudan and the other flew a reconnaissance flight over the Red Sea. That night three S.81s set off to bomb Aden, but one turned back, and one of the other two hit a hill near Massawa while coming into land.

The following day seven S.81s of 29 *Gruppo* (Assab) attacked the port of Aden and Khormaksar airfield during daylight hours. That night ten Caproni Ca 133s returned to hit the same targets, while three others attacked Cassala airfield in the Sudan.

To the south an Allied column of half a dozen trucks and 200 men was attacked by three Ca 133s of 66 *Squadriglia* (Yavello). They had come in to carry out a reconnaissance of Moyale and Dibbandibba. Ca 133s of 65 *Squadriglia* (Neghelli) attacked the Allied positions around Moyale on two occasions, each time attacking with three aircraft. There were other Italian reconnaissance flights along the coast, near Mogadishu and over Buroli.

The RAF launched nine Blenheims, belonging to 8 Squadron (Aden) against the Macaaca airfield at Assab. One of the Blenheims was badly damaged as it came in to land. In the afternoon twelve Blenheims of 39 Squadron (Aden) attacked the airfield at Diredawa. They managed to damage a hangar and five Fiat CR.32 fighters. Gura was attacked by nine Wellesleys operating out of the Sudan with 223 Squadron. Asmara was hit by nine Wellesleys of 47 Squadron. The Italians managed to scramble some CR.42s of 412 *Squadriglia* to intercept, and shot up one of the bombers, and a second was hit by Italian anti-aircraft fire. Both aircraft were written off when they landed back at base. The Wellesleys had managed to force down a CR.42 after they hit it with machine-gun fire.

Hartebeests of 11 South African Air Force (SAAF) Squadron launched an offensive sortie from Kenya. Three aircraft, led by Maj Preller, refuelled at Garissa. Their move was part of a larger operation to attack Italian Air Force bases in the south. At night on 12 June, eight Vincents of 8 Squadron (Aden) dive-bombed Macaaca airfield.

The Italians were first off the mark on 13 June. Four S.81s belonging to 4 *Gruppo* lifted off from Diredawa in the early hours. They were headed for Aden. At around 0440 four Gladiators belonging to 94 Squadron were scrambled to intercept them. The S.81 flown by *Sottotenente* Temistocle Paolelli and Mario Laureati was shot down off Ras Imran by Flg Off G.S.K. Hayward. A second Italian bomber, having hit its target, began suffering from engine trouble and made a forced landing in Italian territory. They believed incorrectly that they had actually landed in French Somaliland, and destroyed their own aircraft and headed back to base on foot. A third

S.81 was hit by anti-aircraft fire over Aden. It was flown by *Colonnello* Mario Pezzi and *Capitano* Parmeggiani. This aircraft actually managed to land safely at Assab. The fourth S.81 ran into technical difficulties and was forced to land at Husu Balid, a British emergency airfield to the east of Aden.

Despite the poor showing of the first attack, another bombing raid was under way three hours later. Nine S.79s of 44 *Gruppo* (Diredawa) were also making for Aden. Again the Gladiators scrambled to intercept, and as they closed, one of the Italian aircraft, flown by *Sottotenente* Ruffini, was hit by anti-aircraft fire from a British warship. The aircraft crashed and the remaining eight Italian aircraft droned over their target. As the Italians made their first pass they had to abort, as the leading aircraft's bomb-doors would not open. The bombers circled round to make a second attempt, and this time the Gladiators closed.

There were just two Gladiators up, one flown by Sgt Price, who attacked two bombers, while Plt Off Stephenson dealt with the other six. Stephenson closed on an S.79 flown by *Capitano* Serafini. His aircraft had been hit by anti-aircraft fire and his port engine had failed and his undercarriage had dropped down. He had desperately tried to keep up with the other aircraft. As Stephenson closed in, the dorsal gunner of the S.79 fired at him. A lucky shot hit Stephenson's top wing and managed to puncture the air cooler. Stephenson had to abort his attack and make a forced landing at Makhnuk. Serafini's S.79 continued to struggle towards Eritrea. He was aiming to land at Assab. As his undercarriage touched the ground it collapsed and the aircraft was written off. One other damaged S.79 managed to land at Assab.

CR.42s intercepted some Blenheim IVFs of 203 Squadron over Assab. One of the Blenheims was damaged in the attack. Blenheims of 8 and 39 Squadrons attacked Macaaca and managed to destroy three Ca 133s on the ground belonging to 27 *Gruppo*. In the south, Kismayu, Jelib and Afmadu were all hit by Ju86s belonging to 12 SAAF Squadron.

The Italians had also not been idle in the south, as before dawn, lifting off from Lugh Ferrandi, three Ca 133s of 9 *Squadriglia* led by *Capitano* Piva made for Wajir. They spotted half a dozen aircraft belonging to 237 Squadron. It was barely dawn, but they swept in to attack, coming under anti-aircraft fire. The Ca 133s pressed home and they later claimed to have destroyed three aircraft, set a petrol dump on fire and destroyed several buildings. One of the Ca 133s was slightly damaged. According to British sources a pair of Audaxes were damaged, 5,000 gallons of fuel destroyed and five of the ground crew killed.

Half a dozen Blenheims lifted off from Aden to attack the K14 satellite landing-ground near Assab on 14 June. The Blenheims, belonging to 8 Squadron, managed to knock out the Italian radio station. They were then pounced on by a pair of CR.42s of 413 *Squadriglia*.

A pair of Wellesleys of 14 Squadron were also intercepted when they tried to attack Massawa. One of the Wellesleys, flown by Plt Off Plunkett, was shot down. This was to be the first victory for *Tenente* Mario Visintini. During the rest of the Sunday three S.79s, operating out of Diredawa, attacked Berbera, and there were a number of reconnaissance flights by Ca 133s and S.81s. In the south, three Hurricanes of 1 SAAF Squadron were brought up to Port Reitz airfield, close to Mombasa.

On 15 June half a dozen Blenheims of 8 Squadron struck Diredawa. They managed to damage a CR.32 and destroy a dump of mustard-gas bombs. The same target came under attack from three Blenheims of 39 Squadron.

Three Ca 133s of 9 *Squadriglia* attacked Wajir and claimed to have destroyed a fuel dump and three aircraft. One of the Ca 133s was damaged by anti-aircraft fire. A pair of S.81s struck Erkowit airfield in the Sudan, damaging a Wellesley belonging to 47 Squadron.

That evening, five Wellesleys belonging to 223 Squadron launched an ill-fated attack on Gura and Difein Island. The first Wellesley burst into flames even before it lifted off, when faulty flares ignited. Four of the Wellesleys managed to take off at 1630. At 2330 one of the Wellesleys force-landed on the coast, sixty miles north of Port Sudan, another crashed on landing as it returned home, and a third was claimed by Italian anti-aircraft guns over Difein Island.

There was considerable movement of aircraft on 15 June. The Italians pulled out most of their units from Assab: the 18th and 52nd *Squadriglie* of 27 *Gruppo* moved to Dessie, the 118th *Squadriglia* was shifted to Sardo, 29 *Gruppo* moved to Mille; at Addis Ababa three

CR.42s of 413 *Squadriglia* joined five S.79s of 7 *Squadriglia* (44 *Gruppo*); three CR.42s of 414 *Squadriglia* shifted from Assab to Gura.

In Aden five Blenheim Is of 11 Squadron arrived at Sheik Othman. No. 11 Squadron also had two more aircraft that were still undergoing inspection and it had lost a pair when the Blenheims had been converted into fighters and given to 30 Squadron in Egypt.

On 16 June the South Africans were busy in the south. C Flight of 12 SAAF Squadron launched four Ju86s. The first pair, led by Maj Martin, refuelled at Wajir and then attacked Neghelli. Below them they found three CR.32s and ten Ca 133s. They bombed the Ca 133s and machine-gunned the three fighters. The South Africans claimed that they had damaged a number of the Ca 133s, but the Italians claimed that only one of their Ca 133s, belonging to 65 *Squadriglia*, had been destroyed.

Meanwhile the other pair, led by Capt De Toit, having refuelled at Lodwar, struck at Wavello. Again they found a number of Italian aircraft sitting out in the open. They bombed half a dozen Ca 133s and would later claim to have destroyed three Italian aircraft, but the Italians only admitted to one loss.

A pair of S.81s carried out a night attack against Erkowit in the Sudan. Much later in the day, a pair of S.81s tried their luck against Summit, but they were driven off by Gladiators (112 Squadron).

Maj Preller, the commanding officer of 11 SAAF Squadron, had something of a personal adventure on 17 June. He had taken off in a Fairey Battle, along with Air Corporals Petterson and Ackerman, to carry out a reconnaissance flight over Mogadishu. After he had taken his photographs he flew on towards Afmadu. Here he saw an Italian Ca 133 belonging to 8 *Squadriglia* on the ground. Preller dived down to make an attack, damaging the Italian aircraft with his machine-guns. Unluckily for Preller and his two crewmen, a stray Italian bullet hit the radiator and the glycol started draining away, which caused the engine to seize up. Preller managed to crash-land. He and the crew got out, set fire to the aircraft and then proceeded to head home on foot with just a single water bottle.

The adventure was nowhere near its end. The South Africans launched intensive search missions to find Preller and the two other men. After a week of searching they had found nothing and assumed that Preller and the other two were dead or had been captured by the

Italians. An aircraft belonging to 237 Squadron buzzed over a track between Garissa and Liboi on 1 July, and the pilots saw Preller on a camel.

Preller was quickly picked up and was able to explain that he had left the other two men at a waterhole and had pressed on to find help. All three men were brought back safely and Preller was awarded the Distinguished Flying Cross.

The Italians had also been very active during 17 June. They had launched no fewer than sixteen sorties. Three S.81s belonging to 18 *Squadriglia* (Sardo) attacked Aden. One of the aircraft was hit by anti-aircraft fire and had to land at Debra Sina. Berbera was also bombed that day by an S.81, and it too was believed to have been damaged by anti-aircraft fire.

The first Italian ground action took place on the Kenyan border. A sizeable force of Italian ground units, supported by Italian aircraft, attempted to overrun the British part of the border town of El Wak. This region had seen several cross-border attacks on a small scale for the past few days. On one occasion members of the King's African Rifles had carried out a raid against some Italian wells and had 'liberated' an Italian flag. On 17 June there had been a night attack by the King's African Rifles. The troops were under explicit instructions not to try and hold the place, but to destroy as much as they could. Each time the Italians tried to close with the raiding parties, they just slipped away into the bush.

This time the situation was rather more serious. As the Italian ground forces moved in, 237 Squadron attacked the Italian airbase. One of the Audaxes, flown by Flg Off Walmisley, carried out a forced landing after being hit by a bullet in the radiator at El Wak. He landed just in time to see British troops withdrawing. They tried to tow the aircraft but the undercarriage collapsed and the Audax was burned.

Further north three S.79s attacked Port Sudan, three S.81s bombed Aden and three more hit the British airfield at Zeila in British Somaliland. One of the S.81s of 29 *Gruppo* attacking Aden was made to force-land at Dancalia after being hit by anti-aircraft fire. One of the S.81s of 4 *Gruppo* attacking British Somaliland was also lost when it fell out of the sky, presumably due to engine failure.

More SAAF reinforcements were being sent to Kenya. Maj J.T. Durrant, commanding officer of 40 SAAF Squadron, with

Hartebeests, left all but four of their aircraft and flew up to take over the Ju52s and 53s of 11 SAAF Squadron. Meanwhile, 11 SAAF Squadron was re-equipped with Fairey Battles.

There was considerable alarm off Aden on 16 June when the Italian submarine, *Galileo* Galilei, torpedoed the Norwegian tanker *James Stove*, and sank her. The submarine intercepted a Yugoslav merchantman, *Drava*. The Italians forced her to stop by firing shots over her bows, and boarded her. But then they allowed her to continue on her way. The submarine was spotted by Flg Off Haywood of 94 Squadron in his Gladiator. Haywood called for help and it arrived in the form of a Vincent and a Blenheim. Together they attacked the submarine. The attack was an unmitigated disaster: the Blenheim's bombs missed the target and the Vincent was nearly destroyed by its own depth charges. Two Royal Navy ships were sent to intercept the submarine, but the destroyer HMS *Kandahar* and the sloop HMS *Shoreham* arrived too late and the submarine slipped away in the darkness. At 1830 the submarine surfaced to make a radio report. HMS *Kandahar* closed but once again the submarine slipped away.

The operation against the Italian submarine resumed the following day, with Blenheims of 203 Squadron mounting patrols to find her. The anti-submarine trawler *Moonstone* managed to pick up the submarine with its Asdic at 1137. The *Moonstone* moved in to drop depth charges, but yet again the submarine disappeared. The *Moonstone* found her again at 1230, and this time the Italian submarine surfaced and fired at the trawler with her twin 100 mm guns. The *Moonstone* turned to attack, firing an ancient 6 in. deck gun. Meanwhile, as she closed, her Lewis gunners opened up. The Italian gun crew dived for cover. By now the *Moonstone* was no more than 550 yards from the submarine, and everyone on board with a weapon was firing at the Italian craft. The 6 in. gun scored a pair of hits on the conning tower. The Italian captain was killed and shortly afterwards the crew surrendered.

As it transpired, the *Galileo Galilei* was one of four Italian submarines operating in the area. The commanding officer, *Capitano di Corvetta* Nardi, had been killed and several of the officers and crew wounded. This had prevented the crew from destroying copies of their orders and enabled the British to find two of the remaining three Italian submarines and sink them. The third Italian submarine was already wrecked near Port Sudan. The submarine was taken back to Aden under her own power, arriving there the following day.

Diredawa found itself under attack from five Blenheims of 39 Squadron and a Blenheim from 11 Squadron. The six Blenheims managed to destroy a hangar and blow up a petrol dump.

To the south the South Africans launched an attack against Wavello. Two Hurricanes of 1 SAAF Squadron escorted three Ju86s of 12 SAAF Squadron. Their target was the Ca 133s of 66 *Squadriglia*. Unbeknown to the South Africans, a flight of CR.32s of 411 *Squadriglia* had been moved to Yavello. The CR.32s scrambled as soon as the South Africans were spotted. Two CR.32s got aloft in time, flown by *Tenente* Aldo Meoli and *Maresciallo* Bossi. They pounced on one of the Ju86s and shot it up before turning their attention to a Hurricane, flown by 2/Lt B.L. Griffiths. They shot down the Hurricane and killed Griffiths. The second Hurricane, flown by Capt St E. Truter, got to grips with one of the CR.32s. He must have hit it, as he saw it pull away belching smoke, and when it landed it flipped over onto its back. Understandably the CR.32 was a write off, but *Tenente* Meoli was only slightly wounded. All three of the Ju86s got home, along with the remaining Hurricane.

The loss of Griffiths's Hurricane forced 1 SAAF Squadron to move six Furies up to Port Reitz on 20 June. The Italians were also reinforcing with three CR.32s transferred from Addis Ababa belonging to 411 *Squadriglia*. They would now be based at Yavello.

The French signed an armistice with the Germans on 20 June, and to test French resolve the Italians mounted a number of reconnaissance flights over French Somaliland. They would soon discover whether the French intended to fight on.

On 21 June eleven Ca 133s of 27 *Gruppo* (Dessie) attacked Djibouti in three waves. If anti-aircraft fire was anything to go, by the French did intend to resist. Only three of the Italian aircraft returned safely to base, having carried out their mission. Two had had to abort, two had been shot down and four had landed at alternative airfields.

British Somaliland was also a target for the Italians on 21 June. Two S.81s fell on Berbera. One of the Italian aircraft had to make a forced landing to the south of Berbera. Local tribesmen slaughtered the crew.

The British also launched their own limited attacks on 21 June. Three Vincents belonging to D Flight of 47 Squadron had moved up to Malakal in the Sudan the day before. They now launched an attack on the Italian strongpoint at Asosa. One of the Vincents had to make a forced landing after running short of fuel, but on 24 June the British managed to clear a runway to bring in fuel for him and his crew, and he was able to take off and fly back to Malakal.

The Italians struck against French Somaliland once again on 22 June. This time the target was Djibouti airfield. A CR.32, four CR.42s and five Ro.37bis were involved in the attack. It seemed that the main purpose was to prevent the British from reinforcing French Somaliland with their own aircraft. The port itself also came under attack. Three S.81s had attacked the port before dawn and eight more during the day. The Italian submarine that had beached near Port Sudan received a supply of food and equipment from an S.81. The submarine's position was relayed to another Italian submarine to come to her help.

In Kenya a photographic flight, the beginnings of 62 Squadron (later 60 Squadron), had arrived in Nairobi, and twenty-one crewmen of 11 SAAF Squadron were bound for South Africa to pick up their new Fairey Battles.

Italian operations against French Somaliland were terminated on 24 June when word arrived of the armistice that had been signed between Italy and France.

Four Blenheims belonging to 39 Squadron and two more of 11 Squadron approached Diredawa at around noon. Flying top cover over the airfield was *Sergente Maggiore* Giardinà in a CR.32 of 410 *Squadriglia*. He informed the ground control that there were incoming enemy bombers and then dived onto the leading three Blenheims. Giardinà managed to damage all three of them and then gave chase and closed on a stricken Blenheim flown by Plt Off Hunter. As the Italian pilot moved in for the kill his guns jammed and he was forced to peel off. Rather belatedly, but responding to Giardinà's appeals for help, a pair of CR.42s appeared. The Blenheims immediately jettisoned their bombs and moved in to engage. The pair of CR.42s made an initial sweep against Hunter's aircraft, which was by now virtually crippled. It would later manage to land in British Somaliland.

Ten Wellesleys attacked Asmara and managed to slightly damage a Ca 133, and an intercepting CR.32 caught fire when it tried to land after having to give up the fight due to an overheating engine.

There were further attacks by both the RAF and the Italians on 25 June. The sole loss of the day was a Wellesley piloted by Sgt F.A. Sanders of 47 Squadron. He and his crew were on a photo-reconnaissance mission over Asmara. The aircraft experienced mechanical problems and he was forced to make a landing in Italian East Africa. Sanders and the crew managed to set fire to their aircraft before the Italians took them prisoner.

On 26 June the RAF hit Gura. Leading the attack were four Wellesleys of 14 Squadron, followed by five Wellesleys of 47 Squadron. They were intercepted at around 0730 by seven CR.42s. Three of 14 Squadron's Wellesleys were hit. In the ensuing battle one of the CR.42s was also hit and the pilot was wounded, but he managed to land safely.

The Italians shuffled their air fleet once again on 27 June. From Diredawa three Ro.37bis of 110 *Squadriglia* were sent to Assab (three CR.42s of 414 *Squadriglia* would join them there the following day).

In the south a number of Ca 133s attacked Wajir and some British warships in the Red Sea were attacked by a number of S.81s. Late in the afternoon Sqn Ldr Bowman, flying a Blenheim of 39 Squadron and accompanied by three Gladiators of 94 Squadron, flew in to Perim Island. They were due to refuel and then attack a petrol dump at Assab shortly after dawn on Sunday 28 June. Bowman lifted off at dawn, accompanied by two of the Gladiators, one flown by Sqn Ldr Wightman and the other by Plt Off Carter. As Bowman's Blenheim came into attack the bombs missed the target, but the Gladiators swooped in and managed to blow up 100 drums of fuel. They were then able to escape without being intercepted.

Assab came under attack again later that morning. No. 39 Squadron had dispatched three Blenheims to destroy the Italian bomb dump. As the Blenheim attack came in, an Ro.37bis, piloted by *Sergente Maggiore* Mario Di Trani, had just landed. The Italian pilot got his aircraft back up to speed and took off again. He found himself being chased by one of the Blenheims, which peppered him with shots. The Italian tried to turn but the Blenheims were too fast. Instead he tried to ram one of the attackers. He missed and his aircraft was buffeted by the slipstream, which put his aircraft out of control. He managed to wrestle with the controls and open fire on one of the Blenheims. By now he had virtually no fuel left. To add to his complications, the undercarriage had been shot up, as had the cockpit and instruments. As he hit the ground both of his tyres were flat and the brakes did not work. For his pains the Italian pilot remained out in the blazing sun and had to be treated for sunstroke.

The fuel depot at Massawa was attacked by four Wellesleys on the same day, but later that night three S.81s of 10 *Squadriglia* were launched to attack Port Sudan. Poor weather meant that they were still close to the target at dawn, and Plt Off Hamlyn was scrambled at 0500 hours on 29 June. Hamlyn was flying a Gladiator from a detachment of 112 Squadron. He climbed to intercept and fired approximately a thousand rounds at one of the S.81s. Suddenly the Italian aircraft exploded and a piece of the debris hit Hamlyn's aircraft. Miraculously two of the Italian crewmen survived, including the commanding officer of 10 *Squadriglia*, *Capitano* Umberto Barone.

The Italians launched three S.79s at Port Sudan later in the day and three more against Aden. British Blenheims bombed Harar and a single Blenheim attacked Assab but was chased away by a pair of CR.42s and an Ro.37bis.

The Italian fuel depot at Massawa came under attack once again on 30 June by five Wellesleys belonging to 223 Squadron. They were followed by four more Wellesleys of 14 Squadron, who were bound for Acico Bay. The 14 Squadron's Wellesleys ran into trouble; one had to turn back, and the lead Wellesley was hit by anti-aircraft fire, but all four managed to get back to base. The bombers attacking Massawa also ran into heavy anti-aircraft fire and the unwelcome attention of Italian fighters. One of the Wellesleys, piloted by Sgt Poskitt, was shot down.

The Italians continued to shuffle their pack, with three Ca 133s (49 *Gruppo*) moving to Neghelli from Jimma, and two CR.32s of 411 *Squadriglia* moving to Neghelli from Yavello. Similarly, seven Wellesleys belonging to 47 Squadron were sent to Khartoum to use that as their base of operations for the next few days.

To the south, just inside Kenya, was a British fort at Moyale. It was garrisoned by 150 officers and men of the King's African Rifles.

Throughout June there had been barely a company holding Moyale, but there had been several clashes with Italian troops along the border. The Italians had made several half-hearted attempts to dislodge the British from their garrison fort. It was a long, low, red set of mud buildings surrounded by barbed wire entanglements. Within, the garrison had worked hard to reinforce the mud brick walls with concrete and to create pillboxes, dugouts and communication trenches.

On 1 July Capt Drummond and his company of the 1st King's African Rifles were rudely woken up by an Italian bombardment. The Italians made several attempts to attack the fort over the course of the day. Reinforcements were on hand, notably in the shape of 237 Squadron, whose biplanes attacked the Italian *banda*. This was not to be the last that Moyale would hear from the Italians.

There were other significant Italian moves on 1 July. No 29 *Gruppo* shifted all of its S.81s from Mille to Dessie and then on to Shashamanna. These were clearly to be used in operations against either Kenya or British Somaliland.

On 2 July the British determined to try and destroy the Italian fighters that were based at Assab. The first attack came in at 0645, launched by a Blenheim of 39 Squadron. As the Blenheim came in it saw a CR.42 taxiing on the runway. A little later a Blenheim from 11 Squadron dive-bombed Assab and reported seeing a CR.42 on its nose. The 11 Squadron's Blenheim never made it back to base, as it was hit in one of its engines and had to crash-land short of its base at Ras Arar. More Blenheims of 39 Squadron attacked Assab at 0750. The three raiders were chased out to sea by a pair of CR.42s. One of the Blenheims, however, saw a CR.42 taking off from Assab and attacked it.

Three Gladiators of 94 Squadron joined in the attacks, arriving over Assab at 0836. Sqn Ldr Wightman saw a CR.42 on the ground and shot at it until it burst into flames. Then Wightman saw a pair of CR.42s above him and immediately attacked, shooting down one of them, but the other managed to escape.

One of the other Gladiators, flown by Sgt Dunwoodie, busy attacking ground targets, found himself being chased by a CR.42. He turned to attack it and shot at it until its engines stopped. He chased it down and fired at it until it crashed. The Italians would later admit that two of their pilots had been shot down over Assab, belonging to 414 *Squadriglia*. One of the pilots had been killed.

Five Wellesleys of 47 Squadron, now based at Khartoum, made attacks on ground targets around Metemma in the afternoon. By incredible bad luck one of the Wellesleys, flown by Plt Off Bush, was hit by rifle fire. The crew was lost when the aircraft crashed.

There were further raids the following day, on 3 July, but there was only one loss – a single Wellesley of 14 Squadron. The aircraft was shot down by a CR.42 of 412 *Squadriglia*, flown by *Tenente* Visintini. The Wellesley was flown by Flg Off S.G. Soderholm.

There was considerable ground action on 4 July 1940. One of the principal targets was Cassala. It was of great symbolic significance to the Italians, as it had once been under Italian rule.

The Italians had mustered a sizeable force to deal with the pitifully small Sudan Defence Force garrison of 320 men. In effect this was two Sudanese motor machine-gun companies, and against them would be arrayed well over 6,500 Italian and colonial troops, including two squadrons of tanks and ten batteries of artillery. In support were three *squadriglie* of bombers (two more were assigned to cover the attacks on Gallabat).

The Italians bombed Cassala for twelve hours. The Sudan Defence Force held on all day for the loss of one dead and sixteen missing (although several turned up later). The Italians admitted to forty-three dead and 114 wounded, although the British at the time claimed 500 casualties and six Italian tanks. The Cassala garrison slipped away during the night.

The Italians also attacked Gallabat on the same day. This lay just across a dry river-bed from Metemma. The British garrison consisted of a single platoon, and the Italians attacked with some 2,000 men, supported by artillery and aircraft.

Three days later sixty Sudan policemen were forced to abandon Kurmuk, as the Italians advanced with a full battalion. These attacks were not designed to precede an all-out invasion of the Sudan. They were merely to block any British attempts to transport arms into Italian East Africa for the rebels. Throughout these operations, although none of the Italian aircraft were shot down, a number of them were hit by ground fire.

Ground combat was still continuing in northern Kenya, but on a relatively limited scale. No. 237 Squadron, based at Isiola, received reinforcements from 40 SAAF Squadron in the shape of three Hartebeests. The newly arrived Hartebeests would not have to wait long for their first taste of action.

Led by Capt Scravesande of 11 SAAF Squadron, six Hartebeests took off, heading for Wajir for refuelling. They would fly on and attack enemy ground units with 120 lb and 20 lb bombs. They made their first attack successfully and then flew back to Bura for refuelling before launching a second attack.

Four Wellesleys belonging to 14 Squadron attacked Zula on the coast of Eritrea at around midday on 8 July. As they turned for home they spotted an S.81 belonging to 10 *Squadriglia* (28 *Gruppo*). It was to the east of the Dahlak Archipelago. The aircraft was being flown by *Sottotenente* Salvatore Suella. Acting as his observer was a naval officer, *Sottotenente* Goffredo Franchini. One of the Wellesleys, flown by Flg Off C.G.S.R. Robinson, attacked. The first attack failed, and as he came in for a second run his gun jammed and the S.81 began firing back. Robinson got in closer to allow his upper and starboard gunners to engage. In the attack the co-pilot of the Italian aircraft, *Sergente Maggiore* Piero Violetti, was wounded, along with Franchini and the aircraft's engineer, Primo *Aviere Motorista* Fiorindo Reggioni. The Italian aircraft broke away and tried to land on a small island. It hit the ground with considerable force, killing Suella. The S.81 then bounced off the ground, and Violetti took over the controls. Robinson chased, trying to finish off the S.81. After ten minutes the Italian aircraft fell into the sea. Amazingly, some of the crew survived. In fact three managed to get into a life-raft. At that point they saw that Franchini was still alive. Franchini refused their suggestion that he get on board the raft, believing that if he did it would sink and they would all die. He ordered the three men to make for the closest island. Franchini was never seen again (later he was posthumously awarded the *Medaglia D'Oro*). The three survivors found themselves washed up on an uninhabited island. They subsisted on birds' eggs and then decided that they must try to make for Dahlak Island. It took them two weeks to reach their destination. Locals looked after them until an Italian destroyer came to pick them up. They returned to base three weeks after being shot down.

On 8 July five Blenheims attacked the Italian base at Diredawa, and on the following day it was the turn of Sardo and Macaaca to receive unwanted British attention.

On the night of 9 July the garrison at Moyale was relieved by D Company of the 1st King's African Rifles. Their commander was Capt David Henderson. Henderson had been a regular soldier in a Scottish regiment, and he was to soon win the Military Cross. He had barely been in charge for half a dozen hours when shelling erupted at 0545 on 10 July. By the time the day was out over 1,000 shells had landed on his positions. The buildings were wrecked, but only one section post was hit. One of the shells went straight through the sergeants' mess. Throughout the bombardment most of the men were safely hidden underground, all except for the cook in the kitchen. The African cook continued to prepare meals throughout the bombardment, and as soon as there was a lull he would aim to feed the garrison.

The Italians tried an attack from the east and attempted to swing around to attack from the south-east. They attacked with at least a brigade, but did not press home their efforts, and the fort held on, now surrounded on three sides by the enemy.

Three S.81s of 63 *Squadriglia* attacked Berbera airfield on Friday 10 July. On the same day the British launched attacks by Blenheims of 39 Squadron against Assab, beginning at 0700. At 0820 a Blenheim of 8 Squadron and three Gladiators of 94 Squadron attacked Assab. Flg Off Haywood claimed a pair of CR.42s which he had shot up and seen burn on the ground. By the end of the day 414 *Squadriglia* had lost every single one of its aircraft. Two had been lost in combat and four had been destroyed on the ground.

Throughout the night at Moyale the Italians tried to break through the barbed-wire entanglements. Each time they were met by bren-gun fire. Throughout the night the garrison attempted to mend the damage inflicted on the defences by the daytime bombardment. The day opened at Moyale with sporadic enemy shelling. It was clear that the Italians had moved their artillery up during the night and were now shelling from a closer range. Italian infantry were trying to encircle the fort. A British relief column was trying to break through, but there were simply too many Italians, and they gave up a mile and a half from the fort.

During the evening of 10 July three Hartebeests of 40 SAAF Squadron flew into Wajir to join up with 237 Squadron. They were to be involved in attacking Italian ground units the following day.

In the early morning of 11 July three Ca 133s belonging to 9 *Squadriglia* (Lugh Ferrandi) approached Wajir. A pair of the Hartebeests were scrambled to intercept. The pair picked on one of the bombers, hitting it several times, and the pilots reported seeing smoke coming out of the centre and starboard engines. In fact the Ca 133 managed to get back to base, but one of the crew-members had been killed and two others had been wounded. The Hartebeests now turned to attack the other two bombers, which had managed to drop their bombs on their target and were now returning fire against the South African aircraft. One of the Hartebeests, flown by Lt N.K. Rankin, took damage and was put out of action for some hours.

By now the Italians had occupied much of the native village of Moyale. As the South African aircraft came in to provide air cover, the garrison gave them what little help they could with mortar and machine-gun fire. At this stage the garrison had barely four days' water left. When Henderson contacted the relief column they suggested that he should try to slip out of the fort that night.

The two Hartebeests (minus Rankin) carried out the ground attack, but one ran out of fuel and had to force-land on its return, and the second had to make for Bura. As the Hartebeest was being refuelled, a pair of Ca 133s came in to strafe the aircraft and the ground crew. The Hartebeest's air gunner, Sgt Lewis, jumped into a truck and drove it onto the airstrip to try and decoy the Italian aircraft from the Hartebeest. It seemed to work, as the Hartebeest was successfully refuelled and was able to fly back up to Wajir.

In the late morning three more Hartebeests had arrived at Wajir. They were ready to take off and make ground attacks by early afternoon. By this time Rankin's aircraft had been repaired and he was able to join them. Aloft over Moyale they encountered three Ca 133s (66 *Squadriglia*, Yavello) and three CR.32s (411 *Squadriglia*). The Italian fighters peeled off to intercept the South Africans. One of the CR.32s managed to get onto the tail of Rankin, and Rankin's aircraft was shot down, killing him and his gunner, Air Sgt D.H. Hughes. The Italians also managed to hit and damage Lt H.G. Shuttleworth's Hartebeest and do minor damage to Lt Jubber's aircraft.

There was a distinct possibility now that the Italians would completely encircle Moyale and advance beyond it. The British plan was now to launch a counter-attack to allow the garrison at Moyale to break out.

To the north a single Blenheim, flown by Flg Off P.A. Nicholas (8 Squadron, Aden), flew a reconnaissance mission over the Italian base at Jijiga. The Blenheim was intercepted by a pair of CR.32s of 410 *Squadriglia*. The CR.32s were flown by *Sottotenente* Veronese and *Sergente Maggiore* Giardinà. The Blenheim was badly damaged in the attack and it had to force-land at Djibouti.

Sunday 12 July dawned at Moyale. The garrison could hope that it would be a quiet day, as it had become something of a tradition for the Italians not to launch any offensive action on a Sunday. Once again Henderson was urged to evacuate the fort. South African aircraft attacked Italian positions in the afternoon, but the sun finally set without any offensive action being launched by the Italians. By 1900 the garrison could see the Italian cooking-fires.

Henderson had noted this trend, and rather than attempt a breakout in the early hours of the morning, after the moon had set, he proposed to break out now. One by one the garrison began leaving their posts from 1930, and formed up in single file along a communication trench. The men stood there in their stockinged feet, carrying their rifles, bren-guns and as much ammunition as they could bear. They were wearing black jerseys and looked like shadows. Led by Lt De Toit, they crept out of the west gate of the fort. De Toit cut through five rows of barbed wire in the outer defences, and then in a long line they crept through a gully straight through the Italian lines. They could see the Italian machine-gun posts above them, and Italian soldiers talking and smoking. Three of the most seriously injured men had to be left in the fort. They were given morphine and left in a bomb-proof dugout.

The three men woke in the early hours of the morning and found themselves alone. They decided that they would also try to break out. One of the men was captured. The other two made it to a maize field before one of them, suffering from a broken leg, collapsed. His companion left him and tried to find the British lines. He was shot at by British sentries, but he waved a bandage as a white flag. The sentries went back with him to the maize field, but they could not find the man that he had left there.

The garrison had marched into safety. One group, led by

Henderson, made a long detour and joined the relief force close to the Marsabit Road. The other party, led by Lt De Toit, took his men straight to the British headquarters.

When the Italians woke on Monday morning the garrison was gone. Anything that could not be taken out had been destroyed. Even the tattered Union Flag had been removed. Britain had lost Moyale. The Italians had gained just a few square miles of Northern Kenya; it would be of no strategic importance.

Elsewhere on Sunday twelve Italian fighters intercepted eleven Wellesleys (14 and 47 Squadrons) attacking Massawa airfield. They managed to shoot down one of the Wellesleys, flown by Sgt F. Nelson. There were two other items of interest in the northern part of the theatre. No. 47 Squadron gave its single Supermarine Walrus to 14 Squadron, based at Port Sudan. It would be used for reconnaissance flights over the Red Sea. Also, Erkowit airfield was renamed Carthago.

On Monday 13 July, 8 Squadron (Aden) received welcome reinforcement in the form of a pair of *Armée de l'Air* Martin 167F bombers and a Blenheim. The aircraft were flown by French pilots in RAF uniforms. The Martins had been flown in from Syria and the crews were keen to avoid the armistice restrictions.

A fuel dump to the south of Assab was attacked by a Blenheim belonging to 39 Squadron (Aden). The Blenheim was accompanied by Plt Off Carter (94 Squadron) in a Gladiator as close support. Unfortunately for Carter, CR.42s of 413 *Squadriglia* intercepted him and shot him down.

On 15 July, 94 Squadron lost another Gladiator in the morning, when Plt Off Sanderson's Gladiator was stricken by a broken oil pipe. He had to make a forced landing. There was worse to come when the aircraft flown by Plt Off Bartlett and Plt Off Hogg collided with one another while they were on patrol to the south of Little Aden. Plt Off Hogg managed to nurse his aircraft back to base, but Bartlett had to bale out and he was later picked up.

There were ominous developments in French Somaliland. The commander, Legentilhomme, was replaced by *Général* Germain. The Petain government was determined to abide by the terms of the armistice. This meant that any help from French Somaliland could no longer be expected by the British. Indeed, within a few days

Germain was talking to the Italians about the use of the railway in French Somaliland.

Four Wellesleys belonging to 223 Squadron attacked Agordat, dropping a number of 250 lb bombs. Later in the day Wellesleys from 14 and 47 Squadrons made an attack on Asmara. There was disaster over the target, when two of the Wellesleys collided with one another in their attempts to evade Italian fighters. One of the aircraft managed to get back home, but it was written off. The other aircraft crashed over Asmara. This was piloted by Sgt W.C.H. Style.

To the south, a number of SAAF Junkers Ju86s were fortunate enough to have just lifted off from Wajir for refuelling at Nanyuki when the airfield was bombed by the Italians. It is believed that the bombing was carried out by a trio of S.81s out of Neghelli. Wajir received more unwelcome guests the following day, 17 July, when three S.79s bombed 237 Squadron's base. A pair of Hawker biplanes managed to attack a solitary C133 (65 *Squadriglia*) over Bura. Later three S.79s and a pair of Ca 133s attacked Bura and they managed to damage an Audax that was parked up beside the runway. Wajir and Bura were hit again on 18 July, this time by three S.79s operating out of Neghelli. One of the S.79s was hit by anti-aircraft fire.

The SAAF returned the compliment when four Ju86s strafed and bombed Neghelli. They managed to set fire to a fuel dump and wreck one of the barracks. There was a problem for Maj De Toit on the return flight. His Ju86 developed a problem with its oil pressure, and he was forced to land short of Nanyuki. Maj De Toit was able to deal with the problem and make it back to base the following day.

The Italians suffered an own goal on Saturday 18 July when a CR.32 crashed on landing at Addis Ababa. It was one of five aircraft belonging to 411 *Squadriglia* returning from Yavello.

There was little activity the next day, 19 July. Bura was bombed by a pair of Ca 133s in the evening. One of the aircraft made a forced landing and the crew marched through the bush, arriving back at base on 21 July.

There were small-scale raids over the next few days, with very little damage achieved by either the British or the Italians. But a major operation was launched by the British on 23 July. Four Wellesleys belonging to 14 Squadron and three from 223 Squadron hit Massawa at around noon. The Italians managed to scramble some

CR.32s. Two of the Italian aircraft chased the Wellesleys of 223 Squadron for nearly half an hour. They picked on Plt Off Ellis's Wellesley, which was trailing behind. It was losing height and the Italian pilots broke off, believing that it was about to crash. In fact Ellis managed to get back to base safely. On their return to home the Wellesleys of 14 Squadron were pounced on by a CR.42. As the CR.42 closed, the Wellesley's rear gunners opened up. They claimed that they hit the engine and that the Italian aircraft stalled. In fact it dived away out of range.

With the possibility of assistance from French Somaliland gone, the British could no longer rely on French air cover, and so they had to redeploy aircraft into British Somaliland to provide air cover for the ground troops. Consequently, on Friday 24 July half a dozen Gladiators belonging to 94 Squadron (Aden) were detached to Berbera.

Massawa was attacked by four Wellesleys belonging to 14 Squadron on 25 July. The Wellesleys encountered three CR.42s over their target and in the ensuing dogfight one of the Wellesleys was badly damaged.

The Italians launched a bombing raid against British installations near Zeila in British Somaliland. The attack was carried out by three S.81s operating out of Diredawa.

A pair of Blenheim IVFs belonging to 203 Squadron (Aden) spotted a tempting target sitting on Mille airfield on Sunday 26 July. There were three Ca 133s sitting on the ground in close proximity. In the strafing attack made by the Blenheims two of the Ca 133s were damaged. A Blenheim returned the following day to finish off the job. A single Blenheim of 203 Squadron led in three Blenheims of 8 Squadron. One of the Ca 133s was destroyed this time, and the other two were damaged.

The port of Aden came under attack from the Italians when three S.79s of 44 *Gruppo* bombed the harbour. They managed to damage the steamer *Mathura*.

Five Wellesleys belonging to 223 Squadron launched an early-morning raid against Massawa. They were met by extremely accurate anti-aircraft fire, and one of the Wellesleys was damaged. As the Wellesleys made good their escape a pair of CR.32s closed with them at 0805. The CR.32s picked on the two trailing Wellesleys. Both of the Wellesleys were badly damaged, and in fact one was written off.

Operating out of Aden in a Blenheim, Sgt J.J. Barry of 11 Squadron made an attack against Assab and Macaaca at 1115. Anti-aircraft fire riddled the Blenheim and Barry was shot down, and he and his crew were killed.

The port of Aden once again received visitors in the form of five S.79s of 44 *Gruppo*. They made attacks on ships and on the petrol dump. During the day a number of Blenheims of 45 Squadron (Egypt) arrived as reinforcements at Carthago. Three Gladiators of 112 Squadron were moved to Gedaref on the Sudanese border.

The three Gladiators were in operation the following day, Thursday 30 July. Their job was to escort an attack on Kassala airfield, which was now of course held by the Italians. They were escorting five Wellesleys belonging to 47 Squadron and three Blenheims of 45 Squadron. The Italian positions at Kassala came under attack from 223 Squadron and by Wellesleys of 14 Squadron. In the last attack, just after noon, the three Wellesleys were all hit by anti-aircraft fire.

In the south, Wajir was bombed, as was Bura. But the Italians were making more elaborate plans, as their intended invasion of British Somaliland was now imminent. As a consequence 411 *Squadriglia* shifted nine of its CR.32s to Diredawa from Addis Ababa to join the existing 410 *Squadriglia* at the base. The Italians made further movements on 31 July. Six Ca 133s of 18 *Squadriglia* moved up from Dessie to Diredawa. On Saturday 1 August *Generale* Collalti set up the *Comando Tattico Aeronautico* for the impending invasion of British Somaliland.

The British were patently aware of the vulnerability of British Somaliland. Lt Col Chater of the Royal Marines was overall commander of British troops in Somaliland. Back in July 1939 he had asked the Colonial Office to provide him with necessary funds to construct defences to protect the two main approaches to Berbera. They had given him £900. He had managed to squeeze out some reserve water tanks and a handful of concrete pillboxes. As early as January 1940 he had asked for another battalion to be brought up from Kenya. It was agreed in principle by March, and the battalion finally arrived on 15 May. By the time the Italians declared war on 10 June 1940 all Chater could muster was a battalion of the King's

African Rifles, the Somaliland Camel Corps and a handful of irregulars.

As far as the British were concerned there appeared to be three alternative strategies for British Somaliland: they could reinforce British Somaliland so that it could resist any invasion; the second option was to evacuate without a fight; and the third option was to hold for as long as possible, inflict maximum damage on the Italians and then withdraw. In actual fact there was really only one alternative; given the strategic situation and compelling reason for troops to remain in Britain, Kenya and Egypt, strong reinforcement was impossible. The prospect of abandoning British Somaliland without a fight was totally unacceptable. All it would do was to allow the Italians to shift their troops quickly to Kenya or the Sudan and apply pressure there.

Once the French had changed their stance and could no longer be relied upon for support, Wavell had to seriously reconsider his options. It now meant that the entire Italian Eastern Army, thought to be around 25,000 strong, could now fall on British Somaliland. It was believed that the Italians mustered some twenty colonial battalions, four Blackshirt battalions, four artillery groups, thirty tanks, two sections of armoured cars and eleven groups of African irregulars. This was an enormous force.

Chater had, in fact, received a Punjabi battalion from Aden, a second King's African Rifles battalion and a light artillery battery. He desperately wanted two more battalions. Wavell ordered the 2nd Battalion of the Black Watch to move from Aden to Berbera and a second Punjabi battalion to accompany them. This now meant that Chater had the 1st Northern Rhodesia Regiment, the 2nd Battalion of the King's African Rifles, the 3rd Battalion of the 15th Punjabi Regiment, the 1st Battalion of the 2nd Punjabis, the 2nd Battalion Black Watch, the 1st East African Light Battery (with just four 3.7 in. howitzers) – in all, just under 6,000 men.

Chater needed to organise his defences. The main road out of Italian East Africa to Berbera ran through Hargeisa. There was, however, a longer route that went east from Hargeisa to Burao and then to the Sheikh Pass and then to Berbera. Mercifully, there were good defensive positions on each of the roads. The Sheikh Pass, which was narrow, could easily be defended and perhaps blocked entirely by using explosives. But the direct route could only be protected at Tug Argan. This was a sandy, dry river-bed approximately 150 yards wide. It lay about halfway between Hargeisa and Berbera. Chater would set up defensive positions on the four hills behind it. Chater also had to consider the possibility that the French might allow the Italians to pass through French Somaliland and attack along the coast.

The forward positions were held by the 1st Northern Rhodesian Regiment, minus one company, the 2nd King's African Rifles, the 3rd Battalion of the 15th Punjabi Regiment and a machine-gun company from the Camel Corps. Chater placed the Black Watch in reserve at Laferug. The Sheikh Pass and the approaches to Zeila were held by the 1st Battalion of the 2nd Punjabis. Patrols were mounted by detachments of the Camel Corps around Zeila, Burao and Hargeisa. The remaining company of the Northern Rhodesian Regiment was also placed at Hargeisa.

As far as the Italians were concerned, the reinforcement of British Somaliland tipped the balance where their offensive actions were concerned. The British forces represented a considerable threat, and in any case the Italians needed a quick and cheap victory for morale purposes.

The early afternoon of 1 August found three S.81s attacking shipping at Zeila. Six Blenheims of 8 Squadron, six from 39 Squadron and two from 203 Squadron were launched against the new Italian airstrip at Chinele, close to Diredawa. As the Blenheims approached they were attacked by Italian fighters and fired at by anti-aircraft guns. The Blenheims pressed home their attack, and as the second wave from 8 Squadron approached, the commanding officer of 410 *Squadriglia*, *Capitano* Corrado Ricci, shot down Sgt Franks's Blenheim. He and his crew were later captured by the Italians. As the Blenheims passed over Zeila on their way home they spotted the S.81s attacking the shipping. One of the Blenheims, flown by Plt Off J.E.S. White and Sgt Crehan (39 Squadron), dived down to attack the Italian aircraft. Two of the S.81s made a swift exit, but the third was engaged by the Blenheim and hit in its starboard engine. In flames, the S.81 made a forced landing. Two of the crew were killed when it crashed, and the rest made their way safely back to the Italian lines.

Ju86s attacked Yavello and Wellesleys struck at Asmara and Massawa. At Asmara a Ca 133 and an Italian fighter were both hit and destroyed on the ground.

The Italian forces began their slow move into British Somaliland, skirmishing with British troops near Hargeisa. However, the Italians did not launch any major aerial attacks on British Somaliland on Sunday 2 August. A detachment from 45 Squadron, flying Blenheims, hit Asmara, and Chinele was hit by 39 Squadron. Once again Italian CR.42s attempted to intercept them, but they met with failure, and the only casualty was *Capitano* Corrado Santoro, the commanding officer of 413 *Squadriglia*. His aircraft was hit in the engine and he had to make a forced landing.

Aerial activity stepped up considerably on Monday 3 August. Italian S.81s and Ca 133s hit several targets in Kenya. On the ground their troops moved forward and took Debel, but as soon as they heard that British reinforcements were moving up they pulled back.

Over Wajir, a single Ca 133 (8 *Squadriglia*) was spotted. Three Furies belonging to 1 SAAF Squadron were ordered to scramble. As it was, only the aircraft of Flt Lt Robert S. Blake and Lt Rushmere managed to get up. Rushmere closed first, but his machine-guns failed to operate. Blake fired straight into the cockpit of the Italian aircraft and the Ca 133 swooped down to land, but instead it crashed and burst into flames. Only the pilot survived the crash, but he died in his attempts to rescue his crew.

Berbera became the target of Italian S.81s at around 1400 on 3 August. Flt Lt Reid on board a Gladiator of 94 Squadron scrambled to intercept. He picked on an S.81 flown by *Capitano* Parmeggiani (the commander of 15 *Squadriglia*). He attacked it until he saw it belching smoke; it managed to land at Jijiga, but one of the crew members had been killed.

Additional reinforcements arrived in the Sudan with the creation of 430 Flight, formerly D Flight of 47 Squadron. They were equipped with Gauntlets and Vincents. The Gauntlets had been flown down from Egypt.

There was increased fighting near Hargeisa on 4 August when the motor company of the Camel Corps attacked the lead elements of the Italian invasion force. They managed to destroy an armoured car and damage two others. By 1500, however, the British forces had withdrawn and the Italians were able to enter Hargeisa.

Earlier in the day five Wellesleys from 14 Squadron and five from 47 Squadron had attacked Italian installations and stores on Sheik Said Island. They were accompanied by three Blenheims of 45 Squadron, who had been tasked with attacking three Italian submarines alongside Abdul Kadir jetty. The Blenheims managed to hit a submarine depot ship. A pair of CR.42s managed to intercept 14 Squadron's Wellesleys. They managed to damage one of the bombers so that its undercarriage collapsed when it landed back at base. WO Trecan, flying a French Martin 167F out of Aden, made a ground attack on Italian aircraft at Dogahbur airfield. He managed to damage one of the Ca 133s.

A pair of Gladiators of 94 Squadron was brought up to a temporary landing strip at Laferug so that they could provide closer support against the Italian columns moving into British Somaliland. The Italians were content to consolidate their positions around Hargeisa on 5 August. They now needed to know precisely where British forces were lying in wait for them. Consequently, reconnaissance missions were flown by Ro.37bis belonging to 110 *Squadriglia*. Meanwhile, S.79s hit Berbera, Zeila, Burao and Aden. The Italians also moved more S.79s and Ca 133s closer to the new front.

The airstrips in British Somaliland were very vulnerable. The only anti-aircraft defences were based around Berbera, and the other strip at Laferug could easily be compromised. The British were perfectly well aware that they would find it difficult to provide fighter support to the bombers out of Aden, or to give the ground forces valuable air cover. As if to prove the point, when Blenheims of 8 Squadron attacked Italian columns to the west of Hargeisa, Plt Off Felstead and his crew were lost when they were pounced on by a CR.32 flown by *Sottotenente* Folcherio (410 *Squadriglia*).

During 6 and 7 August the Italians failed to make any further advance into British Somaliland. The road out of Hargeisa was covered by British strongpoints, and they would have to move across country in order to make any progress. On 6 August the Blenheims of 8 Squadron and 39 Squadron continued to harass the Italians. Again the Blenheims came up against CR.42s.

Elsewhere, British bombers operating out of the Sudan struck at the submarine base at Massawa, and they badly damaged an Italian torpedo boat, *Acerbi*, killing fifteen and wounding several more. The bulk of the Italian casualties were caused when an anti-aircraft gun exploded. To the south, a pair of Ca 133s of 9 *Squadriglia*, operating out of Baidoa, hit the airfields at Wajir and Harbow.

The Italians were determined to seize control of the air over British Somaliland, and as a consequence they moved up more CR.32s and CR.42s. Unable to reinforce British Somaliland, nine Gladiators belonging to 1 SAAF Squadron were brought down from Egypt. Instead of being flown south into Kenya or east to Somaliland, they were retained at Khartoum in case of increased Italian activity.

The Italian columns resumed their advance on 8 August. They immediately ran into a delaying company of the North Rhodesian Regiment. But there was worse news for British Somaliland: at 0600 at Berbera a pair of CR.32s and a CR.42 caught two Gladiators belonging to 94 Squadron on the ground. The CR.32 of *Capitano* Ricci wrecked one of the Gladiators, setting it alight. Attacks by *Sergente Maggiore* Tellurio and *Sottotenente* Komienz smashed the second Gladiator, burning off its tail. It was now clear that British aircraft remaining in British Somaliland were too vulnerable, and as a consequence the pair that had been brought up to Laferug were ordered to fly to Aden.

At the very least, the British had to contest the skies over Berbera, and at around midday Blenheims belonging to 203 Squadron encountered three S.79s that were bombing the port. One of the Blenheim IVFs, flown by Plt Off Corbould, shot up one of the S.79s and killed one of the crew. The Italian aircraft managed to limp home. The Godojere Pass was attacked by three S.81s. Two more S.79s attacked Berbera. Three Ca 133s struck the Karim Pass. Italian fighters were overhead, searching for targets. A small consolation was the action of four Ju86s belonging to 12 SAAF Squadron. They hit Neghelli airfield and destroyed one Ca 133 and damaged two others.

The Italians were under enormous pressure, from both Rome and Addis Ababa, to press on. But in their defence the force commanded by *Generale* Carlo De Simone was trying to push forward an enormous number of men and equipment for 165 miles from the closest railhead at Diredawa. He was linked to Diredawa by a single, disintegrating road. He was perfectly aware that the British were digging in about fifty miles ahead of him, at Tug Argan. He had already won air superiority and knew that any British air cover had to come from Aden, around 200 miles away. As soon as he was ready he could now push on and close with the British defences at Tug Argan.

In preparation for the attack, Italian aircraft struck at Berbera airfield to make it totally untenable. They shot up a crash-landed Blenheim, but were greeted by anti-aircraft fire from both ground units and from the Australian cruiser, HMAS *Hobart*.

There was little chance that the four battalions holding the Tug Argan positions (Black Hill, Knobbly Hill, Mill Hill and Observation Hill) could hold out against the massive strength of De Simone's Italian force. One of the Italian columns had already reached the coast, but progress was held up by cruisers of the Royal Navy and British aircraft flying out of Aden. The Italians moved up even more aircraft. CR.42s and CR.32s were flown into Hargeisa and aircraft from Addis Ababa moved up to Diredawa.

But the Italians were not getting everything their own way. Three of 8 Squadron's Blenheims made dive-bombing attacks on Italian positions in the Tug Argan area. They were met by CR.42s, but this did not dissuade the British. They returned again, this time to dive-bomb Dubato. Tragically, on the return flight, two of the three Blenheims in this last attack collided with one another. Plt Off A.G. Curtis and Plt Off A.J.G. Bisson were lost.

The main Italian ground attacks came in on 11 August against Tug Argan. Initially some of the outer positions were lost, but they were regained by determined counter-attacks. Italian troops were infiltrating around the flanks of the position.

Six Ca 133s and three S.81s attacked British positions in the Godojere Pass. British bren-gunners managed to shoot down one of the S.81s. The Italians launched three CR.32s against the Black Watch positions and a fuel dump at Laferug. Later an S.79 bombed the battalion headquarters.

Plt Off Rowbotham of 39 Squadron took off at dawn from Aden on 12 August, along with Flt Lt Smith of 11 Squadron. Their target was the Darboruk area. Smith's aircraft was attacked by a CR.42. He managed to nurse his badly damaged aircraft back to Aden.

Rowbotham was not so fortunate: he drew the attention of two CR.42s, and his aircraft was so badly damaged that he had to crash-land at Berbera. Unperturbed, 39 Squadron launched three more Blenheims against the same target. *Sottotenente* Alberto Veronese (410 *Squadriglia*) in a CR.32 attacked the lead Blenheim. Reacting rapidly, the third Blenheim, flown by Flt Sgt Thomas, dropped his bombs and attacked the Italian aircraft. The two protagonists flew straight at one another, firing. Thomas's observer was killed and Thomas himself took a bullet in the shoulder. In desperate pain he managed to nurse the aircraft to Berbera, where he crash-landed. Thomas was awarded the Distinguished Flying Medal. He could have drawn some consolation from the fact that he had also wounded Veronese.

While Thomas was engaged with Veronese, three S.79s were bombing Berbera airfield. A single Blenheim IVF (203 Squadron) was covering the landing ground. The Blenheim chased off the three Italian bombers, but a lucky shot wounded the pilot and the observer.

The Italians concentrated most of their activity on 12 August around Laferug and Mandera, with six Ca 133s making attacks. The Italians set up a new *Comando de Gruppo Tattico* at Yavello and moved 65 *Squadriglia* from Neghelli. They were clearly considering further offensive action against Kenya. Kenya had received fifteen Fairey Battles for 11 SAAF Squadron, having been flown up from South Africa.

Although the Italian assaults on 12 August had been fairly aggressive, only Mill Hill had been captured. On the night of 12 August the 2nd King's African Rifles had been forced out of Mirgo Pass. The road to Berbera was open.

Although Italian attacks were not as aggressive on 13 August, there were further attacks. Throughout 13 August Ca 133s and CR.32s launched attacks on the ground units. More Italian aircraft were moved up, and it became obvious that unless the British troops began to withdraw then they would be outflanked and cut off from Berbera.

Four of the Fairey Battles that had come up to Kenya launched a mission against Jimma. They ran into heavy anti-aircraft fire and some CR.32s. The Fairey Battle flown by Capt J. De Wet was hit by an anti-aircraft shell and by a CR.32. He crash-landed at Lokitaung, writing the aircraft off.

On 14 August three S.81s and three Ca 133s attacked British troops retreating towards Berbera and a fort near the Godojere Pass. Vehicles were strafed on the road to Berbera by three CR.32s, and S.79s attacked vessels off Bulhar. In the south, three Ca 133s operating out of Baidoa attacked Wajir. A Gladiator flown by Lt A. Colenbrander (1 SAAF Squadron) damaged one of the Ca 133s.

The British began to withdraw from the Tug Argan positions on the night of 15 August. The withdrawal was covered by the Black Watch and a pair of companies of the 2nd King's African Rifles. This was just thirty-five miles from Berbera. Italian forces had overrun an outpost on the road to Laferug and had taken prisoners. Ca 133s bombed Laferug, S.81s Mandera and S.79s Berbera. The British were desperately trying to provide air cover, and ordered six Blenheim Is of 84 Squadron (Iraq) to be flown to Port Sudan and then on to Aden. The aircraft were over Kamaran on the morning of 15 August when they saw an S.81. The six Blenheims swooped down to attack, led by Flt Lt Cattell. The S.81 attempted to escape but its starboard wing caught fire and then it folded back and broke up. Then the tailplane fell off and the S.81 went straight into the sea. Two of the crew managed to get out before it hit the water. The Blenheims then flew on to Aden.

In effect the bulk of British troops in British Somaliland had withdrawn to Berbera by 16 August, and the evacuation had begun. This now meant that the Italians were determined to stop the British forces from slipping away, so they concentrated on the shipping in the port. At dawn a pair of S.81s came in over the port, but both of them were hit by anti-aircraft fire. At noon two S.79s appeared and one was hit by anti-aircraft fire. Later in the afternoon three S.79s came in but were intercepted by a pair of Martin 167Fs (8 Squadron). It is believed that Flt Lt Ritoux-Lachaud shot one of them down. Another S.79, flown by *Sottotenente* Luigi Conti, was shot down, but this may have been the one claimed by the Martin pilot. More Italian aircraft moved up from Addis Ababa to Diredawa, in the shape of two S.79s, three CR.32s and three S.81s.

The desperate struggle for British Somaliland continued into 17 August. Five Ca 133s and a pair of CR.32s attacked Berbera, while five Blenheims hit the Italian airfield at Hargeisa. A Blenheim belonging to 39 Squadron was hit by anti-aircraft fire over Zeila. The pilot managed to ditch the aircraft into the sea, and he and his crew were picked up by HMS *Ceres*.

All white civilians, Abyssinian refugees, many of the police and the Camel Corps had already been embarked from Berbera bound for Aden. The struggle for British Somaliland was coming to an end. Yet still the British resisted. At 0535 on 18 August three Blenheims of 11 Squadron attacked Italian columns near Laferug. They were intercepted by a pair of CR.32s flown by *Sottotenente* Veronese and *Sergente Maggiore* Volpe (410 *Squadriglia*). Sgt Gay's Blenheim was shot down by Verones to the north-west of Laferug. Meanwhile five Wellesleys of 223 Squadron struck Addis Ababa. They encountered anti-aircraft fire and a single CR.42. The CR.42 hit four of the Wellesleys, but the attack was a successful one, as they had destroyed three Ca 133s, one S.79 and one S.75, and damaged two other aircraft. Berbera still came under Italian attack, even though the Italians were literally knocking at Berbera's door.

As dawn broke on 19 August the evacuation was complete. Some 7,000 men had been extracted from British Somaliland. The very last raid by the Italians was launched by three S.79s, but the Italian columns were still under attack from aircraft flown out of Aden. The Italians had captured British Somaliland. The cost to the British was thirty-eight killed, 102 wounded and 120 missing, most of whom had become prisoners of war. The Italians had lost 465 killed, 1,530 wounded and thirty-four missing. It had been a desperate time, and the RAF aircraft based in Aden had fully played their part in trying to protect the ground forces. In the period 5–19 August they had flown 184 sorties, and they had lost seven aircraft, while ten had been badly damaged. Between 16 and 19 August they had flown seventy-two bombing sorties and mounted thirty-six fighter patrols over Berbera.

With the battle for British Somaliland over, the Italians could now disperse their aircraft once more to present less of a tempting target for the British. Three CR.32s of 411 *Squadriglia* were sent to Addis Ababa, Gura received three S.79s of 10 *Squadriglia*, and three Ca 133s of 52 *Squadriglia* moved to Miesso. The *Comando Tattico Dell Settore Aeronautica Ovest* was disbanded on 26 August.

CHAPTER THREE

Interlude

The British were in a 'lose–lose' situation over British Somaliland. If they had given up the territory without a fight the Italians would simply have claimed that they were too frightened to face the Italian might. By defending it all they managed to achieve was to allow the Italians to boast that they had routed the British back and into their ships. It is far from certain whether substantial reinforcement of British Somaliland would have made any difference at all. Winston Churchill was certainly beside himself with anger, losing British Somaliland at a time when Britain itself was fighting for her life against the *Luftwaffe* during the Battle of Britain. A victory of any kind would have been so valuable to the British cause.

Churchill was certainly determined for action. According to the War Office he thirsted for action, and his head was full of projects that had no attraction for the Chiefs of Staff. He fretted at the delays which were unavoidable in the preparation of modern fighting forces, and he pressed them incessantly to grapple with the enemy.

It was an impossible time for Britain, alone, outnumbered and with shortages in every piece of equipment. Of the twenty-six infantry divisions in Britain at the time, only three had their full complement of field artillery, and fifteen had less than half. There were shortages in anti-tank guns, bren-gun carriers, tanks, mortars and machine-guns; in many cases what the troops had was obsolete, and much had proved to be inadequate in France in 1940. In truth British forces could barely defend themselves at home, let alone launch any major offensive in another part of the world.

Wavell himself had one incomplete armoured division and two infantry divisions to defend Egypt. Churchill would not be dissuaded by such trifling matters. He wanted a seaborne invasion of

Eritrea to be launched, and as early as 27 July he had summoned Lt Gen Marshall-Cornwall, commander of III Corps, and presented him with his plan of attack. III Corps had a pair of inexperienced territorial divisions.

According to a report of the meeting:

> The PM placed his finger on the Italian port of Massawa. 'Now, Marshall-Cornwall,' he said, 'we have command of the sea and air; it is essential for us to capture that port; how would you do it?' I looked hard at the map for a moment and then answered, 'Well, sir, I have never been to Massawa; I have only passed out of sight of it, going down the Red Sea. It is a defended port, protected by coast defence and anti-aircraft batteries. It must be a good 500 miles from Aden, and therefore beyond cover of our fighters. The harbour has a very narrow entrance channel, protected by coral reefs, and this is certain to be mined, making an opposed landing impracticable. I should prefer to wait until General Wavell's offensive against Eritrea develops; he will capture it more easily from the land side.' The PM gave me a withering look, rolled up the map and muttered peevishly, 'You soldiers are all alike; you have no imagination.'

In fact the options were very limited. In order to mount an offensive from Kenya, troops would have to cross 300 miles of desert. From the Sudan there was at least a railway, but there were no troops. Egypt might ultimately provide extra troops, but after mid-September 1940, when the Italians crossed over the frontier into Egypt, there was renewed danger. Wavell was firmly of the opinion that the Italians would make further advances into Egypt in October, possibly co-ordinating these attacks with a thrust into the Sudan from Kassala.

It was hard to see where any reinforcements could be found to send to Maj Gen William Platt, Commander-in-Chief in the Sudan. He had the Sudan Defence Force (mainly for internal order) and three British battalions to protect a border that stretched for 1,200 miles. There were two brigades of Indian troops, known as the 5th Indian Division, in Aden, but Churchill and the Cabinet had earmarked them to be sent to Basra to protect the Iraqi oilfields.

Wavell argued with Churchill and the Cabinet about their deployment, desperate to have them in the Middle East. Churchill and the Cabinet finally relented, and Wavell, rather than taking them for himself in Egypt, directed them to land at Port Sudan. At a stroke Platt now had six more battalions; two field regiments of artillery and a mechanised cavalry regiment. The Sudan could now be protected, but taking the offensive was another matter.

Eritrea was the most obvious target, but it was riddled with disease. Massawa, for example, was believed to be rife with malaria, typhus, meningitis, tropical ulcers, smallpox, worm infections, rabies, typhoid and a host of other diseases. Viruses and bugs would be as much of a challenge to British forces in Eritrea as the Italian garrison.

Churchill was certain of his priorities in East Africa. He said:

The defence of Kenya must rank after the defence of the Soudan. There should be time after the crisis in Egypt and in the Soudan is past to reinforce Kenya by sea and rail before any large Italian expedition can reach the Tana River. We can always reinforce Kenya faster than Italy can pass troops thither from Abyssinia or Italian Somaliland.

In fact Churchill determined to send South African troops to Egypt and the two West African brigades to the Sudan. This would then release the 5th Indian Division for operations in Egypt.

Wavell was keen to ensure that the Eritrean coast posed no threat to shipping in the Red Sea. For now he would concentrate on supporting the rebels in Abyssinia and in launching spoiling attacks from the Sudan and Kenya to tie down the Italian army.

Emperor Haile Selassie arrived in Alexandria on 25 June 1940. His position was somewhat unknown. It was not clear whether the native rebels supported him. Britons who had lived in Abyssinia before the Italian invasion were firmly of the opinion that there was widespread support. Many Abyssinian refugees had now been armed by the British with a variety of weapons from a wide spread of different sources. They were formed into infantry battalions and trained by British and Sudanese officers and NCOs. The idea was that they could be slipped into Abyssinia to operate with the rebels, who had been renamed at Selassie's insistence as Patriots.

The operation was put into action by Brigadier D.A. Sandford. He had been a consul in Addis Ababa in 1914 and had been a Gunner during the First World War and won the Distinguished Service Order and bar. He had then worked for the Sudan Political Service. After that he had become a farmer near Addis Ababa and was close to Haile Selassie. Sandford's operation was called 101 Mission. Haile Selassie was determined to accompany Sandford across the border, but Wavell forbade him to do so. Sandford led the first group across the frontier on 6 August, bound for Mount Belaya. Three weeks later another party left, and shortly afterwards a third party crossed, but this was ambushed and wiped out by Italian irregulars.

With the departure of Sandford, Maj Orde Wingate arrived in Khartoum on 6 November. He had already established something of a reputation. Wingate was often portrayed as melancholy, opinionated, bullying and arrogant. He did not bathe but instead he scrubbed himself with a dry brush and he ate raw onions, but many found him charming. Wingate became the liaison officer to 101 Mission, and because Sandford was already in Abyssinia he was virtually in command. He inspected two new Abyssinian battalions, organised the purchase of 18,000 camels and had many meetings with Haile Selassie. Wingate also flew to visit Sandford, meeting him thirty miles to the south of Lake Tana. Both men believed that Haile Selassie should re-enter Abyssinia at the closest opportunity.

After the fall of British Somaliland air operations continued in all of the theatres adjacent to Italian East Africa. On 20 August five Wellesleys belonging to 223 Squadron bombed Dessie. Less than an hour later four Blenheims of 39 Squadron, accompanied by one from 11 Squadron, hit Diredawa. They damaged an S.81 and a C32. The Blenheims were attacked by a pair of CR.42s from 413 *Squadriglia*. *Capitano* Corrado Santoro managed to shoot down the Blenheim flown by Plt Off Jago. Santoro also managed to hit the 11 Squadron's Blenheim sufficiently to make it crash-land back in Aden.

On 21 August half a dozen Fairey Battles of 11 SAAF Squadron struck Mogadishu. They managed to destroy two Italian aircraft that were under repair and damage four others. They also hit the hangars and wrecked two trucks. Mogadishu was hit again on 24 August. This time the Italians responded by scrambling three Ro.37bis against them, but they were too slow.

Dessie was also hit on 24 August by three Blenheims of 11 Squadron. The Gallabat Fort was attacked by a pair of Vincents and a pair of Gauntlets of 430 Flight. Asmara was attacked on 26 August by five Wellesleys of 223 Squadron. A pair of Italian fighters intercepted them and shot down the Wellesley flown by Plt Off J.C. Smitheram.

Three raids were launched against Mogadishu on 28 August by 11 SAAF Squadron. Once again the Ro.37bis fighter support failed to catch the Fairey Battles. The pilots of the Battles were delighted to report that they had destroyed several hundred trucks, but much later, when Mogadishu fell, the trucks were revealed to be ancient and worn out, and had been dumped there for some years.

Assab naval base was attacked on 1 September 1940. The attack was launched by Blenheims belonging to 8, 11 and 39 Squadrons. They managed to destroy a barracks, a shell store and damage a tug and make good their escape. Sgt Norris, flying a Wellesley of 14 Squadron, was engaged in photo-reconnaissance over Harmil Island. Italian fighters from Massawa pounced on him and shot him down. He landed on the island and he and his crew were taken captive.

There was an encounter between a pair of CR.42s and three Gladiators (1 SAAF Squadron) over Kassala. The Gladiators came out on top; both Maj Van Schalkwyk and Lt J.J. Coetzer managed to shoot down a CR.42.

The Italians responded the following day, on 2 September, when a number of S.79s attacked Aden. These aircraft, operating out of Diredawa, would attack Aden again at noon on 4 September. Other S.79s made an attack on the steamship *Velko* in the Red Sea, and she was quite badly damaged.

To the south, on 3 September, 12 SAAF Squadron launched three Ju86s against Yavello. They caught three Ca 133s on the ground and destroyed them. Unfortunately anti-aircraft fire hit and destroyed the Ju86 flown by Lt R.G. Donaldson. He crashed and there were no survivors.

Five S.79s attacked a shipping convoy in the Red Sea on 5 September. They damaged a Blenheim IVF that was escorting the convoy. The convoy was attacked once again the following day, Sunday 6 September, by a single S.79.

Meanwhile three S.79s struck Aden. Six Gladiators were sent up to intercept and they succeeded in damaging two of them; one managed to land at Adigolla, and the second was clearly damaged enough to hit a tree when it made a landing at Diredawa.

There was a bizarre incident on 7 September. A pair of Gauntlets, each carrying eight 25 lb incendiary bombs, took off with a pair of Vincents to attack Metemma airfield. One of the Vincents did not even make it off the ground, as it hit trees and was badly damaged when the pilot landed again. None the less, the three aircraft were over the target at 1305. They spotted a Ca 133 dropping supplies to the Italians by parachute. Flt Lt A.B. Mitchell attacked, and the Ca 133 dived straight into the ground. Mitchell then regained height and dropped all eight of his bombs on the target, but to no apparent effect.

Mogadishu was attacked once again by the aircraft of 11 SAAF Squadron. They were intent on destroying what remained of the wrecked trucks, but instead they spotted twelve Ca 133s on the ground and homed in on them. They actually managed to damage one of them, which was in fact unserviceable.

On Tuesday 8 September Adjutant M.R. Rowland, piloting a Martin 167F of 8 Squadron (Aden), attacked Moggio airfield. Unfortunately he was attacked by a CR.42 from 413 *Squadriglia* and shot down. The only survivor was Flg Off P.C. Rupert, who was taken prisoner. Port Sudan had been raided on 7 September, and it was attacked again the following day. They concentrated on the airfield. Elsewhere, flying out of Gobwen, three Ca 133s attacked the airfield at Garissa.

On 9 September, 11 SAAF Squadron attacked Shashamanna airfield on two occasions, hoping to destroy a reported fourteen Italian aircraft on the ground. They did destroy one S.81 and damage two more, and also a Ca 133. The Fairey Battle flown by Capt R.A. Blackwell and Air Sgt F.A. Van Zyl was shot down. Dessie was raided by five Blenheims belonging to 11 and 39 Squadrons. Six Blenheims belonging to 45 Squadron were flown in from Egypt to take up station at Summit in the Sudan, and in South Africa Maj L.A. Wilmot began organising 3 SAAF Squadron, which would ultimately see service in Kenya.

British ground forces made limited moves against Kassala in the early hours of 10 September. In support of the ground attack, three

Wellesleys of 14 Squadron bombed the Italian positions. They were attacked by a pair of CR.42s, and Plt Off J.A. Ferguson's aircraft was shot down.

On the morning of 12 September, 12 SAAF Squadron launched four Ju86s against Jimma airfield. A number of Ca 133s were damaged. Shashamanna was attacked by three Fairey Battles of 11 SAAF Squadron, and they destroyed an S.81 and damaged another. Unfortunately, four CR.32s were already aloft as the attack came in, and the Battle flown by Lt E.G. Armstrong was shot down. The South Africans lost another aircraft in the operation: the Battle flown by Lt J.E. Lindsay, Air Sgt L.A. Feinberg and Air Gunner V.P. McVickar was attacked by a CR.32 flown by *Maresciallo* Gobbo (411 *Squadriglia*). The Battle hit the ground, killing a local villager, and then burst into flames. The crew managed to get out, but they were captured by Italian troops.

The newly arrived Blenheims at Summit launched their first operation on 14 September. They made raids on Asmara and Gura. The Italians, meanwhile, launched three Ca 133s from Jimma against a fort at Boma. Gura was again attacked on 16 September, this time by Wellesleys of 223 Squadron. The aircraft flown by Plt Off Walker failed to return to base, and its fate was unknown.

On 18 September, with 40 SAAF Squadron in place in Kenya, 237 Squadron shifted to Khartoum. The following day five S.79s attacked a British convoy in the Red Sea, where a pair of Gladiators of 94 Squadron failed to catch them. Massawa was attacked on 20 September by three new Blenheim IVs of 14 Squadron. One of the aircraft was hit by anti-aircraft fire and it had to make a forced landing; the crew was captured.

Flt Lt Mitchell of 430 Flight and three pilots of 1 SAAF Squadron attacked the Tessenei landing ground on Sunday 20 September. Again, the Italians tried to attack the convoy in the Red Sea, but they were intercepted by escorting Blenheims.

The Italians were by now frustrated by the continued attacks by the Fairey Battles against their positions in Mogadishu and Shashamanna, and moved aircraft up to attack Archer's Post, 11 SAAF Squadron's base. Raids were carried out against Aden by day and by night on 22 September. S.79s returned again on September 24, but no appreciable damage was caused.

The rest of 45 Squadron arrived in the Sudan from Egypt on 25 September. They had already launched three Blenheims against Gura and Mai Edaga. The squadron was ready for operations by 27 September, and three of its aircraft attacked Assab. On Wednesday 30 September three more Blenheims attacked Gura, but they were pounced on by CR.32s and CR.42s. In the ensuing air battle the Blenheim flown by Flt Lt G.J. Bush was shot down. It is believed that he had fallen victim to *Tenente* Visintini of 412 *Squadriglia*.

An S.79 attacked Aden on 30 September. It was intercepted by two Gladiators of 94 Squadron. The Gladiators believed that they had shot it down, but in fact it had escaped. The two remaining flights of 1 SAAF Squadron in Kenya became 2 SAAF Squadron.

Six CR.42s of 412 *Squadriglia* intercepted three inbound Blenheims of 45 Squadron at dawn on 2 October. The Blenheims' target was Gura. The CR.42s picked on the lead Blenheim, flown by Sqn Ldr J.W. Dallamore. Dallamore's Blenheim quickly burst into flames and he jettisoned his bombs and ordered the air gunner to bale out. Dallamore wrestled with the aircraft to give the navigator time to bale out too. By this time the aircraft had dropped so low that Dallamore could not get out in time, and he was killed when the aircraft exploded on the ground. The two remaining Blenheims were then chased by the fighters; certainly the CR.42s scored a number of hits on them, but they escaped. Blenheims were also launched against Assab and Afmadu on the same day.

On Sunday 4 October three CR.42s were spotted over Metemma. Three Gladiators were scrambled to intercept them. One of the CR.42s was shot down by Lt S. De K. Viljoen, and the pilot was seen to bale out. Capt Boyle, despite his aircraft having suffered damage, caused significant problems for another one of the CR.42s, and it is likely that this aircraft was made to force-land. To the south, Fairey Battles of 11 SAAF Squadron dropped propaganda leaflets over Yavello.

On Monday 5 October three Wellesleys of 47 Squadron accompanied a pair of Gauntlets of 430 Flight, flown by Flt Lt Mitchell and Plt Off A.N. Johnstone. Their target was the fort at Gallabat.

For the next ten days there was very little air activity. The Italians shifted a number of aircraft from Yavello to Addis Ababa, and on 12 October some Wellesleys of 47 Squadron moved up to Gedaref.

Gura was the target of 45 Squadron's Blenheims once again on 13 October. Three Blenheims were launched, but one had to turn back due to engine problems. The two others, one flown by Flg Off G.C.B. Woodroofe, and the other by Plt Off G.A. Cockayne, were both shot down by CR.42s of 412 *Squadriglia*. Both aircraft were lost, with all their crew members. Over Aden three Gladiators of 94 Squadron were scrambled to intercept a single S.79. Flg Off Haywood managed to damage the bomber and kill two of the crew.

At around noon on 14 October three Fairey Battles attacked Jimma airfield. The Battles were followed by a fourth aircraft to take photographs of the damage. A pair of CR.32s managed to cause minimal damage to one of the Battles. On the night of 14 October major raids were launched against Diredawa. The British claimed to have damaged a pair of S.79s and S.81s and a Ca 133. This did not prevent the Italians of 6 *Squadriglia* at Diredawa from launching an offensive operation of their own the following day, when they struck against a convoy moving up the Red Sea. Three S.79s were involved in the attack. They were intercepted by a pair of Gladiators and a Blenheim.

An unfortunate incident occurred on Friday 16 October when Flt Lt Mitchell of 430 Flight, in a Vincent out of Gedaref, attacked Tessenei airfield. After his mission he was followed home by a Ca 133. The Italians now knew where the new landing-field was based, and at 0525 *Generale* Piacentini on board an S.79 led nine of 412 *Squadriglia*'s CR.42s to hit the new British base. The CR.42s managed to destroy eight of 47 Squadron's Wellesleys – all they had – and also two of 430 Flight's Vincents.

Two days later, on 18 October, 1 SAAF Squadron sent three Gladiators, flown by Capt Boyle, Lt Duncan and Lt Pare, to attack Barentu airfield. They were making a low-level attack when they spotted three CR.42s belonging to 412 *Squadriglia* lifting off. They also noted an S.79 and five Ca 133s parked in the open. The Gladiators set all three of the CR.42s alight and then shot up the bombers. According to Italian records none of the aircraft were written off.

Another convoy was approaching the Red Sea on 20 October, and the Italians made a number of individual attacks with S.79s. Garissa airfield was attacked by three Ca 133s operating out of Gobwen later on in the day. Only one Fury of 2 SAAF Squadron managed to lift off in time to intercept. It was flown by Lt H.J. Burger, the commander of the squadron's H Detachment. He attacked one of the Ca 133s and managed to damage it sufficiently to make it force-land. The crew set fire to their aircraft shortly before being captured.

Five Blenheims flew in from Aden to bomb Alomata. The Blenheims were intercepted by a CR.32 flown by *Sergente Maggiore* Ugo Zoino of 411 *Squadriglia*. As Zoino manoeuvred to open fire, he pressed the firing button and one of his explosive shells detonated. The explosion punctured his oil tank and covered him with hot oil. Zoino tried to disengage and realised that he could not land, as the airfield was being plastered with bombs. He then spotted one of 8 Squadron's Blenheims and tried to work around it and open fire with his other gun. The gun jammed, so he attempted to chop at the tail of the Blenheim with his propeller. At this point his goggles fell off and his eyes were smothered in oil: he was virtually blind. He broke off and headed to land, but as he did so the Blenheims shot at him. He leapt out of the aircraft and hid in a ditch. With 8 Squadron gone he tried to get his CR.32 into safety, but another two Blenheims arrived and he once again had to hide. Miraculously neither he nor his aircraft suffered any further damage.

On 22 October the Italian Air Force was told that henceforth there would be strict fuel rationing. Ground movement of supplies and ammunition would now be horse drawn.

Nine Hurricane Is arrived in Kenya on Saturday 24 October. The new 3 SAAF Squadron was to be deployed on a number of airstrips from the frontier down to Mombasa. This would allow Gladiators of 2 SAAF Squadron to be moved up to the Sudan. There was immediate work, however, for the newly arrived Hurricanes. Flt Lt R.S. Blake and Lt D.H. Loftus (2 SAAF Squadron) borrowed a pair of 3 SAAF Squadron's Hurricanes and flew them up to Lokitaung, near Lake Rudolph on the border between Kenya, Abyssinia and the Sudan. Intelligence suggested that there would be a major raid against Lokitaung. The reports were correct, as on Sunday 25 October three S.81s out of Yavello approached the target. The aircraft were flown by *Capitano* Tito Zucconi, *Sottotenente* Argento and *Sottotenente* Titi. Their target was in fact Lodwar. They were actually hunting for Hurricanes, having received their own intelligence reports that these new aircraft had arrived in the area. Blake and Loftus scrambled as soon as the S.81s were spotted. Blake shot down Argento's S.81. Only one of the crew managed to survive the crash. Loftus attacked Titi's S.81 and he knocked out two of the engines and smashed up the instrument panel. Titi jettisoned his bombs and tried to make a forced landing in a dried-up river-bed at Lokitaung. Titi managed to land his aircraft and set fire to it, and then tried to make good his escape, but he was captured by British police. Meanwhile Blake had closed in on Zucconi's S.81. He shot it up and believed that he had shot it down, but this was not the case, and it managed to get home. Three more Italian aircraft, this time S.79s operating out of Gobwen, bombed Port Reitz on the same day.

By late October 47 and 223 Squadrons had begun receiving 14 Squadron's Wellesleys, that squadron now being supplied with Blenheim IVs. There was an unfortunate incident on 26 October. A Gladiator spotted what it believed to be an S.79, but it was in fact one of the new Blenheims. The Gladiator pilot shot up the Blenheim and wounded the pilot in the arm. The Blenheim was subsequently written off. The new Blenheims hit Massawa on 30 October in a raid led by Flt Lt J.K. Buchanan.

On the last day of October 1940 the Italians launched an audacious raid into the Sudan. They were bound for Rosières. The expedition was led by *Colonnello* Rolle, who was at the head of 1,500 men in some ninety trucks. The attack was quickly dealt with by the Sudan Defence Force and air attacks by Wellesleys and Vincents, covered by Gladiators of 1 SAAF Squadron. Around ten of the lorries were destroyed.

There was near-disaster in Kenya on that Saturday when Gen Cunningham, accompanied by Air Cdre Sowrey and Gen Jan Smuts, the South African Prime Minister, were nearly shot down. The visiting dignitaries were being given a tour of inspection on board a pair of Ju86s and a Rapide. They were escorted by two Hurricanes. The convoy was *en route* to Nanyuki, and passed over Archer's Post and failed to use the correct recognition signal (waggling wings and lowering undercarriage). No. 2 SAAF Squadron's detachment at Archer's Post mistakenly believed that the aircraft were Italian, and launched three Furies to intercept. The leading Ju86 was hit several times before the attack was called off.

CHAPTER FOUR

The Northern Front

On 1 November 1940 Lt Gen A. Cunningham assumed command in Kenya from Lt Gen D.P. Dickinson. Wavell had laid out general policies. As far as Lt Gen W. Platt in the Sudan was concerned, he was:

> To prepare an operation for the recapture of Kassala, which had been occupied by the enemy soon after the outbreak of war with Italy, to be carried out in early 1941 if the necessary reinforcements could be made available from Egypt; this depended mainly on the success of the desert offensive. To maintain pressure in the Gallabat area. To further the rebellion in Abyssinia by all possible means.

As far as Cunningham was concerned:

> In the south to advance to the frontier on the line Kolbio–Dif as soon as possible. On the northern frontier west of Moyale to maintain pressure on the enemy by means of small mobile columns. In May or June, after the rainy period, to advance on Kismayu; I had hoped for an advance on Kismayu before the rainy season but General Cunningham at this meeting informed me that after careful examination he did not consider it possible owing to water difficulties and the lack of sufficient transport. In the spring and summer of 1941 to penetrate into Abyssinia in conjunction with operations from the Boma area of the Sudan.

Platt had assessed the situation in December 1940 for the prospects of offensive action from the Sudan. He proposed to prepare for the capture of Kassala by February 1941, to maintain pressure on Gallabat but not to attempt any large-scale operations. He would also support rebellion within Abyssinia by any means at his disposal.

On Sunday 1 November 1940 three Gladiators belonging to 1 SAAF Squadron were escorting some Gauntlets of 430 Flight on a mission to bomb Italian troops and transports in the north. They spotted Ca 133s bombing British troops around Gallabat. One of the Gladiators, flown by Lt R. Pare, made an attack and shot up one of the Ca 133s. The rest of the Gladiators and Gauntlets moved onto their target and came under heavy anti-aircraft fire. They all managed, however, to return safely to Azzoza. By this time the whole of 1 SAAF Squadron was based at Azzoza, and a few days later three more Gladiators of K Flight also arrived there.

Five Gladiators attacked a single S.79 over Noggara at 0930 on 2 November. The Italians were later to claim that they shot down one of the Gladiators, although British records do not substantiate this claim.

The British were gearing up now to launch an offensive against Gallabat Fort. They had mustered some twenty-seven aircraft, and against them in the air alone were thirty-two bombers and seventeen fighters. The ground attack was to be launched by Brigadier W.G. Slim's 10th Indian Infantry Brigade Group. His force would be supported by half a dozen light tanks and six cruiser tanks. Slim's troops were moving up to their start positions and were due to launch their assault at dawn on 5 November.

Local air superiority was vital, and early in the morning of 4 November over Metemma three Gladiators of 1 SAAF Squadron engaged four CR.42s of 412 *Squadriglia*. Lt L. Le C. Theron, Capt Boyle and Lt A. Duncan all claimed a kill, although it was likely that only Theron's claim was correct.

An S.79 tried its luck against a convoy in the Red Sea when it was attacked by a Blenheim of 203 Squadron. The Blenheim's pilot, Flt Lt Pike, shot up the S.79 and it fled home. Two of the crew were killed.

Neghelli was plastered with bombs and then covered in leaflets by Fairey Battles of 11 SAAF Squadron. The Battle, flown by Lt B.L. Hutchinson, was shot down by anti-aircraft fire. The crew managed to get out and set fire to the aircraft, but by this time a number of local villagers had arrived and the bombs still on board detonated and killed twenty of them.

The first major offensive of the Second World War by the British was soon to be under way, but the Italians had not been idle. They had considerably strengthened the little stone and mud fort at Gallabat; they had surrounded it with walls of logs and stones and a thorn hedge (Zariba). The ground around the fort had been cleared to give good fields of fire. The small frontier post of Metemma had also been fortified and manned with troops from the 4th Colonial Brigade. The local Italians were split between Gallabat and Metemma. The commander, *Tenente Colonnello* Castagnola, had placed one of his battalions in the old British fort and the rest of his troops back at Metemma.

The Italians had mortars, anti-tank guns and rifles and a mix of artillery. At its full strength it was broadly equivalent to the brigade group that Slim would be launching against it.

Slim had one Baluchi battalion, one Garhwali battalion and the 1st Essex, which had replaced the original Punjabi battalion. In addition to the twelve tanks of the Royal Tank Regiment, he had the 28th Field Regiment of the Royal Artillery. His troops were in position by midnight on 5 November, ready to launch their pre-dawn attack.

Throughout the night Italian sentries fired Very lights, but it seemed that the Italians were largely unaware of the build-up. At 0530 Wellesleys and Vincents began dropping bombs on the fort and on the radio station. Shortly afterwards the Royal Artillery opened up, and while the bombers were still making their attack runs three Gladiators of K Flight appeared overhead to patrol over the heads of the advancing British troops.

The Italians did respond quickly. Around six or seven CR.42s of 412 *Squadriglia*, led by their commander, *Capitano* Raffi, appeared out of the sun and attacked the Gladiators. Flt Lt Savage was shot down, Plt Off Kirk's aircraft was badly damaged and he had to bale out, and Plt Off Hamlyn was also hit, and he had to make a forced landing.

Shortly afterwards the bombardment of Gallabat lifted and shifted to Metemma. Indian infantry scrambled through the gaps ripped in the barbed wire by the tanks, and by 0730 Gallabat had been captured.

Rocks and mines had put five of the six British cruiser tanks out of action, and four of the six light tanks needed repair. This now meant that the attack on Metemma could only be led by one cruiser and two light tanks. It would take at least four hours after the repair troops arrived to get the tanks back into action. The momentum of the assault was being lost.

Overhead Maj Van Schalkwyk (1 SAAF Squadron) had lifted off from Azzoza. He arrived over Gallabat and was pounced on by CR.42s. It was eight against one, and Capt Boyle immediately lifted off in his Gladiator to assist him. Unfortunately he was too late, and his commanding officer was shot down and killed. Boyle was now involved in a life-or-death struggle himself, and he too was shot down and crash-landed. He was later to be awarded the Distinguished Flying Cross.

So far the British had lost five Gladiators for no return. Gallabat ridge had been taken, but now Italian aircraft were appearing over the battlefield in increasing numbers. Wave after wave of Ca 133s attacked the ground troops, who had no air cover and nowhere to hide.

There was more action in the air at midday. A Gladiator of K Flight linked up with four from 1 SAAF Squadron and pounced on five Ca 133s. Just as they came in to attack, the Gladiators were attacked by six CR.42s. Flg Off Haywood (not G.S.K. Haywood of 94 Squadron) was shot down. The other Gladiators responded quickly; Lt Duncan and Lt J.L. Hewitson chased the Ca 133s, while Lt Pare and Lt Coetzer held off the fighters. Duncan shot up one of the Ca 133s, and he saw it crash onto the road leading to Gondar. The Ca 133 that Hewitson attacked also lost control and crashed into the ground. Meanwhile, Pare and Coetzer had succeeded in holding off the CR.42s, and had in fact driven them away.

Throughout the evening and into the following morning the British positions were under continual attack from Ca 133s. The Italian bombing was precise and caused a number of casualties. Slim knew he had to try to take Metemma, as this was the route into Abyssinia.

Throughout the day on 7 November the Royal Artillery bombarded the Italian positions. They managed to destroy a petrol dump, but the Italian Air Force, with outstanding performance, was making the area around Gallabat untenable. In fact the day had again not been good over the battlefield. Five Wellesleys of 47 Squadron, accompanied by four Gladiators, had come to provide some assistance. They chased off four CR.42s, but the Gladiator flown by Lt R. Pare, having managed to shoot down one of the CR.42s, was then attacked by four more. He dived down to escape, but his aircraft's engine seized and he had to force-land. While the Gladiators chased off the first four CR.42s, five Ca 133s and five S.81s attacked the ground forces.

It was decided that rather than continue to be pummelled by the Italian Air Force, the attack would be terminated, and in fact Slim would pull back to his start positions. In all the British had lost 168 men, but the Italians had lost 428. Castagnola reported to his commander, *Generale* Martini, in Gondar that he could not hold for much longer, not knowing that the British planned to withdraw. The operation had failed to open the road into Abyssinia.

The British were determined, even though they were evacuating Gallabat, that the Italians should not reoccupy it, and that if they tried they would suffer heavy casualties. Slim set up a semicircle of troops and sent patrols to probe the Italian lines.

On 9 November the Baluchi battalion reoccupied the fort, withdrawing at nightfall and then returning the following morning. The Italians had attacked the fort when the Baluchis were not there, and instead had been punished by the Royal Artillery. As the new front settled down, the ground troops got used to the noise of Ca 133s, and would scramble for cover on hearing it.

Further to the north, from 5 November, the 12th Frontier Force Regiment had been attacking Italian positions at Tehamiyan Wells, close to Kassala. It had managed to take the position by the afternoon, and on 6 November it moved up to tackle the main Italian defence line in the area. There was no RAF air cover and consequently the regiment was set upon on at least three occasions by CR.42s escorting Ca 133s. As a result of the air cover and the tenacious defence of the Italians, the British fell back.

Air Cdre Slatter flew down on 7 November to take control of the air operations over the front. K Flight's five remaining Gladiators flew into Azzoza. Four of the five accompanied three Gladiators of 1 SAAF Squadron on patrol the following day. A modicum of air cover had now been established. On 9 November, 2 SAAF Squadron gave up three of its Gladiators from Kenya to 1 SAAF Squadron. There was a near-disaster. The three Gladiators were accompanied by a Lodestar transporter, in which the pilots were due to fly back to Kenya. As the aircraft came in to land, Sudanese Home Guards opened up and wrecked the Gladiator flown by Lt Dimmock.

Air operations began to slacken, but on 11 November there was an aerial tussle between Gladiators of 1 SAAF Squadron and CR.42s of 412 *Squadriglia*. This was 1 SAAF's last action, as they were posted back to Khartoum on 13 November.

The British went back on the air offensive on 14 November, launching three Blenheim Is of 8 Squadron against Diredawa. As the aircraft came in to attack, the one flown by Plt Off Young was hit by anti-aircraft fire. He made a forced landing on the Arabian coast.

On Sunday 15 November Plt Off Wolsey (K Flight) scrambled to intercept a pair of S.79s attacking Port Sudan. He riddled both of the bombers with hits but they both managed to escape.

Flt Lt Buchanan DFC (14 Squadron) flying a Blenheim IV attacked Gura at around midday on 16 November. He had just dropped his bombs when he was attacked by three Italian fighters. He lost them in the clouds and then circled round to check to see where his bombs had fallen before he returned to base.

No. 237 Squadron was now deployed with its Hawker Hardies to support action around Gallabat. Plt Off Campbell, attacking Italian positions at Metemma, was hit by ground fire and he crashed into woodland. No. 223 Squadron lost a Wellesley to anti-aircraft fire over Massawa, and to the south a Battle flown by Lt Van Vliet was shot down over Callam, near Lake Rudolph in Kenya, by anti-aircraft fire. The pilot force-landed, set fire to the aircraft and then escaped enemy patrols and linked up with elements of the King's African Rifles.

There was an interesting diversion in tactics on 18 November. The cruiser, HMS *Dorsetshire*, launched a Walrus flying-boat against targets in Massawa. It bombed the area with little effect. The following day a Ca 133 was shot down, presumably by ground fire, over Gedaref.

A pair of CR.42s of 412 *Squadriglia* attacked a Blenheim belonging to 45 Squadron over Keren. They riddled the Blenheim with shots and wounded the pilot, Sqn Ldr Ray. No. 203 Squadron lost a Blenheim on 19 November. The aircraft, on escort patrol, crashed into the Red Sea and its crew were killed. That night and on 20 November S.81s attacked Aden.

In the early hours of Friday 20 November the S.81 flown by the Diredawa base commander, *Colonnello* Francesco Via, was attacked at 0430 by a Gladiator of 94 Squadron, flown by Sqn Ldr Wightman. Wightman shot down the bomber, and Via and two other crew members were taken prisoner by the Royal Navy.

Port Sudan was attacked by a pair of S.79s on the afternoon of 21 November. A pair of Gladiators belonging to K Flight scrambled to intercept, while the Royal Navy cruiser, HMS *Carlisle*, provided anti-aircraft support. The Gladiators, flown by Flg Off Green and Plt Off Smither, shot at both of the bombers. One of the S.79s was so badly hit that it was thought it had to force-land at Karet. The report that it had force-landed there was wrong, as when 14 Squadron sent Blenheim IVs to finish it off it was not there. It had actually managed to get back to base.

Flying over Italian Somaliland in a Fairey Battle, Capt D.W.J. Allam (11 SAAF Squadron) was attacked by two CR.42s scrambled out of Kismayu. His aircraft was hit several times and he crash-landed, set fire to his aircraft and was then taken prisoner. Interestingly, when he was released in April 1941 he could report that the South African aircraft had actually been attacking dummy aircraft at Shashamanna and that the real aircraft were hidden.

On the same day, 22 November, three Hurricanes of 3 SAAF Squadron intercepted three Ca 133s that were attacking Bura. The lead Ca 133 was shot down by Lt Allen. One of the other Ca 133s had been so badly shot up by both 2/Lt Glover and 2/Lt Kershaw that it crash-landed on the border with Italian Somaliland. The crew tried to head back to their base, but they were captured by an African patrol and made prisoner.

The Italians had received considerable aircraft reinforcement. S.79s had been flown in from Libya. This meant that 14 *Squadriglia* were now equipped with S.79s, passing its S.81s over to 15 *Squadriglia*. There was also considerable change in the Sudan. No. 8 Squadron's sixteen Vincents were handed over to a special general-purpose flight based at Khormaksar. No. 8 Squadron, for the moment, retained its Blenheim Is and Swordfish. Nos 11 and 39

Squadrons were ordered to Egypt, as they would be needed for the British offensive in the Western Desert.

There was an exciting rescue for Flg Off Mackenzie and Sqn Ldr Selway on 26 November. Six Blenheim IVs of 14 Squadron were tasked with a raid on Nefasit, but as they approached Dessie Island they were attacked by three Italian fighters. The bombers tried to slip away by heading out to sea, but Mackenzie's Blenheim was hit. The rest of the Blenheims outpaced the fighters and bombed the island of Sheik El Abu, which was an Italian listening-post. Selway, having jettisoned his bombs, swung round to find Mackenzie. The latter had force-landed, but Selway landed alongside him, took the crew on board and flew them home.

A Hardy flown by Flg Off P. Holden Garde, accompanied by Sgt A.P. Burl of 237 Squadron, was over Metemma on 27 November when it was ambushed by a pair of CR.42s of 412 *Squadriglia*. In the attack Burl was killed, but Holden Garde nursed the aircraft until he reached Guriangana, and managed to force-land.

The Royal Navy sent another Walrus to attack Italian positions on the coast of the Red Sea on 29 November. The Walrus bombed what it believed to be a military installation, and then the cruiser finished it off with its shells. But all they had managed to destroy was a fish-tinning plant. Three CR.42s attacked Gedaref on 30 November, and they believed that they had destroyed a Wellesley, but in fact it was a dummy aircraft.

An Italian column near Metemma suffered heavy casualties when British bombers attacked it the following day. Other RAF aircraft attacked Kassala.

On 2 December Gladiators flown by South Africans were assigned escort duty for three Hardies of 237 Squadron. They attacked an Italian bomb dump on the Gwanda river, and a number of Italians were killed and wounded.

Two of 14 Squadron's Blenheim IVs set off on 4 December. One of the aircraft mounted a diversionary attack between Agordat and Keren. The other aircraft, flown by Flg Off Rhodes, headed for Mia Atal and Ghinda. Rhodes's aircraft ran into CR.42s of 412 *Squadriglia*, and they managed to shoot the Blenheim down.

There was a rescue mission in motion on 5 December. Three Fairey Battles of 11 Squadron were dispatched to try to find a Ju86 of

12 SAAF Squadron that had gone down to the south of Mega after having been hit by anti-aircraft fire. One of the three Battles crashed and Lt M/ MacDonald and his crew were killed. Some of the Ju86 crew stayed beside the aircraft and were found on 10 December. The body of the pilot, Lt Vermeulen, was discovered later.

A new squadron arrived at Nanyuki which was to become 14 SAAF Squadron. Its initial aircraft were three Martin Maryland Is. The new commanding officer was Maj C.E. Martin DFC. They immediately began training, but there was an early mishap when a Hartebeest landed on top of one of the Marylands just as it was taking off.

On 6 December four of 47 Squadron's Wellesleys were launched to attack enemy positions at Burye. One of the four Wellesleys turned back, but the other three were attacked by some CR.42s. The Italian fighters shot down Plt Off Witty.

In the south, the South African pilots had been warned to prepare to support a forthcoming attack on the Italian frontier at El Wak, and photo-reconnaissance missions were a daily affair. The attack in the south was being made after constant pressure from Churchill, and to a lesser extent from Wavell. Indeed Gen Cunningham had some 77,000 men at his disposal, 27,000 of whom were South African troops (there were another 6,000 South Africans serving in black regiments). In addition there were 33,000 East Africans and 9,000 West Africans. In fact there were more troops than the entire white population of Kenya. The problem was that the Italian frontier posts were so remote and distant from the British supply bases that any attack was going to be incredibly demanding. As it was, the date set for the attack would be 15 December.

Meanwhile, on 11 December, six Battles of 11 SAAF Squadron attacked Yavello. They destroyed three Ca 133s and damaged five others. On the 12th, 412 *Squadriglia* attacked the airstrip at Gaz Regeb. This was the base of B Flight, 237 Squadron. The attack came in led by *Tenente Colonnello* Liberati in an S.79. He was followed by five CR.42s. They caught a number of Hardies parked on the airfield and managed to destroy four of them. One of the CR.42s was hit by fire from the Sudan Defence Force defending the airfield. He headed for home but was forced to land to the east of Aroma. One of his fellow pilots spotted him and flew down and landed alongside. Then, throwing out his parachute, *Tenente* Mario Visintini pulled Rafi, the downed pilot, aboard and they made it home.

Plans were under way for the offensive from the Sudan. The 4th Indian Division was transferred from the Libyan front and embarked for Port Sudan. It was due to arrive on 16 December. Fearful that this convoy would attract the attention of the Italian Air Force, aircraft were shifted from Kenya to cover them. A pair of Hurricanes from 3 SAAF Squadron, flown by Maj L.A. Wilmot and Capt K.W. Driver, flew up to join 1 SAAF Squadron. Wilmot was the commander of 3 SAAF Squadron, and now he took that position with 1 SAAF Squadron.

Operations were also under way for an offensive out of Kenya. The initial ground attack was to be made by the 1st South African Brigade, the 1st South African Light Tank Company and the 24th Gold Coast Brigade. Carefully husbanded air cover consisted of 40 SAAF Squadron's nine Hartebeests, three Ju86s of 12 SAAF Squadron and four Hurricanes of B Flight, 2 SAAF Squadron. The target was El Wak. It was held by three battalions of Italian colonials with some artillery support.

The tiny little Vickers tanks found it difficult to even burst through the barbed-wire entanglements. A Bangalore torpedo was used by 2/Lt Christopher Ballenden (Gold Coast Brigade) to blow a hole in the defences. The light tanks poured through, followed by infantry with fixed bayonets. They found, among other things, an Italian bakery, and inside one of the flour bins was an Italian colonel. The Italian fort and village had been dive-bombed by Junkers Ju86s, and overhead the Hartebeests flew seventeen ground support sorties. The Transvaal Scottish broke around the flank to cut off the retreat road to Bardera. They captured the Italian brigade headquarters of the 191st Colonial Infantry Regiment. Natal Carbineers charged the defences, led by Corporal Frank Foxon, who led the charge with his bren-gun over 150 yards of open bush. As one of the Carbineers said:

> We were into that blazing village, the smoke drifting, the Italian colonial soldiers sprawled in their rifle pits, the ground scarred by our artillery and the deadly flat craters of our mortar fire. Foxon, firing from the hip, was at the forefront of

the bayoneteers, probing dugouts for fugitives. Then suddenly all was quiet again. We stood, smoke-grimed and sweating, gulping water from Italian water bottles.

Throughout the day the Hurricanes had worked tirelessly overhead, and the Hartebeests were constantly aloft. Three arrived just before dawn on 17 December just in time to see three S.81s beginning to bomb the village. The S.81s were followed by three Ca 133s, led by *Capitano* Raoul Gamba. The three Hartebeests attacked Gamba's aircraft. Capt Gardner shot up the bomber. The attack was then taken over by Maj Durrant, and the Italian aircraft peeled away to crash-land. Capt Gardner flew over the site of the crash, dropping his medical kit and some cigarettes to the Italian crew. The Italians set fire to their aircraft and then set off through the bush, with Gamba wounded in the leg, and eventually made it home. Italian losses in the attack on El Wak were eight officers, 200 colonial troops and twelve guns. Just two South Africans were killed.

Sure enough, the Italians became aware of the imminent arrival of the 4th Indian Division. No 44 *Gruppo* moved up ten S.79s to operate out of Gura on 15 December. They needed to know precisely what was happening at Port Sudan. At 1145 on 16 December three S.79s approached Port Sudan on a photographic mission. Capt Driver was already aloft, testing out one of the newly arrived Hurricanes. Immediately he was joined by three Gladiators and the other Hurricane. Driver made for the second S.79, but it eluded him in the clouds. He then fired at the third S.79, shooting it down. Forty-five minutes later three more S.79s came over and bombed the harbour, and another three forty-five minutes later repeated the attack. The tenth S.79 came on its own at 1335. This time two Gladiators and a Hurricane were scrambled to attack it. Maj Wilmot was credited with knocking it out of the sky.

Two more Hurricanes arrived from 1 SAAF Squadron, flown by Capt Boyle and Lt Duncan. They were ready to respond when three more S.79s appeared at 0915 on 17 December. Three of the Hurricanes and two Gladiators scrambled to intercept. The bombers eluded all of them except Capt Driver. He followed them for nearly forty miles, and then he opened fire, shooting up the starboard engine, but had to break off his attack. The S.79 and its two companions managed to make it back to Gura.

Shortly afterwards four S.79s from Asmara attacked the port. Again the British scrambled two Gladiators and two Hurricanes, but once again the bombers eluded them in the clouds.

Elsewhere, on 16 December, there was an early-morning reconnaissance mission by the only remaining French Martin 167F left in Aden. It was over Diredawa when it was attacked by a pair of CR.32s. The fighters climbed to get above the intruder, and then one of the CR.32s, flown by *Sottotenente* Veronese, dived into attack and riddled the starboard engine of the Martin. Severely impaired, the Martin dropped speed and was now attacked by *Sergente Maggiore* Athos Tieghi. He managed to shoot up the Martin and set it on fire. The observer was killed and two of the crew managed to bale out, but the parachute of the pilot, *Adjudant* Chef Y. Trecan, was caught by the tail of the aircraft, and he plunged to his death. Only one crew member survived.

The end of operations around El Wak and the safe arrival of the Indian Division at Port Sudan caused a temporary lull in aircraft activity. There had been some movement, with Italians concentrating aircraft at Bardera, on the River Juba, in Italian Somaliland. Three CR.42s had come down from Addis Ababa, three more from Vittorio d'Africa and a pair of Ro.37bis from Mogadishu.

On the afternoon of 18 December *Tenente* Romano Palmera, piloting an Ro.37bis, was carrying out a reconnaissance mission over El Wak. Palmera spotted the Hurricane of Flt Lt Blake taxiing to take off at the landing ground at Ndege's Nest. Palmera swooped down and fired at the Hurricane and then made good his escape.

Marylands of 12 SAAF Squadron launched reconnaissance missions into Italian Somaliland on 21 December. To the north, on 24 December, a Hardy belonging to 237 Squadron and flown by Flg Off MacIntyre, accompanied by his gunner, Sgt Collins, intercepted three Ca 133s that were bombing British ground targets near Kassala. In the engagement one of the Ca 133s was shot down.

Christmas Day and Boxing Day saw little activity, but on 27 December six CR.42s of 412 *Squadriglia* droned towards Gedaref to make a strafing run. The 1 SAAF Squadron detachment at Azzoza scrambled five Gladiators. Only three managed to lift off in time, and they soon closed with two additional CR.42s that were flying cover for the strafing aircraft. Capt Le Mesurier and Lt T. Condon homed in on one of the CR.42s. The captain's guns jammed and the CR.42 fired back and hit Condon's aircraft's propeller. Condon, however, pressed on, shooting down the CR.42, which crashed, killing the pilot some five miles from Gedaref.

Three CR.42s of 413 *Squadriglia* intercepted a Maryland photographing Bardera. The Maryland had spotted three S.81s parked beside the runway on 28 December. The fighters chased off the Maryland, but could not catch it.

As a result of the reconnaissance mission, four Hurricanes, led by Flt Lt Blake of B Flight of 2 SAAF Squadron, lifted off at 1525 on 29 December. Two of the aircraft were flying at 3,000 ft and the other two at 6,000 ft. The two lower aircraft, flown by Capt A.Q. Masson and Lt A.M. Colenbrander, made the first attack, being fired at by an armoured car. Despite this, they managed to hit all three S.81s, setting them on fire. Three CR.42s were on standby, conscious of the fact that the Maryland reconnaissance almost certainly meant that a raid would be mounted on Bardera. The first two CR.42s lifted off, flown by *Tenente* De Micheli and *Sottotenente* Bartolozzi. The third CR.42 could not take off due to the dust clouds, so *Sergente* Strano lagged behind. The dust clouds attracted the first two Hurricanes, and they both fired at him, damaging his throttle, puncturing the compressed-air cylinder and riddling him with splinters. Despite this, Strano continued to try to take off, but he could not operate his guns. He later managed to land with a pair of flat tyres and no fabric on his rear fuselage. Masson and Colenbrander continued their strafing runs, unaware of the fact that two of the CR.42s had lifted off successfully.

There were no radios in the Hurricanes, and when Flt Lt Blake spotted the Italian fighters heading for him he had to fly close to his wingman, Lt J.A. Kok, to warn him. But it was too late. Kok was quickly engaged by De Micheli, and Bartolozzi attacked Blake. Kok succeeded in shooting down De Micheli and then managed to bale out, but was captured. Meanwhile Blake had been hit in the foot and his fuel tank burst into flames. He could not get out of the cockpit, and so instead he flipped his aircraft over and fell out. He managed to open his parachute in time and was picked up by the Italians. Blake had been one of the most successful pilots in East Africa, and incredibly he had been shot down by Bartolozzi, who had been flying CR.42s for just a week.

As 1940 came to an end it was almost honours even between the Italians and the British and their allies. The year 1940 saw the Italian Air Force in East Africa at its strongest and most potent. From this point on, as ground was lost in the war, its ability to fight back would diminish.

The Italians had managed to get seventy-four new aircraft to Italian East Africa by the end of 1940. Three *squadriglie* were now equipped with S.81s, but most of the new aircraft were S.79s. A pair of S.82s had also been delivered, but one had crashed during December. CR.42s were arriving in increasing numbers; thirty-six of them had been dismantled and brought in on S.82s. Replacements would be fewer in 1941 – just seven more S.79s and fifteen CR.42s. In all, the Italians had lost 137 aircraft since the outbreak of the war: eighty-three of them had been lost due to enemy action and the remainder had been written off, become worn out or had been damaged or destroyed in some other way. The Italians had been able to keep up the pressure on the British by deploying the bulk of their reserve aircraft, and by October 1940 they had just ten left in reserve.

The Italian Air Force would begin 1941 with 132 serviceable aircraft. There were a number of aircraft undergoing repair, in fact eighty-five of them. There were also forty under repair at the various airfields, and there were also nineteen allocated for transport duties. This gave them a total of 276 aircraft, the bulk of which (fifty-eight) were deployed in the north.

After being hopelessly outnumbered at the beginning of the conflict, the air strength of the British and South African squadrons had grown over 1940. In Kenya the SAAF had ninety-four aircraft, a mixture of Hurricanes, Furies, Battles, Ju86s, Marylands, Hartebeests, Valentias, Lodestars and Ansons. In the Sudan, 203 Group had a mix of Hurricanes, Gladiators, Blenheim IVs, Hardies, Lysanders, Vincents and Gauntlets. In Aden there were still Blenheim Is, Blenheim IVFs, Gladiators, Vincents and Swordfish.

The situation in East Africa had radically changed. At the beginning of December 1940 Operation Compass had been launched against the Italians in the Western Desert. The 7th Armoured Division, the 4th Indian Division and a regiment of Matilda tanks had surged forward, and in just two days, on 11 December, had captured 38,300 Italian prisoners and seized seventy-three tanks and 237 guns. The Italians were in full retreat, towards Bardia. This was the root cause for the availability of the 4th Indian Division.

The Duke of Aosta, Commander-in-Chief of Italian East Africa, now realised that he faced possible enemy action on three fronts. He was right in assuming that the most dangerous frontier was the one with the Sudan. He had positioned *Generale* Luigi Frusci in Eritrea, with three colonial divisions and three independent brigades. Covering their flank were three more brigades and five Blackshirt divisions covering the area from the Setit river to around Gallabat. On the southern border there were ten brigades; four brigades were allocated to deal with the rebels. Each of these field forces was supported by irregulars, and there were two divisions, the Savoia and Africa, in reserve at Addis Ababa.

Platt's plan was to launch an assault at the beginning of February 1941. He knew that even with the Indian Division it would not be easy.

The Duke of Aosta was already asking for permission to pull back from his exposed positions along the Sudanese border, and in fact from early January the British were aware of the fact that the Italians were intending to evacuate Kassala. Indeed, the Duke of Aosta telegraphed Rome and told them that his northern front now faced at least 60,000 enemy troops. His men had suffered enormously from malaria and other diseases. He could not be certain that his men were strong enough to stand against a determined assault. He wanted to withdraw towards Agordat and form a line in Eritrea from there to Barentu. The Duke eagerly awaited Rome's consent before he dared move his men.

The air war kicked off in 1941 on 4 January. A pair of Hardies of 237 Squadron dive-bombed Italian positions around Metemma. One of the aircraft, flown by Flg Off Christie, was hit by anti-aircraft fire. The Hardy caught fire, and while Christie struggled with the controls Sgt K. Murrell fought the blaze. They managed to get back to a landing-strip near the front lines. Murrell was awarded the Distinguished Flying Medal.

The British attacked Massawa on 8 January, and anti-aircraft defences shot one of the raiders down. To the south, Yavello was hit by six Fairey Battles on 9 January. They managed to destroy two Ca 133s parked beside the runway.

On 12 January the 4th and 5th Indian Divisions were moved up towards Kassala. They would strike on 17 January.

Meanwhile, on Sunday 12 January a pair of Gladiators intercepted an S.79 and three escorting CR.42s over Aroma. The CR.42s managed to shoot down one of 1 SAAF Squadron's aircraft, flown by Lt J.S.R. Warren. Meanwhile a 237 Squadron Hardy, flown by Plt Off Simmonds and Sgt Gray, was attacked by a CR.42 over Tessenei. The Hardy was badly shot up, but it managed to land in the bush and the crew escaped on foot.

With the Italians gearing up for an expected push from the Sudan, they were caught unawares with 'a sudden attack from the south. Cunningham struck against the south of Italian Somaliland.

On 16 January a Blenheim crew would discover the changed attitudes of the French, and suffer as a consequence. A Blenheim of 8 Squadron left Aden alone to attack targets in Eritrea. It seems likely that the Blenheim over Jijiga was attacked by a CR.32. Two days later a British reconnaissance flight confirmed that the Blenheim had force-landed in French Somaliland and that the crew had been interned by the French.

On 17 January aircraft began to be moved forward for the big assault from the Sudan. Six Wellesleys of 47 Squadron moved up, along with detachments of 1 SAAF Squadron. However, during the night of 18/19 January the Italians withdrew from Kassala.

But Platt was determined not to let the Italians get away unmolested. He brought forward his planned attack from 9 February to 17 January, although ultimately he postponed it. But when the attack on Kassala was made it was an enormous anti-climax. A two-battalion assault was planned, but the garrison had slipped away.

Platt started the pursuit straight away, pushing his mobile Gazelle Force Unit forward, supported by Sikh infantry, who were in turn supported by the rest of the 4th Division. These units took the road to Keru and Biscia, while the 5th Division headed along the road to Aicota. Overhead 223 Squadron and 47 Squadron launched their Wellesleys against Barentu and Agordat, as well as the aircraft workshops at Mai Edaga.

By 20 January the British were advancing on Agordat and

catching up with Italian rearguard units. The Italians threw CR.42s at the advancing columns, but ground fire hit two of them and they were compelled to make forced landings. Another attack was made by S.79s and Ca 133s. Four of the Ca 133s were hit and three of them force-landed.

During 20 January Haile Selassie was flown from Khartoum aboard a 46 Squadron Wellesley, escorted by 1 SAAF Squadron Hurricanes, down to Umm Idla on the border.

Dawn on 21 January found Gazelle Force making probes into the Keru gorge. The road here snaked for a mile and a half through a cut in the cliffs. The Italians had mined it and they had also demolished some of the cliffs. *Generale* Fongoli's 41st Colonial Brigade had been deployed to hold the narrow roadway. The lead commander of the British forces, Brig Frank Messervy, threw his Sikhs against them, supported by artillery. They were beaten back with 150 casualties. Suddenly, breaking out of cover, came two Italian officers on white horses, leading a squadron of Abyssinian cavalry. The gunners had to fire at the cavalry over open sights. The Italian cavalry were held off and retreated, re-formed and charged once again. By the time they were beaten off for the second time the cavalry had taken nearly forty casualties.

On the southern road the 5th Division reached El Gogni, some ten miles beyond Aicota. The Italians had dug in here along a low ridge.

Throughout 22 January the Italian Air Force made a number of raids in the north. They bombed Tessenei airfield, British transports near Keru and other targets. The two Ca 133s with fighter escort that attacked Keru were intercepted by two Hurricanes and two Gladiators of 1 SAAF Squadron. Lt O.B. Coetzze in a Hurricane riddled one of the Ca 133s, and then he came under attack by CR.42s. Meanwhile Lt H.J.P. Burger also attacked and apparently shot down another Ca 133. There was considerable confusion as to whether the two Hurricane pilots had in fact shot down the same aircraft, or whether this was indeed two Ca 133s. An Italian survivor from the encounter gave his own account:

> On the morning of 22 January 1941 a formation of three Caproni Ca 133s of the 18 *Squadriglia*, 27 *Gruppo*, took off from Asmara to bomb the enemy advancing from the north.

Tenente Passetto was in command and I, a *sergente*, was the second pilot. The aircraft on the right was flown by *Sottotenente* Nicoletti and *Serg* Belcaro, while that on the left was flown by an officer whose name I do not remember, and *Serg* Dichino. After take-off I took over control from *Tenente* Passetto who gave me the course and altitude. Over Agordat we received an escort of two Fiat CR.42s which stayed 200 metres above us. Not long after, the Observation Commander of the aircraft came into the cockpit and, staying between the two pilots, indicated to the *Tenente* to look down to the left. After a moment I saw a shower of flak coming from below and I then saw two Hurricanes. The *Tenente* ordered us to jettison the bombs, took over control and started to bank in the direction of home. A Hurricane attacked us from behind and the aircraft on the left crashed in flames, while that on the right was hit, dived away and disappeared from our view. We were alone in the sky, the *Tenente* banked again, increasing speed. I saw the needle of the tachometer move forward and stop at 175 km/hr. The Hurricane turned back, attacking us again. We were hit by one bullet after another and the Observation Commander was wounded in the thigh. Our radio operator was very good; he was firing with a Lewis gun to the rear and was managing to reload very swiftly. In the meantime the engineer was manning another Lewis but was only getting off single shots. The next thing that happened was that the petrol tank was hit by a burst of fire. I saw a torrent of fuel pouring over the engineer, the floor, and eventually disappearing through the doors, leaving a grey trail behind us. I was looking at all that fuel and worrying about the engine exhaust. We were then attacked again from the right – the Hurricane was determined to finish this old Caproni that was still flying! The right engine was hit. I heard the sound of bullets hitting metal parts all around the aircraft, but fortunately none of us was shot. Our escort did intervene, but from my seat I could not see a thing. Those who could see said there were four Gladiators present also. The *Tenente* landed at Agordat, the tyres burst and the Caproni ran on wheel rims with a terrible noise; after that it drew to a halt. A moment later *Sottotenente* Nicoletti's Caproni also landed, damaged and with one wounded. When banking I had thought I saw for a moment a very, very small Caproni far below. It was *Sottotenente* Nicoletti; up higher something bright was coming down very slowly. These images disappeared very quickly from my vision. When we landed a mechanic explained the mystery. It was the radio operator of the plane that had been shot down in flames; he had been soaked in fuel and caught fire as he baled out, falling like a burning torch on his parachute – ironically his surname was Fuoco [*fuoco* – fire]. The ambulance arrived and picked up the wounded. The engineer complained that he was very sore because of being showered with fuel and was longing for a proper shower! After this action the 18 *Squadriglia* had no more aircraft. The officer, *sergente* and engineer from the aircraft shot down had been able to bale out and arrived in our lines on foot. Out of the three crews there was one person dead and three wounded. The mechanics were able to repair the damage to *Sottotenente* Nicoletti's Caproni just sufficiently to allow the aircraft to fly back to Asmara. However, I confirm that in the afternoon the Hurricanes returned and blew up my Caproni.

In fact it was Lt Burger and Lt Hewitson who attacked Agordat airfield and destroyed the Italian airman's Caproni.

On the ground both British columns pressed on, and on 23 January 1 SAAF Squadron was covering the advancing units. The Italians resorted to high-level bombing to avoid more aircraft losses. On 21 January more raids were made on British forces near Metemma and Gallabat. Both sides claimed kills, but in fact they only damaged one another's aircraft.

As the advance continued, new airfields were set up, so that by 27 January 237 Squadron moved to Umtali, and 1 Squadron had moved up a detachment of six Gladiators and six Hurricanes to Sabderat. They struck at Gura airfield, scoring hits on aircraft on the ground. Even the Italians were later to confirm that four S.81s and three S.79s were badly damaged.

Generale Frusci had determined to dig in at Agordat and at Barentu. At Agordat there were two forts and defences, the beginnings of an anti-tank ditch and miles of barbed wire. The garrison holding the main line was 4th Colonial Division (three brigades), under *Generale* Baccari, a Blackshirt division and supporting twenty-four tanks and seventy-six guns. They were also supported by a company of Germans, recruited from merchant ships.

To attack them the British had seven battalions, forty-eight field guns, a pair of machine-gun companies from the Sudan Defence Force and Skinner's Horse. The plan was to launch the two Indian battalions of the 11th Brigade to take the crests of Cochen while the 2nd Cameron Highlanders and the 5th Brigade, along with the tanks, struck through the plain. The attack would go in on the night of 29/30 January.

In the early morning of 29 January eight Blenheims of 14 Squadron struck the Italian airfields of Mia Edaga and Gura. Two of the Blenheims were damaged when they were attacked by a pair of CR.42s. The same targets were attacked by eight Hurricanes and five Gladiators of 1 SAAF Squadron at 1400. They arrived just in time to see a number of S.79s and CR.42s over the airfield, returning from an attack at the front. An S.79 was picked on by Capt Driver, who succeeded in shooting it down. Above were three CR.42s of 412 *Squadriglia*. They dived down to join in the fight. Driver, meanwhile, had swooped down and shot up an S.81 on the ground. With their fuel exhausted, the South African pilots headed back, certain that they had shot down at least five CR.42s. In fact none of them had been shot down.

The first phase of the ground assault went in as expected that night. There was tough fighting in the darkness, and the Italians provided a determined defence, counter-attacking when necessary. Despite their actions, the British were in possession of Cochen by dawn.

In the early morning of 30 January Driver led four Hurricanes to hit the same target where he had shot up an S.81 the day before. They fell on the landing field of Adi Ugri. Driver managed to set one of the S.81s on fire and Lt Duncan set fire to a second one. Although Driver did not know it, the aircraft were in fact already beyond repair. Flg Off Miller, piloting a Lysander of 237 Squadron, made a forced landing over Barentu on 30 January. He and his crew were taken prisoner.

On 31 January British troops once again assaulted Italian positions around Agordat. The Italians launched a counter-attack with the Blackshirt battalion and eighteen tanks. The British drew the enemy forward into a trap that would be sprung by hidden Matilda tanks. The Matildas opened fire at point-blank range, knocking out eleven Italian tanks. The infantry now opened up and the Blackshirts fled. By the end of the day the road to Asmara was full of retreating Italian troops. On the battlefield the British scooped up over 1,000 prisoners.

Meanwhile the 5th Indian Division was still struggling to take Barentu. Each time the British made an attack the Italians counter-attacked. But as soon as they discovered that Agordat had fallen they too began to fall back towards Aressa.

Chapter Five

The Southern Front

It was water that changed the course of events on the Kenyan front. A British geological survey section found water at Hagadera, between Garissa and Liboi on the Somaliland border. They drilled down over 350 ft, and by 20 January 1941 600 gallons were being pumped out every hour. Up until this time the dry land between the British bases and the coastal areas of Italian Somaliland were too inhospitable and dry to risk a major offensive. Later, another well would be found at Galmagalla, which could produce 400 gallons an hour.

Nearest the coast the 11th African Division would be aimed at Kismayu in southern Italian Somaliland. The 1st South African Division was ready to strike into Italian East Africa at Mega. Cunningham had decided to give the Kismayu offensive priority, and if he had the opportunity he would press on to take Mogadishu. He knew that there was a major fortress at the river mouth of the Juba, and this would be a formidable obstacle. Timing was vital: if he did not strike quickly then the rains would come and make movement nearly impossible. One of the Italian positions that would have to be taken was the waterholes at El Yibo, El Sardu and El Gumu.

Just before dawn on 16 January Hartebeests of 40 SAAF Squadron struck El Yibo and covered the advance. The fight for El Yibo would last for three days, and in fact when the position was finally carried the strongpoint was held by just seven Italians and 100 irregulars.

On 17 January a pair of Marylands attached to 12 SAAF Squadron carried out photo-reconnaissance flights into Italian Somaliland. On 19 January, 12 SAAF Squadron launched six Ju86s against an Italian vehicle park at Neghelli. They managed to destroy or damage upwards of 150 vehicles. Fairey Battles of 11 SAAF

Squadron launched pre-emptive raids against Italian airfields, striking at Yavello and Shashamanna. They burned one S.81. On 22 January a reconnaissance flight by an Ro.37bis of 110 *Squadriglia* over Gerill was intercepted, but the Italian aircraft managed to escape.

The 1st South African Brigade began moving from Wajir on 23 January and came under attack from Italian aircraft. There was another contact over Gerill on 26 January when Hurricanes of 3 SAAF Squadron tried to intercept three Ro.37bis that had been strafing the area. By the time the Hurricanes arrived the raiders had gone. There was, however, a combat situation when an Anson flown by Lt E.A. Gebhart of 60 SAAF Squadron was shot down by a Ca 133. The aircraft hit the ground before anyone could bale out, and everyone was killed.

A number of Gauntlets and Hartebeests of 2 and 41 SAAF Squadrons covered the advance of the 1st South African Division from Buna towards Moyale on 28 January. One of the Hartebeests, flown by Lt C.H. Beech, was hit by anti-aircraft fire. He force-landed safely. There was an attack going on that day against Moyale, covering the main thrust towards El Gumu and Gorai. As the British troops moved forward, Ca 133s were launched at the border town of Dif and S.79s at Colbio. Over the same ground that had claimed Beech's aircraft the previous day, Lt A.D. Maxwell also fell victim to anti-aircraft fire.

There was great fortune on 30 January in the discovery of the Italian airfield at Gobwen. A Maryland of 12 SAAF Squadron, flown by Lt Tennant, was attacked by a CR.42 while it was carrying out a reconnaissance mission over Kismayu. In his attempts to avoid the Italian aircraft Tennant flew down to ground level and spotted and strafed some Ca 133s on the airfield.

The following day, with the advance against El Gumu faltering due to the Italian resistance around the fort at Gorai, the attack on Moyale was halted. Hartebeests of 40 SAAF Squadron supported an attack by armoured cars and mortars against the Italian defences. The Italians broke and the pursuit went on into the next day, with El Gumu being overrun. On 1 February the Hartebeests attacked Hobok, to the east of El Gumu.

Hartebeests attacked Hobok again on 2 February, covering an

attack made by armoured cars and infantry once more. The Hartebeests engaged ground targets, and when Lt J.D.W. Human of 40 SAAF Squadron knocked out a machine-gun post and then struck an Italian armoured car, he was hit by ground fire. Even as he was losing height, his gunner, Air Sgt J. Jackson, continued to shoot at the armoured car. The Hartebeest finally gave up and he crash-landed. Human was later awarded the Distinguished Flying Cross and Jackson the Distinguished Flying Medal.

There were major reinforcements of aircraft on Sunday 2 February, with the arrival of the aircraft carrier HMS *Formidable*. She was *en route* to the Mediterranean and was carrying Fairey Albacores of 826 and 829 Squadrons, in all twenty-one aircraft. She was also carrying twelve Fairey Fulmars of 803 Squadron. In the early hours nine of the Albacores bombed Mogadishu. The other Albacores dropped magnetic mines into the harbour.

The 25th East African Brigade, supported by A Flight of 40 SAAF Squadron, struck into Abyssinia and took Kalam, close to Lake Rudolph. The area was somewhat hostile, and was occupied by a tribe called the Merille. They had allied themselves with the Italians because the Turkanas had allied themselves with the British. The two tribes had been rivals for generations. As a result, the Merilles held out in a fort, and flying out of Lokitaung, C Flight of 40 SAAF Squadron plastered the positions at Todenyang at dawn. The camp belonging to the chief was bombed and strafed by a Hartebeest flown by Lt Roberts. Despite the fact that the tribesmen did not have any anti-aircraft guns, they managed to inflict considerable damage on the Hartebeests. Lt Roberts's Hartebeest was hit, as was Lt Smith's, and Capt Stableford's aircraft suffered damage.

Three Fairey Battles were now brought up to put an end to the resistance by the tribesmen. They came in at 4,000 ft, but even then one of the Battles was hit by ground fire. The British resorted to negotiation, and eventually the Merille changed sides.

In the morning of 3 February Hurricanes of 3 SAAF Squadron, now based at Aligabe, mounted patrols over the Dif area. One of the Hurricanes later escorted Hartebeests of 41 SAAF Squadron to attack Afmadu. The Hurricane, flown by Lt Marsh, was attacked by five CR.42s. Meanwhile, Capt Frost, another 3 SAAF Squadron

Hurricane pilot, scrambled to intercept three Ca 133s that were attacking Dif. He managed to work himself into a position behind the bombers and intercepted them as they headed home. He was then pounced on by a pair of CR.42s, which he outmanoeuvred, and then came in again to attack the Ca 133s. Once again the CR.42s intercepted him. He fired at one of them and saw it crash to the ground and burst into flames. Frost then attacked the Ca 133s again, firing at it and noting the pilot bale out. But the rest of the crew remained in the aircraft and managed to crash-land it. Frost now headed for the second Ca 133, which he shot down, and then the third, which crash-landed after he attacked it twice. Eleven of the Italian crewmen were taken prisoner by ground troops.

It was still only morning, and at 1130 three Hurricanes of 3 SAAF Squadron lifted off at Galma Galla to escort three Ju86s on an attack against Gobwen. The Hurricanes attacked first, with Capt S. van Breda Theron shooting up a CR.42 and then a second as it was taking off. Lt Dudley swooped down to shoot up a Ca 133 while his back was covered by Lt Upton. Dudley swooped down again as the Ju86s approached. He shot up another Ca 133, and then Upton destroyed another, turning it into a ball of flames.

By 4 February the 12th African Division had captured Beles Gugani. It was opened as a landing-ground on 7 February and immediately bombed by Italian aircraft. C Flight of 41 SAAF Squadron flew in to occupy it, and they were later joined by three Hurricanes of 3 SAAF Squadron.

The British were preparing to attack Afmadu in Italian Somaliland. Before the ground forces went in the Italian positions were plastered with bombs. Waves of Fairey Battles and Ju86s (six of the former and nine of the latter) took part in operations, covered by Hurricanes of 3 SAAF Squadron. The bombardment was so fierce that the 9th Italian Colonial Infantry Brigade withdrew. British ground forces poured into Afmadu at 0700 on 11 February. Shortly afterwards Hartebeests were able to land there. They were quickly followed by the rest of 41 SAAF Squadron. Quickly the 24th Gold Coast Brigade Group passed through Afmadu and made for Bulo Erillo and Gobwen.

By the morning of 13 February the 24th Gold Coast Brigade Group was attacking Bulo Erillo. The Italians were entrenched behind barbed wire and had armoured car support. After a fierce

Members of the 3rd SAAF Fighter Squadron in Abyssinia with a captured Italian aircraft.

Essential maintenance work being carried out by the SAAF.

A downed Italian aircraft.

Barentu aerodrome.

The burned hangar at Agordat aerodrome, where three Capronis were destroyed.

RAF Bomber pilot examining the damage to his wing inflicted over Keren.

The town of Keren was bombed by the RAF.

S79s burning on Gobwen aerodrome.

Addis Ababa aerodrome under attack from the SAAF. Thirty-two aircraft were destroyed in one offensive.

A Wellesley en route to Keren.

An S 79 near Diredawa on April 3 1941.

Brigadier Fowkes receives an important message, delivered by the Hartebeest, whilst travelling to Addis Ababa.

Bombed Italian planes at Addis Ababa aerodrome.

Ju 86 bombers of 12 SAAF Squadron.

Three Fairey Battles belonging to SAAF Squadron.

One of 40 SAAF Squadron's Hawker Hartebeests.

The alert spotter's perch at Ndege's Nest airfield in northern Kenya.

Briefing time for 11 SAAF Squadron, by Major R L Preller, DFC.

3 SAAF Squadron's Hawker Hurricanes in Kenya.

One of 12 SAAF Squadron's Martin Maryland I reconnaissance bombers in January 1941.

The SAAF used Avro Anson Is for photo-reconnaissance and coastal surveys in 1941 over Kenya.

One of 50 SAAF Squadron's Ju52s.

One of 3 SAAF Squadron's Curtiss Mohawk IVs in Mombasa in July 1941.

Loading the bombs in a Junkers.

The Junkers 86 was one of the
SAAF's long-range bombers.

A few of the SAAF's
Hawker Hartebeests.

Manning the Lewis
machinegun of a Hartebeest.

The Valentia biplane was used for transportation during the East Africa campaign.

The Gloster Gladiator was used extensively by the SAAF.

One of the Royal Italian Air Force's CR42s.

The Italian airbase at Neghelli being bombed.

Haile Sellassie raises the Ethiopian flag (20 January 1941).

The Duke of Aosta surrenders on 20 May 1941.

General Smuts of the Union of South Africa.

Lieutenant General Sir Alan Cunningham.

Brigadier F W
Messervy.

Major Orde Wingate and Haile Selassie.

The cave in Amba Alagi was the home of the Duke of Aosta.

Lieutenant General Sir Alan Cunningham and Major General Wetherall at Addis Ababa after signing the armistice.

The Wolchefit escarpment from the viewpoint of an Italian machinegun turret.

Troops of the 10th Indian Infantry Brigade cross the Atbara into Eritrea.

Captured Italian ammunition at Mogadishu.

The Emperor Haile Sellassie makes his return speech.

Fort Toselli occupied by the allied forces.

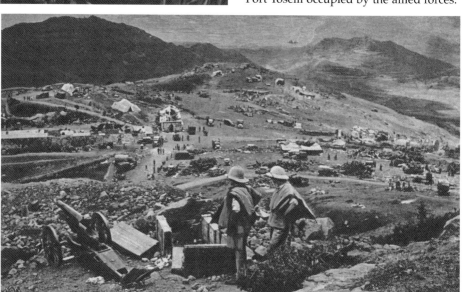

The fortress of Moyale.

fight the Italians were driven out, leaving behind many prisoners, five armoured cars and some artillery. By the evening it was clear that the Italians were abandoning Kismayu, and the 1st South African Brigade redoubled its efforts to catch up with the Italians before they could slip away.

Meanwhile, overhead, in a Maryland, Capt O.G. Davies of 12 SAAF Squadron made a reconnaissance over Mogadishu. He saw a staff car on the road from Mogadishu to Jelib. He opened up on it and saw it crash into trees. He then strafed other road transport. Davies then found himself over the Vittorio d'Africa airfield and some tempting Ca 133 targets. He shot up two of them but was then pounced on by *Capitano* Palmera in a CR.42. The Italian hit him numerous times, and in fact when Davies got back to base they counted 732 holes in his tail.

Fairey Battles of 11 SAAF Squadron hit Berbera, but two were hit by anti-aircraft fire. One of them had to make a forced landing at Beles Gugani and the other at Afmadu. During the night S.81s made an attack on Afmadu, and Kismayu was now also under attack from Fairey Swordfish off HMS *Hermes* and gunfire from the cruiser HMS *Shropshire*.

The 1st South African Brigade, supported by twelve light tanks, attacked Gobwen on the morning of 14 February. The Italian rearguard was beaten back and they fled across the River Gruba, burning the bridge behind them. Cunningham now thrust his men forward once again to seize Kismayu. It was occupied at 1700 hours, and the last Italian defences were occupied by 1900. The Italians had evacuated the civilian population and blown up whatever they could not take with them. Cunningham was ahead of schedule.

For the second day Ju86s of 12 SAAF Squadron hit pontoon bridges over the River Juba, while Fairey Battles swarmed over retreating Italian columns on the Jelib–Bardera road. On 14 February one of the Battles was hit by anti-aircraft fire and had to force-land.

Ground troops were now approaching Jelib, and the Italians tried to slow up their advance by attacking with bombers. In the early hours of the morning on 15 February a Ca 133 was badly damaged, and just after daylight another was hit and had to force-land. Ahead of the advancing British troops nine Ju86s of 12 SAAF Squadron bombed Italian troops at Jelib. HMS *Shropshire* moved towards

Brava under cover of Hurricanes, so that it could shell the Italian army command posts at Modun. The cruiser's gunfire was directed by Capt Davies in a Maryland. He was later to be awarded the Distinguished Flying Cross. A Hurricane of 3 SAAF Squadron, piloted by Lt Glover, intercepted three S.79s attacking ground troops near Jelib. He managed to damage two of them.

The major problem that now faced Cunningham was to cross the Juba. At Gobwen it was 580 ft wide, and it narrowed as it went north. At some points it could be waded, but there the jungle was thick and impossible for vehicles. A good place was found at Yonte. No. 12 SAAF Squadron launched three Ju86s to attack Italian positions on the opposite side of the bank. Meanwhile, Fairey Battles attacked Jelib. The 1st South African Brigade managed to cross during the night, but was immediately counter-attacked by Italian troops. The South Africans moved south to take the fortress Jumbo from behind. By the following day the Gold Coast Brigade had also succeeded in crossing the Juba, at Mabungo. It had had to cut a track for three miles through tropical forest.

The 11th African Division managed to cross the river and by the following day, 20 February, Jumbo had been taken and Gobwen had become a forward base for 12 SAAF Squadron.

Capt Davies of 12 SAAF Squadron flew another photo-reconnaissance mission over Brava and Mogadishu. He was attacked by *Capitano* Romano Palmera, the commanding officer of 10 *Squadriglia*, in his CR.42. This time Davies escaped with less damage – only five holes in his starboard wing.

Cunningham now moved to cut off Mogadishu. His troops would aim to sever the road to the port, a feat that would be accomplished by 22 February. Jelib had been taken by the 1st South African Brigade, supported by the Hartebeests of 41 SAAF Squadron. Italian troops were now streaming away from the front, their lines shattered and their morale broken. Their exit was hastened by an attack from three Fairey Battles of 11 SAAF Squadron that managed to destroy eight vehicles on the road from Lamma Garas to Duduma.

Lt B.S.M. Hamilton was attacked by *Capitano* Palmera (110 *Squadriglia*). Palmera shot down Hamilton, killing the pilot, but Flt Sgt J.W. Dixon managed to bale out in time. Dixon was taken prisoner, and an Italian officer handed him over to a native soldier to take him to headquarters. The local man, angry about the number of civilians that had been killed in raids on Mogadishu, promptly sentenced Dixon to death and shot him.

The Italians tried to counter-attack from Bardera on 22 February, but were beaten off by the 2nd Nigerian Regiment. By this time Cunningham became aware of the fact that the Italians had thrown virtually all of their reserves into the defence of the River Juba, and as a consequence there was very little left between him and the city of Mogadishu. At 0600 on 23 February, the 23rd Nigerian Brigade and the 22nd East African Brigade began advancing towards Mogadishu. In the evening they fought a vicious engagement at Modun.

Capitano Palmera was also in action again on 23 February. He and *Sottotenente* Malavolti, in their CR.42s, attacked a Hartebeest belonging to 41 SAAF Squadron over Jelib and Merca. Sgt McWilliam returned fire as best he could, and as Malavolti came in for an attack Lt Shuttleworth managed to fire a burst at it with the front guns. At this point the two CR.42s broke off.

Over Moyale Capt C.P. Kotze in a Hartebeest of 40 SAAF Squadron spotted that the position had been abandoned by the Italians. This meant that Cunningham would no longer have to assault the position.

On 24 February Allied troops passed through Modun and Brava. The Italians declared Mogadishu an open city. By the evening of 25 February Merca had also been captured, and the same evening elements of the 11th Division entered Mogadishu, not having come across any Italian opposition in the final twenty miles. The Nigerians had covered 275 miles between 0600 on 23 February and 1700 on 25 February.

The capture of Mogadishu was to prove to be a vital breakthrough and an absolute success in terms of its offensive goals. It allowed 12 SAAF Squadron to move first to Gobwen and then to Margherita. The advanced air headquarters shifted from Kismayu to Mogadishu. Mogadishu airfield was occupied by 41 SAAF Squadron. The campaign had succeeded in destroying two entire Italian colonial infantry divisions, the 101st and the 102nd.

The advance was not yet over, however, and the 11th African Division now prepared to head north towards Harar, while the 12th

African Division struck north-west, along the Juba, to take Bardera, Iscia Baidoa, Lugh Ferrandi and Dolo.

A conservative estimate of the number of Italian troops lost in the campaign was around 31,000. The British had captured an enormous amount of stores, ammunition and food, and remarkably, despite the fact they had been told that there was no petrol in Mogadishu, 350,000 gallons of motor spirit and 80,000 gallons of aviation spirit were found. This would enable the advance to continue even before the British had managed to reopen the ports of Mogadishu and Merca.

Despite the capture of so much equipment and fuel, Cunningham's ability to press on would very much depend on his ability to supply his mobile columns. A prime example of this was the attack on Dagabura, some 590 miles to the north of Mogadishu. It was attacked by a handful of armoured cars and two companies from the 2nd Nigeria Regiment. The column was under the command of Lt Col J.A.S. Hopkins. There was an Italian rearguard at Dagabura, and Hopkins had left behind the rest of his battalion, so that he could cut off the retreating Italians before they escaped.

On average the lead troops moving out of Mogadishu were to make sixty-five miles a day. In fact, when the mobile column of Nigerian troops from the 11th African Division left Mogadishu on 1 March, six days later they would be 354 miles up the coast.

Even ahead of the ground troops, 12 SAAF was running Maryland reconnaissance flights as far as Harar. The Maryland could report on 6 March that Italian troops were pulling back to a line from Harar to Jijiga. Reconnaissance missions were now being launched as far as 700 miles. Capt Davies photographed a bridge near Awash on 8 March. This would later allow a Bailey bridge to be built in advance, in anticipation that the Italians would blow up the existing bridge before the British got there.

The Italians desperately needed to know where the 11th African Division was, and on 11 March an S.79 flew overhead at Gabredarre. The bomber was hit by anti-aircraft fire. To stop this from happening again, B Flight of 3 SAAF Squadron was moved to the south of Gabredarre, to Gorrahai.

However, the advance was so rapid that on 12 March Dogabur was taken and Hartebeests of 41 SAAF Squadron flew up to occupy the airfield, which was now within striking distance of the Italian airfields at Jijiga and Diredawa. The Harbeestes were soon joined by the Hurricanes of 3 SAAF Squadron's B Flight.

The war was becoming critical now, and for the Italians the campaign was nearly lost. The theatres were becoming merged, as Cunningham struck north and west and Platt struck east. Soon they would be joined by a new force, striking from Aden itself through Berbera.

Of final interest in this theatre was an engagement in the Dogabur region on the morning of 13 March. A pair of S.79s had been dispatched to bomb vehicles near the airfield and were flying at around 6,000 ft. Just before the bombers approached, Lt Venter of 3 SAAF Squadron, in a Hurricane, had taken off to escort a single Hartebeest of 41 SAAF Squadron that was probing the area over Jijiga. Venter lost sight of the Hartebeest and then lost his own bearings. He was forced to land in the bush some fifty miles to the east of Dogabur, having run out of fuel. He managed to find a couple of Somalis, and he gave them a message to get help. Soon afterwards they ran into a South African armoured car. The South Africans radioed Dogabur to tell them where Venter had landed.

Lt L.R. Dudley was already looking for Venter, but he had run into the S.79s and had chased them for some time. He was then joined by Capt S. van Breda Theron. Dudley had used up all his ammunition on the attacks on the bombers. Theron chased the bombers for 100 miles, and then he returned to base. But in the afternoon he set off to find Venter, managing to spot him, land alongside, and then siphon off his own petrol to put into Venter's aircraft.

Venter and Theron took off together, heading back for Dogabur. Just as they reached there they saw Lt Dudley taking off. He was immediately attacked by a pair of CR.42s, and his aircraft was badly damaged. It crashed and burst into flames. The two CR.42s were flown by *Capitano* Palmera (110 *Squadriglia*) and *Sergente Maggiore* Tominello (413 *Squadriglia*). The Italian pilots now began shooting the six Hartebeests parked on the airfield. They then spotted Theron and Venter, who climbed to escape. Theron got behind Tominello's CR.42 and shot it down. Venter got behind Palmera, and with his aircraft in flames Palmera baled out. He was picked up by the 11th African Division and handed over to the pilots at Dogabur. His war was over.

CHAPTER SIX

The Tough Nut

Immediately after the battle of Agordat on 1 February 1941, Gazelle Force was instructed to pursue the Italians towards Keren. The British were held up at the Barak river, where the Ponte Mussolini bridge had been partially destroyed. The main girders had been severely damaged and it was impossible to get motor transport over it. At this point the Barak was around 150 yards wide and consisted of a strip of very soft, deep sand that, without a temporary track, vehicles had no hope of crossing.

The Italians were not about to make even this difficult task easy for the British, as they had laid a large number of mines around the approaches to the bridge and were covering the minefield with machine-gun posts and an artillery piece. This small rearguard was quickly overwhelmed by field artillery, which allowed the British to lay their track, and by the evening of 2 February Gazelle Force, along with six light tanks and the 11th Indian Infantry Brigade, was just five miles from Keren.

In the skies on 1 February, 1 SAAF Squadron's fighters had broken up an attack by five S.79s near Agordat. By this stage the Italian Air Force was in a parlous state. Since the middle of January it had lost seventeen aircraft due to enemy action, three more had been destroyed in accidents and twenty-four more were out of commission until at least March, due to the severity of the damage. This now meant that the Italian Air Force in East Africa could muster just thirty-seven Ca 133s, fifteen CR.42s, fourteen CR.32s, seven S.79s, six S.81s, two Ro.37bis and one S.82. The Italians by this stage also knew that it was suicidal to launch Ca 133s against any Allied target unless they were protected by fighters. It was the view of the Italian command that if air activities continued at its present level of intensity for another fortnight the Italian Air Force would virtually cease to exist.

There was another Italian casualty on 2 February when a patrol of 3 SAAF Squadron Hurricanes flew a sortie to Afmadu. The pilots, Capt J.E. Frost and Lt Hewitson, saw nothing on their first sortie, but on their second they spotted a Ca 133 on the ground. Frost strafed it and set it on fire. By now 3 SAAF was based at Aligabe and was very much at the forefront of the push.

Meanwhile, on the ground, as Gazelle Force pressed on from Ponte Mussolini they encountered a good road heading north-east over rolling terrain. Ahead of them was an escarpment, literally the entrance into Eritrea. The escarpment seemed to stretch for miles, and indeed for the last few miles before Keren the road ran through a narrow valley, with the escarpment on the left and an enormous spur on the right. It would be in this valley and the surrounding heights that the battle of Keren would be fought. There were Italian observation posts all above the valley, some as high as 2,000 ft. During daylight hours nothing could move without being seen. The valley was bare; a handful of trees and some scrub and no other cover. The valley was wide; between half a mile and a mile and a half. The road itself ran along the south side of the valley as far as Mount Dologorodoc, where it turned sharply to the north over a bridge and then uphill to enter the Dongolaas Gorge, which was no more than 330 yards wide. Above was Fort Dologorodoc, and here was a wide part, known as the Happy Valley. The only entrance for real traffic was over the bridge.

In the north wall of the valley was the Acqua Gap, flanked to the east by Mount Zelale, known as the Sphinx due to its shape. Fort Dologorodoc, guarding the entrance to the gorge, was overlooked to the east by Mount Falestoh, to the north-east by Mount Zeban and to the north-west by Mount Sanchil. Fire could be brought down on the fort from any of these summits.

To the north-west of Mount Sanchil were a series of features that would play an important role in the battle – Brig's Peak, Sugar Loaf, Saddle, Near Feature, Hog's Back, Flat Top Hill, Mole Hill, Mount Samanna and Mount Amba. All of the mountains were steep, covered in boulders and scrub, there were no paths and some took as much as an hour and a half to climb.

The railway running from Agordat to Keren ran along the north side of the valley. When it reached Dongolaas Gorge it had climbed a third of the way up the lower slopes of Mount Sanchil. The railway would be of enormous use, particularly to the 4th Indian Division.

When Agordat fell, Keren was believed to have been held by just a single colonial brigade. The British believed that if they moved quickly they could overrun Keren before the Italians poured reinforcements into it. Unfortunately, intelligence revealed that by 2 February the Italians had in fact already reinforced Keren. A colonial brigade and part of a Grenadier division had been brought up from Addis Ababa.

By now the British were at the first major Italian roadblock in the Dongolaas Gorge. The Italians had sited units to cover the position. Any British that drew close to it came under immediate fire. A reconnaissance was sent out, and although the British tried to rush the roadblock on 3 February, they were unable to get past. The 2nd Camerons worked their way towards Brig's Peak and secured Cameron Ridge. Meanwhile Skinner's Horse was sent around the right flank, and units probed into the Happy Valley to try and find a way around the block.

Storming the Italian positions at Keren was not a task that the British could take lightly. Added to the natural strength of the Italian positions, the temperature was also rising daily. Both the British and the Italians knew that the engagement at Keren would be decisive. A surprise attack by the British was unlikely, as the Italians had good observation posts and the air force was still active. The British knew that this would not be an easy assault. Keren was indeed a tough nut to crack. Any casualties now would be incredibly difficult to replace.

The British hunted for a way past the block; in fact the 3rd Central Indian Horse hunted for a way through some sixty miles to the south, and reached Arresa, which No. 2 Motor Machine-gun Group of the Sudan Defence Force had reached. They found that Arresa was a possibility, but they could see how difficult the route was, as the Italians had abandoned nearly all their vehicles along here in their retreat from Barentu. It would take time to build a road through here, and every wasted hour would give the Italians an opportunity to move troops down and make Arresa as difficult as Keren.

The expected rains would also make the route impossible. The British hunted to the north and found nothing, and they came to the gradual realisation that only at Keren was there any real option.

On 3 February Hurricanes of 3 SAAF Squadron scrambled over the Dif area. Later Lt Marsh escorted Hartebeests of 41 SAAF Squadron on an attack on Afmadu. Marsh engaged one of five CR.42s that came up to intercept, but it evaded him in the clouds. Capt Frost, based at Aligabe, on his third sortie of the day, saw three Ca 133s bombing a British camp at Dif. He dived to attack, making a frontal attack on the third Ca 133. He was then bounced by two CR.42s. Frost evaded them and swung around to try and catch the Ca 133s again. As he came in for another attack the CR.42s tried to intercept him. He fired a burst of machine-gun fire into one of them. The CR.42 pulled up and then spun down, crash-landing in a ball of flames. Frost then turned to attack the bombers again. The Ca 133s broke formation, and as Frost closed with one of them the pilot baled out and the controls were taken over by the co-pilot, who managed to crash-land the bomber. Frost now tackled the second bomber, which burst into flames and crashed. He now moved on the third one, shooting at it in two passes and then seeing it crash-land. British ground troops took eleven Italian air crew prisoner.

Over Eritrea, six Gladiators of 1 SAAF Squadron landed at the new airstrip, codenamed Pretoria. They took off again at 1145 to attack Italian positions around Gondar. They spotted an Italian landing-ground near Azozo, and on it were five Ca 133s. The Gladiators came down and began strafing the Ca 133s, which were being refuelled and loaded with bombs. The Gladiator pilots claimed that they hit and blew up all five, but the Italians later only admitted to one.

Peeling away from the Italian airfield, the Gladiator pilots saw another airfield, with CR.42s taxiing to take off. Also on the ground were a number of S.81s. The Gladiators got in one strafing attack before the CR.42s engaged them. In the ensuing dogfight Capt Le Mesurier and Capt Boyle each claimed to have shot down a CR.42. In the fight Lt Smith's aircraft was badly damaged and he had to make a forced landing at Azozo.

One of the CR.42 victims that day was *Sergente Maggiore* Enzo Omiccioli. Omiccioli was originally of 410 *Squadriglia*, but had been recently flying with 412 *Squadriglia*. He was shot down during the attack on Gondar, and was posthumously awarded the *Medaglia*

D'Oro for his actions while flying a CR.32 on attachment to 411 *Squadriglia*, when he shot down Lt Rankin of 40 SAAF Squadron in a Hartebeest. He had also shot down two Blenheims when he was with 410 *Squadriglia*, and four when he was with 412 *Squadriglia*.

On 4 February, 1 SAAF Squadron launched three Gladiators and three Hurricanes for an attack on the airfield at Bahar Dar. As they approached the airfield they saw three Ca 133s on the ground. Capt Driver shot one up, and Lt White and Lt Coetzer claimed another one each.

Meanwhile, four more Hurricanes of 1 SAAF Squadron were on escort duty with Wellesleys to attack the area around Gura. They encountered three Blenheim IVs of 14 Squadron. Immediately the South African pilots took the Blenheims to be enemy aircraft and launched an attack, damaging one so badly that it had to crash-land at Port Sudan. The Hurricanes then peeled off to attack four CR.42s. Maj Wilmot attacked one at low level over Asmara, believing that he saw it crash among some buildings.

A pair of Blenheim IVFs launched an attack on Makale airfield from Aden. The pilots, Sqn Ldr J.M.N. Pike and Flt Lt Gethin of 203 Squadron, shot up three S.79s, and may well have badly damaged three others that were undergoing repairs. The Blenheims were then set upon by a pair of CR.32s of 410 *Squadriglia*, flown by Verones and Folcherio. The Italians hit both of the Blenheims, and one of them was forced to crash-land back at Aden.

There was considerable activity over Eritrea on 5 February. There were engagements between Hurricanes and Gladiators of 1 SAAF Squadron against as many as six CR.42s. In one of the engagements Capt Driver attacked a CR.42 and saw it crash-land close to Asmara. Meanwhile Lt Coetzer shot down another CR.42, while Capt Le Mesurier claimed a third.

Italian aircraft attacked the 5th Indian Brigade outside Keren on 6 February. From now on, 1 SAAF Squadron was assigned to provide cover for the ground troops over the area.

British bombers struck Keren and Assab, and on 7 February a CR.42 of 412 *Squadriglia* attacked and shot down a Hardy of 237 Squadron over Keren. The crew-members of the Hardy, Flg Off Taylor and Sgt Stowe, were both killed. The British lost a pair of Wellesleys flown by Flg Off Helsby and Sgt E.E. Blofield over Adi

Ugri. The Wellesleys were attacked by CR.42s of 412 *Squadriglia*, and one of the kills was claimed by *Maresciallo* Soffritti. Pike and Gethin were active again on 6 February, and this time they attacked Alomata. They saw nine Ca 133s on the ground and shot up eight of them.

On the ground, the 5th Indian Infantry Brigade, less one battalion, was moved from Agordat to Keren. It was hoped that it could attack around the right flank of the Italian positions, through the Happy Valley and into the Acqua Gap. During the previous night the 3rd Battalion of the 14th Punjabis occupied Brig's Peak, but was driven off on the afternoon of 6 February. The 1st Battalion of the 6th Rajputana Rifles occupied part of Cameron Ridge and held off vicious counter-attacks.

It was clear that the Italians were reinforcing the area. During the night of 7/8 February the 5th Indian Infantry Brigade moved into position in the Happy Valley, and in the early morning of 8 February the 4th Battalion of the 6th Rajputana Rifles launched an attack on Acqua Gap. It was wired and strongly held, and the battalion was only able to consolidate on a ridge just below it. It was a perfect target for the Italian Air Force.

Elsewhere, another attempt was made to secure Brig's Peak, this time by the 3rd Battalion of the 1st Punjabis. It was to take it until 1500 on 10 February to succeed.

No. 14 Squadron launched four Blenheim IVs on 8 February to attack Asmara. One Blenheim was hit by anti-aircraft fire and shot down. Later in the day four Hurricanes of 1 SAAF Squadron launched a patrol over Asmara and were attacked by five CR.42s. Capt Driver managed to shoot one down and Lt Van Der Merwe damaged a second one.

There was disaster on Sunday 9 February when Agordat and the surrounding airfields were attacked by 412 *Squadriglia*. Five CR.42s were involved in the strafing and bombing runs. The Italians would claim five Hurricanes, five Hawker biplanes, two Wellesleys, two Gladiators and two other aircraft. In actual fact just two Wellesleys, two Hardies and two Lysanders were destroyed.

Throughout the period 10–12 February the Italians made numerous counter-attacks against Brig's Peak and Cameron Ridge. The 3rd Battalion of the 1st Punjabis were driven off Brig's Peak once again in the early hours. Meanwhile a second attack on the Acqua Gap was being launched. The 4th Battalion of the 11th Sikhs aimed to take Mount Zalale (the Sphinx) while the 4th Battalion of the 6th Rajputana Rifles attacked Hill 1565. Neither battalion was able to reach its objectives; in fact the 29th Indian Infantry Brigade was then pulled out. The second unsuccessful attack on the Acqua Gap made it clear to the British that shortage of transport, ammunition, rations and petrol was becoming a problem. The 29th Indian Infantry Brigade was pulled back to Barentu, and the rest of the 5th Indian Division was moved back to Subderat and Tessenei, where it could be more easily resupplied.

No. 1 SAAF Squadron was launching offensive patrols over Asmara on 10 February. Six Hurricanes got into a dangerous dogfight with five CR.42s in the cloudy skies. Capt Boyle managed to shoot down a CR.42, and Capt Driver, having chased a pair of CR.42s and then lost them in the clouds, shot at a third one and saw it burst into flames. Driver then received a number of hits and two CR.42s chased him, but he managed to evade and land safely at Agordat. In all probability, the Hurricane pilots had actually only shot down one Italian aircraft – a CR.32, almost certainly flown by Sergente Marlotti (412 *Squadriglia*). His body was found near the wreckage of his aircraft. His parachute had not opened.

No. 1 SAAF was determined to sweep Italian fighters from the skies over Keren, and on 11 February it launched no fewer than eleven fighters. On one of the patrols two Hurricanes were attacked by CR.42s. The CR.42s tried to slip away and were chased by Lt S. de K Viljoen. The South African pilot ran out of fuel and had to land near a village. He was lucky that the village was already in British hands; he managed to obtain some fuel, and took off the following morning, but promptly crashed. He returned to base on foot, and later his aircraft was recovered and repaired.

In all likelihood, the three CR.42s that had been encountered by the Hurricanes were being led by *Capitano* Mario Visintini. He was leading two young pilots. It was a disastrous sortie. Visintini was blown off course and was killed when he crashed into Mount Nefasit. The two young pilots had to make forced landings. Visintini was another desperate loss for the Italian Air Force. He had flown in the Spanish Civil War and had probably shot down a number of

Wellesleys and Blenheims. In total he may have claimed fifteen to seventeen kills. Visintini was posthumously awarded the *Medaglia D'Oro*.

More aggressive combat patrols were launched once again on 13 February. Five Hurricanes engaged five CR.42s, and as one of the CR.42s tried to evade an onrushing Hurricane it began to belch smoke. It was attacked by Capt Boyle and set on fire. The pilot managed to bale out. Meanwhile Lt Duncan saw another CR.42 in trouble, and as he attacked it the pilot also baled out. In fact just one of the two losses was a CR.42 flown by Luigi De Pol (who was badly wounded and later died in hospital). The other aircraft was the last CR.32 in Eritrea, which was flown by *Tenente* Bossi. It was later claimed that Bossi had been machine-gunned while he was dangling from his parachute. In hospital he had to have an arm and a leg amputated, but he died as a result of his injuries.

An S.82 transporter was destroyed when the British raided Zula, and welcome reinforcements arrived with K Flight's return from Egypt. The Gladiator flight was commanded by Flt Lt J.E. Scoular DFC. It would now be based at Mersa Taclai.

Along the Red Sea coast the 7th Indian Infantry Brigade reported that the Italians were pulling back from the Karora area, and requested permission to launch an assault on the area. The British had considered this to be an option some time before, and thought it would be useful, as it would divert enemy attention from the Kassala region. The area was thought to be capable of sustaining a brigade-sized group, which could strike from Port Sudan via Suakin into Karora, and then on to Nakfa and Cub Cub before approaching Keren from the north.

The 7th Indian Brigade was minus one battalion, the 4th of the 11th Sikhs, which was now a motorised unit and operating with Gazelle Force. To compensate, the 4th Battalion of the 16th Punjabi Regiment was released from garrison duties in Khartoum. To support the thrust was a battery of 25-pdrs, No. 4 Motorised Machine-gun Company of the Sudan Defence Force, the 12th Field Company of Sappers and Miners and the 170th Light Field Ambulance Unit. Supporting this force was the 14*éme Battalion Etranger* of the French Foreign Legion and *Battalion* Garby (*Troisiéme Battalion de Marche* Tchad). These were Free French forces. The Foreign Legion had seen action in Norway, and *Battalion* Garby had taken the long route overland from French Equatorial Africa. They were commanded by *Colonel* Monclar and were known as the *Brigade D'Orient*. It was hoped that this force would be able to threaten Massawa and Marsa Kuba.

On 10 February the small port of Mersa Taclai was occupied by the 1st Royal Sussex, and the troops moved on towards Nakfa and Cub Cub. Here there was serious resistance by the Italians, and a successful attack was led by *Battalion* Garby. By 1 March the 7th Indian Brigade and its supporting units had forced the Mescelit Pass, just twenty miles to the north of Keren.

Meanwhile, overhead, the Italians managed to shoot down by ground fire a Vincent of 430 Flight over Eritrea on 14 February. No. 223 Squadron lost a Wellesley flown by Flg Off Willing when he was shot down by anti-aircraft fire as he and two other Wellesleys attacked aircraft workshops at Mai Edaga. On the following morning, 15 February, a 47 Squadron Wellesley flew over Mai Edaga to see how successful the previous night's attack had been. Three CR.42s intercepted and attacked the bomber. Luckily three Hurricanes of 1 SAAF Squadron were already aloft over Gura, and flew to attack the CR.42s. In the dogfight Capt Boyle claimed that he had shot one down.

Capt Driver, leading four Hurricanes and two Gladiators, attacked Asmara. Six CR.42s came up to intercept and Driver shot down the leading aircraft, seeing it crash on the airfield.

The Hurricane sweep by 1 SAAF Squadron on 15 February had been in preparation for a major attack by Wellesleys against the Gura airfield. Nos 47 and 223 Squadrons mustered eleven Wellesleys to attack Gura, supported by the fighters. They reported having set two S.79s on fire.

Two Blenheim IVFs of 203 Squadron in Aden attacked the Makale airfield, claiming to have destroyed one S.79 and damaging two others. The Blenheims were then attacked by a single CR.32 of 410 *Squadriglia*, flown by *Sottotenente* Veronese. He shot down the aircraft flown by Sqn Ldr A.L.H. Solano before chasing the other Blenheim, flown by Sqn Ldr Scott. Scott managed to crash-land at Aden.

In the last month the Italians had suffered enormous casualties – some fifty-three aircraft destroyed and twenty-three damaged. This was around seventy-five per cent of their aircraft strength. In the same period, 17 January to 16 February, the Italians had claimed twenty-two kills, eight probable kills and eighteen enemy aircraft destroyed on the ground.

According to Lt Gen Platt on 17 February, the situation at Keren was as follows:

> 5th Indian Infantry Brigade had relieved 11th Indian Infantry Brigade on the hills. 11th Infantry Brigade was resting in reserve. The enemy had been reinforced by the majority of the Savoy Grenadier Division, in addition to the 1st Division, and was aggressive. He held the highest ground, and was continuing to extend his right around the northern flank of the 5th Indian Infantry Brigade. On the other hand there was a steady flow of deserters at the rate of 150 a day. The enemy was known to have suffered heavily in the recent attacks. 7th Indian Infantry Brigade, from the north, was closing on Cub Cub, which, if taken, would allow this brigade to make its presence felt against Keren. The Foreign Legion, which had reached Suakin, was awaiting a ship to carry it forward to join 7th Indian Infantry Brigade. Administrative activity in building up the necessary reserves in the forward areas continued.

The 4th Indian Division was taking casualties at a rate of around twenty-five a day. A plan would need to be put in place in order to break the Italian resolve and to push forward.

Meanwhile Italian bombers attacked Tessenei and Agordat airfields along with troops on the front on 19 February. The Italian commander in the region had been advised that it was no longer tenable for Italian aircraft to operate from Eritrean airfields; they would have to be withdrawn into Abyssinia. In recognition of this, 1 SAAF Squadron was assigned escort duty for ten Wellesleys to attack Asmara, where the Italians were massing their aircraft prior to their being shifted south. The Hurricanes came in first, shooting up three S.79s, two CR.42s and two Ca 133s. At noon on 20 February the Hurricanes struck at Massawa, Decamere and Adi Ugri. This time they wrecked four CR.42s and two each of Ca 133s and S.81s.

There was ominous news on 21 February: a reconnaissance

aircraft had reported that new CR.42s had been delivered by transport aircraft to Massawa. Seven Hurricanes of 1 SAAF Squadron, led by Maj Wilmot, lifted off from Agordat at 0800 hours. They refuelled en route and were over the airfield at noon. The Hurricanes attacked the six hangars, coming in virtually at ground level. They strafed half a dozen Ca 133s and a CR.42. Lt J.J. Coetzer was shot down by anti-aircraft fire. The Hurricanes were joined by seven Albacores launched from HMS *Formidable*. They bombed Massawa Harbour. Four of them were hit by anti-aircraft fire but they all managed to get back home. Chinele airfield at Diredawa was also hit by six Blenheim IVFs of 203 Squadron and six Blenheim Is from 8 Squadron; all were from Aden. The Blenheims' bombs peppered the area, but in the clouds they missed the airfield and hit the town instead.

Meanwhile, over Keren, a pair of S.79s attempted to bomb British positions. Both of them were hit by anti-aircraft fire, and one was destroyed when it had to force-land.

Seven Hurricanes of 1 SAAF Squadron flew into Tole for refuelling in the morning of 23 February. They took off again in the afternoon, to attack Makale. Four of them were to cover three that would carry out a strafing attack. The covering aircraft would also be there to protect a Wellesley that was expected to join in. Maj Wilmot led in the three strafing Hurricanes. They shot up a CR.32 on the ground. Inside was *Sottotenente* Folcherio (410 *Squadriglia*), who was about to take off. Suddenly, *Sottotenente* Veronese in a CR.32 attacked Wilmot's aircraft and shot him down. Lt Duncan then promptly shot down Veronese. Wilmot survived the crash and became a prisoner of war. Veronese was wounded. His wounds in fact prevented him from taking any further part in the fighting, and he was eventually evacuated to Italy. He would later fly with the Italian Co-Belligerent Air Force for the Allies. He was shot down and killed when he was strafing German artillery in Greece in a Spitfire V on 4 November 1944.

Meanwhile, over Makale, the four covering Hurricanes, having given up on the Wellesley, dived and set fire S.79s on fire.

There were more attacks by Allied aircraft on 24 February, when three Blenheims belonging to 203 Squadron struck Addis Ababa airfield. Two days later Plt Off Wells, in a Gladiator of K Flight (now at Mersa Taclai) over Cub Cub spotted a pair of CR.32s above him. The Italians did not see him, so he climbed and managed to shoot one down over Keren. Zula airfield was attacked by Capt A. Duncan of 1 SAAF Squadron. He saw an S.82 and shot it up. He then wrecked a nearby hangar.

On 28 February a pair of Wellesleys of 47 Squadron, now operating from Sennar, attacked Burye. The aircraft flown by Flt Sgt Wimsett was shot down by anti-aircraft fire.

By the beginning of March Albacores from HMS *Formidable* had taken up a position at Mersa Taclai and were bombing targets around Eritrea. Two Ca 133s were spotted at a landing-strip near Alomata. These were both strafed by a Blenheim IVF of 203 Squadron. By the beginning of March, 1 SAAF Squadron had handed over the last of its Gladiators to 237 Squadron as it was now fully up to strength with Hurricanes.

On the ground at Keren, the 4th Indian Division was given the job of seizing Mount Sanchil, Brig's Peak, Hog's Back, Saddle, Flat Top Hill, Mole Hill and Samanna. The Indian 5th Division would attack to the right of the main road. It was decided that the attacks would be consecutive rather than simultaneous, so that each assault could be supported by all of the available artillery. The date fixed for the assault was 15 March, as the 5th Indian Division could not be brought forward until that time. It was imperative that the Italians be kept on the back foot and that they were not made aware of what was being planned. As a result, vigorous reconnaissance patrols were launched.

By 8 March the plan for the 4th Indian Division was taking shape. There would be two attacks: on the right the 11th Indian Infantry Brigade would be made on a three-battalion front. The 2nd Camerons would strike Mount Sanchil and Brig's Peak, in the centre the 1st Battalion of the 6th Rajputana Rifles would strike at Saddle and Hog's Back, and on the left the 2nd Battalion of the 5th Mahratta Light Infantry would tackle Flat Top Hill. The 4th Battalion of the 6th Rajputana Rifles and the 1st Royal Fusiliers would be held in reserve. The left-hand attack by the 5th Indian Infantry Brigade, including 51 Commando, would aim to secure the flank of the 11th Infantry Brigade from any possible counter-attacks from Mount Amba.

The 5th Indian Division would aim to capture Mount Zeban and Fort Dologorodoc. The task of assaulting Fort Dologorodoc itself was given to the 9th Indian Infantry Brigade and the 2nd Highland Light Infantry. The 29th Indian Infantry Brigade was given the job of capturing Mount Zeban.

As many aircraft as possible would be needed over the battlefield, and the three bomber and one fighter squadrons were instructed that they would be required for direct, close support, and would need to fly at least six sorties a day.

On 5 March over Massawa Lt J. Van Der Merwe of 1 SAAF Squadron spotted and strafed a train. He returned later that morning and strafed it again. In the afternoon, accompanied by three Wellesleys, he again attacked the same train. Diredawa was targeted by six Blenheims of 8 Squadron (Aden) on 9 March. Aerial reconnaissance suggested that there were a number of CR.42s and an S.81 on the airfield. This was in fact a decoy, and a trap was sprung by the Italians as the six Blenheims came in. Three CR.32s of 410 *Squadriglia* attacked the bombers. The leading CR.32, flown by *Capitano* Ricci, attacked the aircraft flown by Sqn Ldr Hanlon. As a result of the encounter Hanlon had to force-land the aircraft on Perim Island on the return flight.

On 11 March Keren airfield was strafed by three Hurricanes of 1 SAAF Squadron. An S.79 was shot up by Capt Driver and Lt Hewitson. On 12 March they attacked Asmara and Gura, shooting up an S.81, and then on their return flight they attacked an anti-aircraft position at Massawa.

The 4th Indian Division attacked its objectives at 0700 on 15 March, just half an hour after sunrise. The sun blinded the artillery observers and the attacking troops. It was common practice for the Italians to stand to at dawn and then break for breakfast. In the early hours of the morning the 9th and 29th Indian Infantry Brigades had got into position behind the lower slopes of Cameron Ridge. The 2nd Highland Light Infantry would attack Fort Dologorodoc once Mount Sanchil and Brig's Peak had been taken. It was hoped that this could be achieved by 0900.

By 0945 the 4th Indian Division was making good progress and the order was given for the 5th Indian Division to begin its assault. Unfortunately neither Mount Sanchil nor Brig's Peak had been taken, so when the 2nd Highland Light Infantry was launched at the fort it was held off at a range of about 200 yards by machine-gun fire from the slopes of Mount Sanchil. By 1300 it was clear that the troops were going to make no further progress and that they should shift their axis of attack to the south rather than the south-west. They would assault once more at 1530.

The lack of success by the 2nd Highland Light Infantry was due, not only to the desperate defensive measures of the Italians, but also to the severe heat. It became abundantly clear that the fort was too great an objective for a single battalion. It was decided, therefore, that the new attack from the south would be made by two battalions, the 3rd Battalion of the 12th Frontier Force Regiment and the 3rd Battalion of the 5th Mahrattas. They managed to take two minor features of the fort, known as Pimple and Pinnacle, by midnight. The 2nd West Yorks were then sent between Pimple and Pinnacle to join in the attack.

The Italians launched a counter-attack before sunrise on 16 March. The British had planned to bombard the fort with artillery at this time, and when the counter-attack came in the Italians found themselves caught between the small-arms fire of the entire 9th Indian Infantry Brigade and the artillery behind them. They broke and were chased into the fort. The 2nd West Yorks broke in at 0600 and began extending their attack.

By the time this had happened the 2nd Camerons had still not been able to prise the Italians off Mount Sanchil and Brig's Peak. Consequently the 1st Royal Fusiliers were sent forward to reinforce. The 1st Battalion of the 6th Rajputana Rifles had taken fifty per cent casualties but had seized the Hog's Back. Elements of the 4th Battalion of the 6th Rajputana Rifles were sent forward to reinforce them. Top Hill had been taken by the 2nd Battalion of the 5th Mahratta Light Infantry. Meanwhile, the 4th Battalion of the 11th Sikhs had taken part of Mount Samanna, but could not dislodge an Italian Alpine Battalion. The remainder of the 4th Battalion of the 6th Rajputana Rifles was thrown at Brig's Peak, but it could not force the Italians out.

By the evening of 16 March only a handful of Italians remained on Mount Sanchil, and Brig's Peak had finally been captured. The 10th Indian Infantry Brigade was pushed forward over Cameron

Ridge and through the gap between Mount Sanchil and Brig's Peak to break into the plains to the west of Keren. But the information about the weakness of the Italian positions was premature, and when the 3rd Battalion of the 18th Garhwal Rifles was thrown forward it was beaten back with heavy casualties.

The aerial contribution during the assault on the Keren defences was not inconsiderable. At 0700 on 15 March, as the assault went in, the bombers of 14, 47 and 223 Squadrons began their day's bombing mission, which by the end of the day would see them having dropped nearly 39,000 lb of bombs on Italian defences.

Elsewhere, 3 SAAF Squadron attacked Diredawa. On the night of 15 March, 8 Squadron (Aden) launched Blenheims against Diredawa. The airfield was hit again by Junkers Ju86s of 12 SAAF Squadron and more Hurricanes. In this attack the Italians had managed to scramble three CR.32s (410 *Squadriglia*). *Sergente Maggiore* Giardinà in a CR.32 attacked a Ju86 and was then engaged by a Hurricane. He was then supported by *Sottotenente* Bartolozzi, who attacked the Hurricane. Bartolozzi managed to land his own aircraft eventually, with 188 holes. The Hurricanes were now able to attack the airfield unmolested. Capt Frost shot up an S.79 and a CR.32, as did Capt Theron, and Capt Harvey shot up another CR.32. The Hurricanes swept back toward their airfield at Dogabur and then launched another assault in the afternoon. This time they attacked a machine-gun post. In this attack Capt Harvey was shot down, but Lt Morley and Capt Theron shot up a pair of S.79s. Frost shot up a CR.32, but his Hurricane was hit in the attack and he had to force-land. Moments after he came down Lt R. Kershaw landed alongside to protect him. Frost set his aircraft on fire and then climbed in behind Kershaw.

Kershaw was recommended for the Victoria Cross for his actions, but in the end he was awarded the Distinguished Service Order.

On 16 March Wellesleys of 47 Squadron attacking Italian positions around Keren were intercepted by five CR.42s. They managed to shoot down one of the Wellesleys, flown by Plt Off Leuchars. At around the same time a Gladiator flown by Plt Off P.H.S. Simmonds (237 Squadron) was attacking Italian positions on Mount Sanchil. He was attacked by a CR.42, but managed to evade it, get behind it and shoot it down.

The intensity of attacks on Italian positions was maintained on 17 March. Four Hurricanes of 1 SAAF Squadron strafed Italian lorries and then an S.82 at Danuba.

By the evening of 17 March the Allied positions on Mount Sanchil and Brig's Peak were in jeopardy. Any further assault would lead to irreplaceable losses. As a result the troops were withdrawn, and Mount Sanchil and Brig's Peak were subjected to heavy shelling.

The capture of Fort Dologorodoc was only part of the 5th Indian Division's objectives. The 29th Infantry Brigade was supposed to move forward and capture Mount Zeban, but until Mount Sanchil was captured this would be suicidal. The Italians were still counter-attacking, and the RAF, along with the artillery, was instrumental in breaking up these attacks. The 5th Indian Division was ordered to resume its advance at 2200 hours on 16 March. Due to delays in bringing up supplies and ammunition, zero hour was postponed until 0030 hours on 17 March.

The 29th Indian Brigade immediately ran into heavy Italian fire. The RAF had to be called in to drop food and ammunition to the 1st Worcesters. So far the 29th Indian Infantry Brigade had managed to just advance around 850 yards beyond the fort. Counter-attacks were now coming in from the Italians, who were trying to recapture the fort.

Meanwhile we will recall that British forces had reached Arresa to the north of Keren. It was hoped that the 7th Indian Infantry Brigade with its supporting units could carry Mount Engiahat, but the Italians were holding strong positions and they found it impossible to break through.

There would now be a short lull in offensive actions on the ground until 25 March.

On 18 March five CR.42s of 412 *Squadriglia* had attacked Agordat. They shot up a number of aircraft, including a Wellesley and two Hurricanes. Shortly after the attack a pair of S.79s appeared overhead and bombed another Hurricane. The CR.42s were not idle that day; later they attacked Gladiators belonging to K Flight over Keren, shooting up two of them.

Later in the day a pair of Hardies of 237 Squadron was also over Keren. The aircraft were flown by Plt Off Storey and Flt Lt N.S.F. Tyas. They were attacked by CR.42s, which managed to shoot down the Hardy flown by Tyas.

On the morning of 20 March a Hurricane attacked trains and
Italian ground forces on the road from Harar to Diredawa. The
Hurricane, flown by Capt Theron, attacked a pair of CR.32s and
managed to riddle one of the enemy aircraft.

It was also on 20 March that British troops landed at Berbera
from Aden, as we shall see in Chapter Seven.

On 21 March at 0515 three Hurricanes of 1 SAAF Squadron took
off to mount a patrol over Keren. They were followed by four others
fifteen minutes later. Meanwhile, a Lysander flown by Flt Lt G.A.
Smith of 237 Squadron was over the same target carrying out
artillery observation. Smith and his gunner, Sgt A.K. Murrell, were
attacked by five CR.42s. The Lysander was damaged and the pilot
was wounded. Four of the Hurricanes saw the attack and closed in
on four of the CR.42s. Capt Driver hit one of them, seeing it fall
away and crash, Lt Pare attacked another, but it escaped, and then he
turned on another one, which saw the pilot bale out as his CR.42
crashed into the ground. The final CR.42 then attacked Pare, and in
the ensuing fight this CR.42 also crashed to the north of Keren.

The Italians tried throughout 21 March to dislodge the British
around Fort Dologorodoc. Anti-aircraft fire hit two Ca 133s and two
S.79s. Meanwhile, Diredawa railway was attacked by six Blenheims.

In the early morning of 22 March a Blenheim of 14 Squadron
spotted a force-landed Gladiator of K Flight some thirty miles to the
south of Mersa Taclai. The Blenheim landed alongside and picked
up the downed pilot. Asmara was hit later on in the day by six
Wellesleys and six Blenheims accompanied by a pair of Hurricanes
of 1 SAAF Squadron. To the south of their target the Hurricane
pilots spotted three CR.42s of 412 *Squadriglia*. As they closed, one
of the CR.42s slipped away, but Lt L. Le C. Theron attacked and
shot down one of the other CR.42s. The third CR.42 was shot down
by Lt J.B. White.

At 0500 on Sunday 23 March Lt W.J.A. White and Lt Pare of 1
SAAF Squadron were over Keren. They spotted six CR.42s above
them and Pare attacked one of them, but the aircraft managed to
return to base relatively unscathed.

By now the battle for Keren was reaching a critical phase. It was
time to resume the offensive and open the road to Keren. The 10th
Indian Brigade began its assault at 0415 and rapidly began to secure

its objectives. No. 47 Squadron alone made sixteen sorties over Keren that day, and 14 Squadron also struck at Keren, being intercepted by three CR.42s. No. 1 SAAF Squadron was involved in dogfights against CR.42s in the morning, and in the afternoon two of its Hurricanes, one flown by Lt Pare, shot down one of the Italian aircraft.

By 26 March the British had reached the final Italian roadblock. It was now clear that the Italians were beginning to pull back. During the attack on Keren the 4th and 5th Indian Divisions had lost upwards of 4,000 men. The fact that the Italians were beginning to fall back became abundantly clear in the early hours of 27 March. The 29th Indian Infantry Brigade was advancing well and reporting that there was only light Italian resistance. By 1000 hours Keren was in British hands. Throughout the morning white flags were raised over Mount Sanchil, Brig's Peak, Mount Zemanna and Mount Amba.

It was now a question of pursuit. The engagement had cost the Italians 40,000 prisoners and 300 guns. By 2030 the 5th Indian Division was approaching Ad Teclesan.

No. 1 SAAF Squadron began strafing the columns of retreating Italian troops. Every available aircraft was brought in, but in the engagements Plt Off M.R.C. Dyer, in a Vincent of 237 Squadron, was shot down by three CR.42s. The next target and line of defence would be around Asmara.

CHAPTER SEVEN

Collapse

A small force arrived in Berbera in British Somaliland from Aden on 16 March 1941. Wavell had agreed at Cunningham's request to improvise a force to take it. The line of the River Juba had been broken, Mogadishu captured and the British were now thrusting towards Harar.

The Duke of Aosta had flown down to Harar at the end of February to instruct *Generale* De Simone to deny Harar to the enemy and to make a stand to the north of Jijiga. At his disposal would be 26,000 colonial troops and 5,000 Italian troops. The Italians were a mixed bag – two Blackshirt battalions, East African police, armed customs officials and a unit of armed drivers. Occupying British Somaliland was the 70th Colonial Brigade, which was supposed to be a good formation. But it was to be an enormous disappointment.

HMS *Glasgow*, HMS *Caledon*, HMS *Kandahar* and HMS *Kingston* appeared off Berbera at dawn on 16 March. They bombarded the port and then landed two Punjabi battalions to seize the former British capital. They found that the 70th Brigade had in fact disbanded itself. A colonel and sixty men in parade dress were waiting to surrender.

Meanwhile the 23rd Nigerian Brigade had reached Jijiga and had sent some armoured cars, along with the 3rd Nigerian Regiment, to cut off the Italian retreat. The capture of Jijiga was a real coup, as it provided an ideal base for the South African Air Force units. Up until this point they had had to try to refuel on their way to and back from bombing missions around Harar and Diredawa. It also meant that the capture of Berbera would allow supplies to come in for the rest of Cunningham's forces. By 22 March the 2nd South African Brigade had landed at Berbera after a six-day voyage from Mombasa.

The way out of the area and towards Harar and Addis Ababa was through the Marda Pass. The Italians had fortified the pass and the hills on either side of it with minefields, entrenchments and barbed wire. The approach to the pass was over five and a half miles of open ground, with no cover. The British believed that it was held by four battalions and a group of irregulars.

On 18 March 12 SAAF Squadron had launched Ju86s to attack the Marda Pass and strafe Italian transport on the Harar road. On 19 March South African bombers were moved up to Jijiga. This included the Ju86s and the Fairey Battles. They could now strike at Diredawa and Addis Ababa with impunity. On 20 March the Harar Diredawa road was attacked by three Ju86s and a Hurricane. They encountered heavy anti-aircraft fire and then a pair of CR.32s. Capt Theron managed to shoot up one of the Italian aircraft.

On 21 March Hartebeests of 41 SAAF Squadron struck the Marda Pass once again. This was in conjunction with a two–brigade attack that was being launched against the pass. It was clear by 20 March that the Italians were happy to slip away if it appeared that a determined push might be made to take the pass. The British decided to throw in the two available Nigerian battalions, and rushed some South African batteries up to support them and called for the 3rd Nigerian Regiment to be brought up as a reserve force. One battalion would be sent against Camel Saddle Hill, three miles to the right of the pass. From here they would then head south towards the pass. The other battalion would make diversionary attacks to the left of the pass. The two battalions were brought up in trucks and the assault would go in at noon on 21 March. The South African artillery was brought up to within three miles of the enemy positions and began to shell the entrenchments. A Nigerian light battery was also brought up to add to the firepower. The trucks carrying the infantry surged forward and then disgorged their infantry.

On the left the 2nd Nigerian Regiment advanced against heavy machine-gun fire from Observation Hill. A pillbox was knocked out by the Nigerian howitzers, and the Nigerian infantry surged forward. On the other side of the pass the 1st Nigerian Regiment headed towards Camel Saddle Hill. The colonial Italian infantry drove them back with counter-attacks, but they were then thrown into confusion by massed South African artillery fire. The hill still remained in

Italian hands by darkness, but one Nigerian company had managed to gain a foothold, and this was reinforced.

As the Nigerians began to prepare themselves for a night attack there came the news that at 0135 a patrol had found the Italian positions abandoned. The Marda Pass, supposedly impregnable as Keren had been, had been taken at a cost of seven killed and thirty-seven wounded. It would take another twenty-four hours, however, before the force could press on, due to the large number of mines that had been planted around the positions.

No. 12 SAAF Squadron was already proving to be of great value, having moved up to Jijiga. A Maryland flown by Capt Glynn Davies flew over Harar and Diredawa. He saw a pair of S.79s and then a third flying above. He chased the S.79 and it is believed that in his haste to escape the Italian pilot crash-landed in a valley.

Back at Marda Pass, the Nigerian Brigade was probing towards Harar and was now on a well-built Italian highway. The problem was that the area was believed to have a large number of mines. Instead, they chose to take an Abyssinian track that bypassed the next Italian defensive position at the Babile Gap. This was a narrow defile between cliffs. Armoured cars led the way and they came under fire, but the position was cleared out by the 3rd Nigerians. They then advanced, and by the evening of 25 March they were approaching the last obstacle in front of Harar, the Bisidmo river.

The Italians had declared Harar an open city. They were warned in no uncertain terms that as long as Italian guns continued to fire from the city then it would be considered a legitimate target by the British. The city itself was in chaos, and the Italians had absolutely no intention of trying to hold it. By the end of March it was in British hands, along with 500 prisoners and two batteries of field guns. Colonial troops were in mutiny or deserting in droves.

There was now the question of increasing numbers of Italian women and children and what could be done with them. It seemed that at this stage most were flooding back towards Addis Ababa.

The situation was becoming increasingly desperate for the Italians, but they were not without the ability to cause damage and suffering to the British forces. On the evening of 28 March five CR.42s moved down to Gauani from Addis Ababa. At dawn on 29 March, accompanied by two CR.32s, they launched an attack on

Jijiga. The attack came in at 0700, and they shot up a Ju52, a Valentia and a Hartebeest, as well as damaging another two Ju52s. A pair of Hurricanes of 3 SAAF Squadron, flown by Capt Theron and Lt Venter, took off to intercept. Theron's aircraft ran into immediate problems and he came in to land. As he touched down he was attacked by a CR.32 flown by *Sergente Maggiore* Giardinà, who shot him in the leg and then set his Hurricane on fire. A CR.42 now came down to finish off the Hurricane. Venter was desperately trying to cope with three CR.42s, and he shot one of them down (*Sottotenente* Silvano who was badly wounded). Capt Frost managed to get aloft and chased a pair of CR.42s, flown by De Micheli and *Sergente Maggiore* Danesin. He managed to shoot down Danesin's aircraft.

No. 3 SAAF had lost a considerable number of Hurricanes, and during 28 March five of 94 Squadron's Gladiators were brought down to be given to the South Africans. In fact on the following day the squadron's last three were also handed over.

On 29 March Diredawa was overrun by British troops. The South African Air Force would take over the airfield once they had cleared the wreckage of eighteen aircraft.

On the morning of 30 March the Italians threw another attack in against Jijiga. They were using up their last bombers, this time a pair of S.79s. They dropped bombs across the airfield in the same positions as the CR.42s had done on the previous attack. They did not see 41 SAAF Squadron's Hartebeests, nor did they notice the fact that two Gladiators and two Hurricanes had been scrambled to intercept them. The Gladiators could not keep up, but the Hurricanes closed in and Capt Frost and Lt Hewitson shot up the bombers. One of the S.79s crash-landed and the other, flown by *Capitano* Serafini, managed to make it back to Addis Ababa. His aircraft had 800 holes in it, and only his parachute pack had saved him from certain death. Later that day several Hurricanes were flown to Diredawa, along with elements of 41 SAAF Squadron.

The Italians were still trying to hold at Ad Teclesan, a position with large, round hills and far greener than Keren. There was no flat ground, so most of the offensive action would have to be carried out on foot. By 0900 on 28 March the Italian troops had been pursued as far as possible. The British forces were now running into an area covered by mines, which would have to be cleared. The Italians had set up three roadblocks on the road below Ad Teclesan. Each roadblock was covered by artillery and machine-gun nests. It was clear that the position would have to be outflanked. However, the 29th Indian Brigade rushed the first two roadblocks, and a pair of companies of the 10th Indian Infantry Brigade, along with Skinner's Horse and elements of the Sudan Defence Force, headed along the railway on the Italian flank. The 9th Indian Infantry Brigade moved up to support, and by early morning on 1 April the last roadblock was cleared. At 0630 Italian emissaries arrived to negotiate with the 5th Indian Division. They stated that they had been ordered to cease resistance and that Asmara should be an open town. As a consequence British troops entered Asmara at 1315.

Asmara, of course, was the capital of Eritrea. Up until now the British had lost over 500 killed and over 3,000 wounded. Italian losses were 3,000 dead and 4,500 wounded, plus, of course, thousands more who had surrendered or deserted. Italian columns were under constant attack.

The Duke of Aosta had now concentrated the bulk of his remaining forces in northern Eritrea, and very little was left to face the south. Asmara had a large population of 40,000 Italians and 40,000 locals. It had no police and the bulk of the population was armed. But amazingly there was little difficulty.

The fall of Asmara had left Massawa in jeopardy. The Italian commander at Massawa was warned that the British would take no responsibility for the feeding of the Italian population if the harbour was damaged or ships were sunk in Massawa harbour.

Admirale Bonetti, the Italian naval commander at Massawa, in desperation, launched his destroyer force on a suicidal attack against Port Said and Suez. One ship had barely left the harbour before it hit a sandbank. By 1430 on 2 April the destroyers had been spotted, and HMS *Eagle*, close to the Suez Canal, was ready to strike. It had seventeen Fairey Swordfish torpedo bombers of 813 and 824 Squadrons. These aircraft had just flown in from Alexandria to Port Sudan.

Six of the Swordfish were launched at 0430 on 3 April to hunt for the Italian destroyers. The two squadrons were led by Commander C.L. Keighley-Peach, who was on reconnaissance on his own some twenty-eight miles to the east of Port Sudan at 0511. He called on three of the patrolling Swordfish to accompany him in an attack on the destroyers with 250 lb bombs. The first attack had several near-misses but no hits. One of the Swordfish remained aloft over the destroyers while the rest flew back to refuel and rearm.

At 0813 Lt A.G. Leathan led seven Swordfish into an attack. Midshipman E. Sargent of the Royal Naval Volunteer Reserve hit the *Nazario Sauro* six times with his six bombs. The crippled destroyer sank in less than a minute.

Meanwhile 14 Squadron had launched five Blenheim IVs and homed in on a stationary destroyer. As they moved in to attack they could see that the Italian crew were abandoning ship, and they plastered it with bombs. This is believed to have been the *Cesare Battisti*, which was later found beached.

Lt E.J.L. Sedgwick led another Swordfish attack on the destroyers at 1010. Sub Lt S.H. Suthers hit one of the destroyers between the funnels with a pair of bombs. This was the *Daniele Manin*, and the crew promptly abandoned her. Sedgwick stayed aloft, watching the two remaining destroyers. They were heading east out of range of the Swordfish.

The two remaining destroyers, the *Pantera* and the *Tigre*, were now to the south of Jedda. They were spotted by Blenheims belonging to 14 Squadron, Wellesleys of 223 Squadron and HMS *Kingston*. The bombers hit both vessels and HMS *Kingston* finished them off.

There was only one surviving Italian destroyer; the one that had run aground at Massawa. It managed to limp back into the harbour and was later bombed by 813 Squadron. The crew scuttled her on 8 April.

On 2 April an S.79 dropped a message to British troops at Diredawa. It reported that an Italian envoy would land there the following day. Sure enough, an S.79 piloted by *Capitano* Serafini landed at Diredawa to discuss terms that would guarantee the safety of women and children, and it was agreed that they would be protected. But the British demanded that the Italians unconditionally surrender. As it would transpire, the Duke of Aosta would not accept these terms. It was agreed that if Addis Ababa surrendered then British bombing missions against the town would be lifted.

Surrender terms were being discussed, but for now the airfield at Addis Ababa was still a prime target. In fact the British launched six attacks on the airfield in order to persuade the Italians that any future resistance was futile. Marylands of 12 SAAF Squadron were sent over the target on 4 April, covered by two Hurricanes of 3 SAAF Squadron. The Marylands approached at noon, and 413 *Squadriglia* scrambled a pair of CR.42s, flown by *Sergente Maggiore* Veronese and *Tenente* De Micheli. They attacked the bombers and were then pounced on by Capt Frost and Lt Marsh.

As it was, the Duke of Aosta decided to pull out of Addis Ababa in order to save the civilians from unnecessary deaths. The British now sent over their next wave against the airfield – four Fairey Battles of 11 SAAF Squadron. They dropped more than 200 bombs, straddling eight aircraft on the ground. Next, four Ju86s of 12 SAAF Squadron, escorted by two Gladiators, strafed and bombed the airfield. Then came three Blenheim Is of 8 Squadron, which had flown via Jijiga from Aden; they were escorted by Capt Frost and Lt Marsh. The final wave saw four Ju86s and two Hurricanes flown by Lt Upton and Capt van Breda Theron come in at 1335. In all, in just under three hours, over 1,500 lb of bombs had been dropped on the airfield.

If anything, it was petrol rather than the Italians that was holding up any further advances. Over in the east the South Africans had come to a halt when they had run out of fuel, but by noon on 2 April the King's African Rifle battalions were trying to find their way across the Awash river. The position was being held by 2,000 Eritreans and 4,000 Italians, supported by a company of medium tanks and seventy artillery pieces. This was the last central reserve of the Italians. There were also irregulars, commanded by *Colonnello* Rolle, but their attempts to join up were halted when the trains carrying them were wrecked by the South African Air Force.

The British managed to gain a crossing on the morning of 4 April. Six East African armoured cars had been hauled across the river through a ford. The arrival of the armoured cars spooked the Italians, and they immediately began to withdraw.

The 11th African Division, by the end of the first week of April, had advanced some 1,700 miles from British Somaliland in just fifty-three days. They had lost 135 dead, 310 wounded and fifty-two missing. But they had captured 50,000 prisoners. This was one of the longest and fastest advances in military history. It was a testament of the work of Col Sir Brian Robertson, the Chief Staff Officer in the Quartermaster-General's branch of the East Africa Force.

On the morning of 6 April Maj Gen Wetherall, escorted by an armoured car, drove into Addis Ababa to receive the formal surrender of the city. The Duke of Aosta had fled three days earlier. The Italian flag was hauled down once and for all.

Meanwhile, the previous day, Capt Frost and three other Hurricanes had been over Addis Ababa at 1345. Frost, Lt Kershaw and Lt Glover shot up a number of Italian bombers. Just before dusk Frost made a repeat visit along with Lt Marsh, smashing up another two bombers. It is difficult to be clear whether these were already abandoned aircraft. When the British took the airfield they found thirty burned-out Italian aircraft on the ground.

No. 11 SAAF Squadron had also attacked the Italians on 5 April. They had flown over an Italian convoy on the Sire–Aselle Road, destroying at least twenty vehicles.

A Maryland on reconnaissance suggested that *Generale* Gazzera was trying to set up a new defensive line at Jimma. Hartebeests of 40 SAAF Squadron (now at Neghelli) saw Italian defences at Wadara and reported this to ground forces.

The same day, 5 April, also saw the last mission of 1 SAAF Squadron in Eritrea. Five Hurricanes were dispatched to attack Gondar. Capt Duncan claimed that he had shot up an S.81 at Azozo. The squadron also received welcome news that at Adi Ugri Maj Wilmot had been found. He had been a prisoner of war. Other pilots and crew had also been liberated there, notably some crews of 47 Squadron, although Plt Off Witty had died in captivity. Squadrons would now be leaving for operations in Egypt. The first to leave would be 94 Squadron.

What had certainly helped the British, and in particular Cunningham, was the fact that the Italians had left behind such an enormous amount of fuel. At Kismayu they had left 220,000 gallons, another 350,000 at Mogadishu and incredibly 500,000 gallons at Addis Ababa.

After the loss of his destroyer fleet, it was now clear to Bonetti that further resistance at Massawa would be futile. He had a perimeter of ten miles to protect, but he had two battalions of marines, two battalions of Blackshirts, some customs guards, Grenadiers and 127 guns, including heavy coastal artillery. By 5 April Massawa had been surrounded by *Battalion* Garby and other Allied forces. On the afternoon of 5 April Bonetti sent out a negotiation team. The Allies would only accept unconditional surrender, and only that provided none of the ships or port installations were damaged. Bonetti would have twenty-four hours to consult with Rome, and then the Allies would attack.

Bonetti prevaricated, and the attack came in on the night of 7/8 April. The Italians gave up with virtually no fight. The gunners fought on, and by mid-afternoon on 8 April Massawa was in the hands of the Allies. Bonetti had tried to break his own sword over his knee, but when it did not snap he threw it into the harbour. A diver recovered it and presented it to General Platt. Bonetti and 9,500 men surrendered.

The Italian threat to shipping in the Red Sea was over, and to the great joy of the British effort the USA, not yet directly embroiled in the war, declared that the Red Sea was no longer a war zone and could now be traversed by American merchant ships. This would have an enormous impact on the course of the war. Weapons and supplies could now flood into Egypt.

CHAPTER EIGHT

Liberation

With the Italian situation spiralling out of control, for the Allies it was as much a question of protecting the civilian population as it was to drive the Italians out of their last strongholds. General Wavell had written a personal guarantee to the Duke of Aosta on 31 March:

> I am anxious to avoid any possibility that Italian women and children should be endangered in the course of military operations. Your Royal Highness must realise that your present military situation may make their protection in certain areas a difficult matter. I am prepared to offer co-operation in ensuring their safety so far as is consistent with my military duty of continuing action against your forces still in arms. I have therefore authorised General Cunningham to get in touch with Your Royal Highness by means which he will suggest and report to me any proposals which may mutually ensure the safety of women and children in zone of operations.

The British were keen at this point not to offer to assume responsibility for protecting and feeding Italian non-combatants. A necessary condition for the British to accept this responsibility would be Italian unconditional surrender. As we have seen, at this point the Duke of Aosta was still unwilling to accept the inevitable. Even after the fall of Addis Ababa the Italians were still believed to have at least 40,000 men in the field, along with 200 guns. Following the capture of Massawa, the two key enemy-held areas in northern Italian East Africa were Amba Alagi and Gondar.

Gondar had always been an important military base, and undoubtedly it would be relatively difficult to take it. But the British had their own problems; Wavell wanted as many troops as possible to be withdrawn from Eritrea and Italian East Africa, so that they could be redeployed in Egypt. The Italians were no longer a threat to the Sudan and there was little chance that they could even mount a counter-offensive and threaten Eritrea. It was still in Platt's mind, however, to destroy what remained of the Italian forces around Amba Alagi and Gondar.

At his disposal Platt had the 5th Indian Division, two motor machine-gun groups of the Sudan Defence Force, 1 Commando, a battery from the 68th Medium Regiment of the Royal Artillery and two companies of mounted infantry from the Sudan Defence Force. The British would need a brigade to garrison Asmara. They had sent light forces to pursue the enemy from Asmara. The Central Indian Horse was at Mai Mescic, but this was relieved by Skinner's Horse. No. 1 Motorised Machine-gun Group had reached Tacazze and No. 2 Motorised Machine-gun Group was along the Red Sea coast, at Zula.

The job of dealing with Amba Alagi was given to the 5th Indian Division. It was 235 miles to the south of Asmara. The Italian positions were strong, but it was decided to attack there at the first opportunity. This would then allow South African troops to pass through Italian East Africa and be redeployed in Egypt.

Amba Alagi presented a considerable obstacle. It was 10,000 ft above sea level, and the road running into Abyssinia crossed the spur of the mountain at the Toselli Pass, where there was a fort. The approach was steep and winding and overlooked by Italian observation posts. To the north-west of Amba Alagi was a long range of mountains, including Little Alagi, Middle Hill, Elephant, Pinnacle and Sandy Ridge. To the south-west were Castle Ridge and Castle Hill. Due north was Bald Hill, a huge, flat-topped mountain with vertical sides, and to the south-east and at the other side of the pass two major hills, Triangle and Gumsa. After the Toselli Pass was the Falaga Pass; this was a poor road and very difficult for motor transport.

It was decided that there were three possibilities in attacking the Italians at Amba Alagi. They could attack from the east through the Falaga Pass, but it was difficult to know just how strong the Italian positions were. There was a roadblock that was covered by fire from

Bald Hill. The second option was to approach by the main road. But the real attack would be along the ridge to the west of the road.

It was difficult bringing up troops, let alone supplies. The 5th Indian Division collected mules from the countryside and detached men to bring up the necessary supplies and ammunition. As the troops converged on their start positions, all movement was carried out at night. It took seventy-two hours to move up the 29th Indian Infantry Brigade, along with its supplies and ammunition. The Italians were completely unaware of the build-up.

On the left, operating against the Falaga Pass, was the unit dubbed 'Fletcher Force'. It consisted of Skinner's Horse, 51 Commando, a company from the 12th Frontier Force Regiment, a motorised machine-gun company of the Sudan Defence Force, a troop of 25-pdrs, a troop of 6 in. howitzers, a troop of 3.7 in. howitzers and a section of Sappers and Miners. In the centre the 3rd Battalion of the 18th Garhwal Rifles, along with a detachment of Sappers and Miners, was to deceive the Italians into believing that the main road would be the axis of attack. The main attack itself, however, would be made by the 29th Indian Infantry Brigade. The date set for the assault was 4 May.

Although the situation in East Africa was developing in the British favour, elsewhere there were huge difficulties. Rommel and the lead elements of the *Afrika Korps*, along with reinforcements from Italy, had thrown British forces all the way back to Egypt. In Greece the Germans had sliced through the Greek defence lines and the British Expeditionary Force on the Greek mainland was about to be evacuated. What remained of the force would be on Crete.

Reserves were desperately needed. As soon as Massawa was taken the 4th Indian Division was sent up to Egypt. The 1st South African Division in Kenya was bringing together the 2nd and 5th Brigades and was making for Mombasa and Berbera for embarkation to Egypt.

No. 1 SAAF Squadron, having destroyed more than a hundred Italian aircraft in the campaign, left in its Hurricanes, bound for Egypt on 6 April. Among them were some of the best pilots that had fought in the campaign, including Capt B.J.L. Boyle, who had shot down five, and Capt Andy Duncan, who had claimed four.

On 9 April Blenheims of 14 Squadron were dispatched to Egypt, and on 10 April 203 Squadron left for Kibrit. No. 223 Squadron passed over its last ten remaining Wellesleys to 47 Squadron and also left the East African theatre. K Flight and 1430 Flight both left, B and C Flights of 237 Squadron shifted to Asmara, and A Flight flew into Khartoum to pick up the Gladiators that had been left by K Flight.

Dessie was now the main target for Allied bombing. On 6 April six Fairey Battles carrying 20 lb fragmentation bombs lifted off at 0640. The Italians scrambled their fighters as soon as the attackers were spotted. Capt E.J. Kelly spotted Italian fighters taxiing up the runway to take off, but their progress was halted as two CR.42s came in to land. Kelly attacked, scattering his bombs across the airfield. He later claimed to have destroyed one CR.42 and damaged another pair. While the rest of the Fairey Battles plastered the airfield with bombs, a pair of Hurricanes, flown by Capt Frost and Lt Glover, strafed about twenty Italian aircraft parked around the airfield. Frost's Hurricane was hit so many times by ground fire that it was written off when he returned to base. Glover shot up a Ca 133 and an S.79, while Frost destroyed two CR.42s and two Ca 133s.

Immediately after this attack, Capt Theron, Lt Venter and Lt Van Ginkel, in their Hurricanes, came in to support eight Junkers Ju86s. They encountered three CR.42s and engaged them. Capt Theron and Lt Van Ginkel each claimed a kill. One of the Italian pilots, *Tenente* Caldonazzo (412 *Squadriglia*) was shot down and killed. Another CR.42 was shot down and the pilot managed to bale out, and a third was so badly damaged that it had to force-land. The three Hurricanes now moved in to make strafing attacks, shooting up a CR.42 and an S.79. The Italians would later admit to having lost two S.79s, four CR.42s, two Ca 133s and an S.81. Four other aircraft were badly damaged.

On 7 April the few remaining Italian aircraft in the area left Dessie, bound for Alomata. These amounted to just four Ca 133s and three CR.42s.

On 9 April Blenheims of 8 Squadron bombed the Medani Road, and Hurricanes and Fairey Battles made an attack on the airfield at Shashamanna. More Italian aircraft were lost; Lt Hewitson shot up a pair of S.79s, Capt Frost shot up two Ca 133s and Lt Torr another Ca 133. The weather was so bad on the return flight that the Fairey Battle flown by Lt M.G.T. Ferreira crashed. Later in the day Jimma was attacked by five Hurricanes. Capt Frost led an attack on a pair of CR.32s, while Lt Glover's aircraft attacked ground targets. The CR.32 flown by *Maresciallo* Mottet was attacked by Frost and Hewitson. The Italian aircraft was badly shot up, and it was wrecked when Mottet landed.

Meanwhile Lt Glover, along with Lt Upton and Lt Marsh, fired at four Ca 133s and a CR.32 on the ground. Frost and Howitson now joined in. As they swept away they encountered another CR.32. Lt Upton attacked it and then Lt Glover joined in; they hit it several times and the pilot baled out. The Italian pilot was extremely unlucky; his parachute caught the tail and ripped in half, and he fell to his death.

The Italians in this attack alone had lost two CR.32s on the ground, two in the air and six Ca 133s. The Italian Air Force was now down to its barest bones: just five CR.42s, four Ca 133s and two each of S.79s and CR.32s. In the workshops there were a number of other aircraft that the Italians hoped to be able to repair.

Two Hartebeests of 41 SAAF Squadron spotted an Italian column that was retreating from Debra Marcos and was actually making for Addis Ababa. It was a huge column with over 14,000 troops, both Italian and native, along with their families, and was led by *Colonnello* Maraventano. Capt T. Van Der Kaay led five Hartebeests and two Gladiators in a strafing attack. They shot up the column, and one of the Hartebeests was hit thirty-three times by ground fire. Another attack was launched the following day, and this time another Hartebeest, flown by Lt C. Collins, was so badly shot up it had to force-land. Collins and his gunner were to spend the next six weeks as prisoners of the column.

Dessie was still held, and this was before the main assault against Amba Alagi. There was another large fortress at Gondar, where the Italians were dug in. They still held Jimma and Gambela, and also positions near Soddu. With the loss of so many troops to Egypt there was now a period of reorganisation. Nos 3, 11, 40 and 41 SAAF Squadrons would now be based in the provinces of Galla Sidamo and Gojjam. Ju86s and Hurricanes would be based at Addis Ababa, and in the north, over Amba Alagi and Gondar, would be 47 and 237 Squadrons, the Free French and elements of 51 SAAF Flight.

Dessie was the target on 12 April for 12 SAAF Squadron.

Unfortunately the pilots could not see the target, and on their return the Ju86 flown by Lt N.S. De Villiers ran out of fuel and had to force-land in French Somaliland. He and his crew were interned by the French, but De Villiers escaped and returned to 12 SAAF Squadron on 29 April.

More Italian aircraft were lost on the ground on 12 April when three Gladiators of 237 Squadron attacked the airfield at Alomata. Most of the Italian aircraft that were hit were already unserviceable, but three Ca 133s and an S.79 were now permanently out of action. On the following day Capt Frost in his Hurricane struck Jimma and shot up and destroyed an Ro.37bis and a Ca 148.

The hunt was still on to knock out the rest of the Italian Air Force's dwindling resources. Gladiators accompanied a Lysander over Debarech on 15 April. When the Gladiators of 237 Squadron saw an S.79 in flight, Plt Off Simmonds attacked it, but the bomber eluded him. Dessie was attacked on 16 April by three Ju86s of 12 SAAF Squadron with Hurricane cover. Around eight Italian aircraft were destroyed, four by Lt Hewitson, three by Capt Frost and another by Lt Glover. Once again many of the aircraft that were hit were already badly damaged. None the less the Italians could still pack a punch, as they launched two raids later on in the day. Two CR.42s and an S.79 attacked ground units near Termaber and a Ca 133 attacked rebels near Deca.

On 17 April it was time for 2 SAAF Squadron to move to Egypt. Several pilots from 3 SAAF Squadron were also due to leave and be transferred to 1 SAAF Squadron. Despite the departures, the air offensive against the Italians continued. An Italian column was attacked on 19 April by three Battles and three Hurricanes. They shot up the convoy, consisting of around forty trucks and tankers. In the engagement the Fairey Battle flown by Capt J.F. Britz was badly damaged and he was forced to land at Combolcia. Lt S.W. Murray flew down to pick up Britz and his crew, but the Italians fired artillery at him, and Britz and the crew were taken prisoner (being released six days later).

The Italians were now using their Ca 133s to try to resupply the column led by *Colonnello* Maraventano. Despite this the attacks on Italian airfields continued. Belese was attacked by Wellesleys on 19 April, Alomata was attacked by a pair of Gladiators of 237 Squadron on 21 April; they destroyed a Ca 133 and damaged a Ca 148. Also on 21 April Lt Geraty in a Gladiator of 3 SAAF Squadron shot down a Ca 133 over Debra Marcos. The Italians withdrew two S.79s and two CR.42s from Combolcia just in time before the airfield was overrun. They were withdrawn to Jimma.

Maj J.D. Pretorius and Lt Hewitson of 3 SAAF Squadron, in Hurricanes, were over Jimma on 24 April. They were hunting for an aircraft that the Italians were intending to use to evacuate *Generale* Gazzera. Suddenly Hewitson's aircraft was hit by anti-aircraft fire and he was killed. No. 14 SAAF Squadron left East Africa on 24 April. It was re-formed in Egypt as 24 SAAF Squadron, with Marylands.

Events on the ground were now reaching a critical phase, and on 25 April a pair of Ca 133s were destroyed by 3 SAAF Squadron when they attacked Lekemti airfield. Dessie fell on 26 April, netting 10,000 prisoners, 240 lorries, fifty-two guns and over 230 machine-guns. One of the captured men was an Italian pilot of 412 *Squadriglia*, *Maresciallo* Arnaldo Soffritti. He had shot down eight British aircraft and destroyed another fifteen on the ground.

The assault against Amba Alagi was close. To support the attack 237 Squadron moved to Makale and 41 SAAF Squadron moved to Combolcia. Incredibly, a pair of CR.42 pilots, seemingly unaware that Combolcia had been overrun, tried to land there, but they were beaten off by anti-aircraft fire.

Three Gladiators of 237 Squadron struck Alomata and Cer-Cer on 29 April. At Alomata they shot up a Ca 133. The three pilots, Flg Off Spencer, Flg Off Simmonds and Flg Off Robinson, all claimed to have destroyed an aircraft at Cer-Cer, respectively a Ca 133, an S.79 and a CR.32. Later in the day Flg Off Spencer and Flg Off Kleynhans attacked Cer-Cer again. They shot up another CR.42. At that point the last serviceable S.79 headed for Shashamanna and a pair of CR.42s made for Gondar. Cer-Cer was attacked once again on 30 April, this time by Flt Lt E.T. Smith and Flg Off Simmonds. They were accompanied by a pair of Lysanders, but all they achieved was to shoot up the same aircraft again.

Patrolling alone over Jimma and Agara, Capt Frost of 3 SAAF Squadron spotted the S.79 that had left Cer-Cer. It was making its way along a valley. Frost attacked it twice, and he saw the crew bale out and the pilot, *Tenente* Curcio, just escaping before the bomber crashed. Frost then passed over Jimma airfield and shot up a CR.32, seeing it burst into flames.

The Italians were building up what remained of their ground forces in the west of Abyssinia. By the beginning of May a column led by *Generale* Bertello had reached the area around Shashamanna. *Generale* Liberati was also converging on the same area.

There was a reshuffle of Allied air assets, with 3 SAAF at Addis Ababa, along with 16 SAAF Squadron, which was just forming up, having taken over 12 SAAF Squadron's eight Ju86s. No. 12 SAAF Squadron had withdrawn into Kenya to be re-equipped, 11 SAAF Squadron, with its Fairey Battles, was now based at Jijiga, and 41 SAAF's Hartebeests were also at Addis Ababa. The Close Support Group was now at Combolcia for the forthcoming attack on Amba Alagi.

The attack on Wadara was due to get under way on 3 May, and this would be supported by 40 SAAF Squadron at Neghelli, with its seventeen Hartebeests. The primary concern was to prevent the Italians from massing for a counter-offensive. Italian troops on the ground were broken up by constant air attacks, and in fact on 2 May no fewer than thirteen were made over Shashamanna.

For a week before the attack on Amba Alagi, Fletcher Force pushed its way towards the Falaga Pass. It managed to capture a large number of prisoners and overran Commando Hill. On the night of 3/4 May, 51 Commando and Skinner's Horse launched an attack, but the Italians were resolute in their defence and the British troops withdrew around midnight. It is important to remember that these attacks along the Falaga Pass were to deceive the Italians into believing that this was the main point of attack by the British.

On the afternoon of 3 May the 3rd Battalion of the 18th Gardhwal Rifles arrived at the Enda Medani Alem Valley. It occupied the valley by 1730 and began moving forward. Again the intention was for the Italians to believe that this was a major push. The infantry moved towards Bald Hill and came up against heavy Italian resistance. Throughout the night more movement was made in deliberate view of the Italian observation posts, to continue to delude them.

At 0415 on 4 May the 29th Indian Infantry Brigade moved forward under artillery cover. The brigade stormed Pinnacle and

Elephant Hill. It then moved into an area that was swept by machine-guns from Bald Hill. It was clear that a continued attack in daylight hours would be suicidal, so the infantry dug in to resume their attack at 0145 on 5 May. This time Middle Hill was overrun, but again, as they passed between Middle Hill and Little Alagi, they came under tremendous machine-gun fire. Once again they were pinned. The brigade had been checked.

Other Allied troops were moving towards Amba Alagi. Patriot forces commanded by R.A.S. Seyoum, along with some elements of the Sudan Defence Force, had reached a point some fifty miles to the south-west of Amba Alagi at Socota. They had overrun an Italian fort and captured the garrison. They had continued to move east, advancing on Mai Ceu. Other Patriot units had cut many of the roads in the area.

On 30 April the 1st South African Brigade, which had overrun Dessie, began to advance and reached Alomata on 5 May. Here it was held up by an Italian rearguard. But it pushed forward, and on 8 May it was placed under the nominal command of the 5th Indian Division for operations against Amba Alagi.

Back at Amba Alagi it had become obvious that Fletcher Force needed infantry in order to make any further progress. The 3rd Battalion of the 12th Frontier Force Regiment was allocated to Fletcher Force, as was the 3rd Battalion of the 18th Garhwal Rifles. Fletcher Force now became the 9th Indian Infantry Brigade.

Meanwhile, on 6 May, two Fairey Battles were detached from 11 SAAF Squadron to support 16 SAAF Squadron in attacks against Italian ground force concentrations. On 7 May Capt Frost led an attack by Hurricanes against Jimma. They shot up a fuel convoy, blowing up four oil tankers and five petrol tankers. Effectively this stranded *Generale* Liberati and his 4,800 men and ten tanks.

Castle Ridge was assaulted at 0410 on 8 May by the 6th Battalion of the 13th Frontier Force Rifles and a company of the 1st Worcesters. Diversionary artillery fire was made on Little Alagi and Bald Hill. The attacking troops overran most of Castle Hill except a small part of the north end. The infantry saw a white flag raised as they advanced, but were met by a barrage of fire. Mist then rolled over the hilltops and the Italians massed for a counter-attack. They rolled the British back off Castle Hill.

Meanwhile, on the night of 7/8 May, the 9th Indian Brigade moved towards Falaga Pass. It captured a large number of prisoners. On the following night it managed to secure the pass. It then moved towards Gumsa Ridge. This effectively meant that the Italians were surrounded on three sides. The 1st South African Brigade was still moving forward, and by 13 May it had made contact with British troops around Amba Alagi.

On 14 May the South Africans began to move towards Triangle, aided by Patriot units. They overran Triangle at 0800 on 15 May; effectively the Italians were now completely surrounded. On the following day they would request an armistice; the negotiations would end in unconditional surrender.

Elsewhere there was still air activity. The airfield at Azozo near Gondar was attacked throughout the day by Wellesleys and by 237 Squadron. By this time, 8 May, 12 SAAF Squadron, now re-equipped with Marylands, made its way to Egypt.

The Allies overran Wadara on 10 May, with the Italians falling back to Dalle. There were only a handful of Italian aircraft that were serviceable, including just two Ca 133s. One of the Ca 133s was flown by *Tenente* Case, and his job was to drop supplies to isolated Italian garrisons. His aircraft was hit by anti-aircraft fire on 12 May.

On 10 May, 40 SAAF Squadron assisted the 21st East African Brigade to capture Giabassire. On 14 May Shashamanna was overrun by the 11th African Division. Everything was now falling back towards Jimma.

There was a possible kill for a Blenheim flown by the Free French on 13 May. The aircraft was attacked by a CR.42 over Azozo airfield, but the kill was not confirmed. Azozo airfield was also hit by four Gladiators of 237 Squadron on 15 May. They wrecked an unserviceable Ca 133 and an S.79. Plt Off W.M. Cooper of 237 Squadron, in a Lysander, was shot down over Amba Alagi. He crash-landed and later died from his injuries.

The Duke of Aosta at Amba Alagi finally surrendered, handing over 5,000 men, fifty-four large guns and 250 machine-guns.

There would be one more major attack before Gondar could be tackled. This was at Debra Tabor, some 150 miles from Dessie. It was defended by around 2,500 Italians (although this was to be an enormous under-estimation). The position had field works and barbed wire. It was under constant observation by a Patriot force, known as Begemeder. It had tried to make some attacks but had got nowhere.

One squadron of Skinner's Horse less the carrier troop, a company of the 3rd Battalion 2nd Punjabi Regiment along with a mortar detachment of three captured 81mm Italian mortars, and a field company of Sappers and Miners were sent to help the Patriots.

In spite of the surrender of the Duke of Aosta, Jimma, Gondar and the port of Assab were still under Italian control. On 10 June Operation Chronometer was launched against Assab. It was completed by a single Indian battalion.

Prior to this 237 Squadron had left for Egypt on 26 May. Now the only RAF unit in Eritrea was 47 Squadron. Aircraft in Aden were now out of range of the ground theatre in Italian East Africa, and consequently 8 Squadron was re-formed, with two flights, one of Vincents and one of Blenheims, and returned to policing duties.

No. 47 Squadron struck at Gondar while Jimma was hit by constant Ju86 and Hurricane attacks. Any Italian ground movement immediately drew the attention of Gladiators and Fairey Battles, and now 41 SAAF Squadron's Hartebeests joined in.

The Italians had been using a Ca 133 painted with a Red Cross to bomb Patriot forces. The British warned the Italians to cease this kind of activity. When they received no reply, a Hurricane strafed and destroyed the offending aircraft on 19 May.

After the fall of Amba Alagi the 1st South African Brigade was sent to Egypt, the 11th African Division received a new Close Support Group, consisting of one flight of Gladiators, two flights of Fairey Battles and two flights of Hartebeests. No. 40 SAAF launched its last offensive mission in Italian East Africa on 21 May. It was then recalled to South Africa for refitting. It left behind sixteen Hartebeests, which it turned over to 41 SAAF Squadron.

By 22 May both *Generale* Liberati and *Generale* Baccari had been captured, and British forces were now close to the Omo river. Any chance of Italian resistance was quickly broken up by continued attacks by Fairey Battles and Ju86s. As part of this campaign, on 26 May a pair of Ju86s of 16 SAAF Squadron were attacked by a pair of CR.42s close to the Omo river. On 28 May the two CR.42s were active again, escorting a Ca 148 that was dropping supplies to ground units. One of the aircraft, flown by *Sergente Maggiore* Antonio Giardinà, attacked and shot down Capt D.R. Clyde-Morley's Hurricane over Jimma. Clyde-Morley was the commander of A Flight of 3 SAAF Squadron, and had taken over from Capt Frost. Clyde-Morley hit the ground hard, but was found by Patriot forces. There was another encounter with the same CR.42s, this time over Soddu on 2 June. Lt Venter of 3 SAAF Squadron chased one of the CR.42s but lost it in the clouds. Sadly, Venter was to lose his life the following day. He crashed into a mountainous area to the south of Soddu on a flight from Addis Ababa to Algato.

In the first five days of June 1941, 11 SAAF Squadron (now renumbered 15 SAAF Squadron) dropped 18,000 lb of bombs in the attacks across the Omo river. The 22nd East African Brigade was pushing on towards Jimma. On 3 June Capt G.A. Giles, in a Hartebeest, was shot down by anti-aircraft fire and killed. He had had a long and illustrious career as a pilot and had flown in 1916 with the Royal Flying Corps; he was forty-three.

With Jimma under threat the Italian aircraft evacuated two CR.42s and a Ca 148, and headed to Gondar. The fighters would be grounded at Gondar until 10 June due to the lack of ammunition. They could recommence their offensive actions once an S.75 had flown in from Italy with the necessary supplies.

The final Italian force on the eastern side of the Omo river surrendered. This was the 24th Italian Colonial Division. The Italians flooding away from the river were under constant attack from Hartebeests and Ju86s. There were just four airworthy Fairey Battles now, and one of them, on 11 June, crashed into some mountains, killing the crew, who were Lt E.J. Steyn and Sgt F.W. Kelly.

By 16 June the Italian garrison at Debra Tabor was cut off. Patriot forces had cut the roads to the east and west of the town. There were around 8,000 Patriot troops in the region. It appeared that the Italians were too frightened to surrender to the Patriot forces and were hoping that British regulars would appear. In actual fact the Patriot forces were squabbling among themselves and not co-operating. British troops in the region amounted to just 250 men, and the Patriots did not seem to want to co-operate with them.

On 16 June five Hartebeests attacked anti-aircraft positions. Lt D. Cobbledick attacked three of the anti-aircraft positions. Both he and his gunner were wounded, and they managed to crash-land at Wolchette.

On 20 June Jimma fell. British forces found fifteen Italian aircraft burnt out on the airfield. The Italians still resisted in the region. *Generale* Pietro Gazzera, who had now been pronounced Supreme Commander in East Africa, still had around 5,000 men at his command. He had determined to make a stand at Dembidollo. His retreat was already cut off by a force of Free Belgians. They had marched from the Belgian Congo and across the Sudan.

On 25 June the Italian garrison at Debra Tabor came out under a flag of truce, and an armistice was agreed until 1600 hours on 27 June. However, no surrender arrangements were agreed, so British forces continued to build up in the area and to bombard Italian positions.

Meanwhile, B Flight of 41 SAAF Squadron moved up to occupy Jimma airfield. A Flight continued operating from the east bank of the Didessa. No. 3 SAAF Squadron also moved into Jimma on 1 July. B Flight had already made the move on 24 June.

Generale Gazzera's headquarters at Dembidollo was under continual dive-bomb attack from 16 SAAF Squadron. It was now clear that the Italian position was hopeless. Gazzera contacted the British to negotiate a surrender. He finally acceded and surrendered to the Belgian commander, *Generaal-majoor* Gilliaert, on 6 July.

With the situation at Debra Tabor unresolved, activities against the town continued until 1 July. The Italian commander then contacted the British and requested a meeting at 1100 hours on 2 July. Finally, surrender terms were agreed, and on 3 July British troops entered Debra Tabor. The garrison marched out on 6 July and laid down their weapons. Patriot forces occupied much of the town. Another 2,400 Italians, 2,000 natives, a huge number of trucks, six guns and masses of ammunition were taken.

All that remained was the final Italian position at Gondar. But there *Generale* Nasi had as many as 25,000 troops. It could be another ruinous struggle.

CHAPTER NINE

Gondar and the End

Back in March the 3rd Battalion of the 12th Frontier Force Regiment, less one company, was withdrawn to Gedaref, to join up with the 9th Indian Infantry Brigade. One company of the Frontier Force Regiment, along with the 21st Field Company of Sappers and Miners, was left to continue their pursuit of Italian forces along the Gallabat–Gondar Road. They stopped some miles to the west of Chelga when they ran into enemy positions. On 5 April the 3rd Ethiopian Battalion and C Troop Light Artillery Battery Sudan Defence Force joined them. With some other changes by 15 April, a new force, known as Kerforce, consisting of the 3rd Ethiopian Battalion and a composite battalion made up from various Sudan Defence Force units, took over operations in this sector.

The Italians were holding an escarpment that was five to ten miles to the west of Chelga. They also held a number of smaller defensive positions. It was difficult country to operate in, as there were poor roads, insufficient grass for camels and in any case the British in the region lacked sufficient transport. The rains began to fall in mid-April, making it all the more impossible.

On 22 April there was a skirmish eight miles to the south of Chelga at Tankal. The Italian counter-attack failed and they left eighty dead.

On 18 May the composite battalion worked its way round to a position just 1,100 yards to the north-east of the Chelga Fort. In the operation they captured over 300 Italians. The following day the Italians counter-attacked, and as a result of casualties they withdrew on 22 May. For the time being no further operations could take place on this front.

By the end of June the composite battalion was concentrated around Gallabat, and the Italians took the opportunity to move forward and establish defensive positions some thirty-six miles to the south-east of Gondar, which covered the road to Debra Tabor.

Meanwhile, No. 1 Motor Machine-gun Group of the Sudan Defence Force was pursuing Italian troops retreating towards Gondar. The unit had managed to cross the Tacazze river on 12 April, and a day later had reached the Wolchefit Pass. Here it was ambushed. The road in the region was extremely difficult; it zigzagged up the face of Green Hill and then onto a plateau. The whole area was covered by machine-guns and mortar positions. The Italians had positioned 3,000 Italian troops and 2,000 natives to defend the pass. They were also believed to have light tanks, thirty guns and a large number of machine-guns and mortars. As a defensive position it was better than Amba Alagi and Keren. British troops could not approach without being spotted immediately. Everything in the valley was in full view. There was only one other way onto the escarpment, and that was a mule track that wound eighteen miles through the hills and emerged fifteen miles to the west of Debarech. The track was only any good for mules, and not for other transport.

Beyond Wolchefit there was no serious block on the way to Gondar. It had to be turned, but it was mined, had been blocked by demolitions and seemed impossible. There were Patriot forces operating on the plateau, supported by a company of the 3rd Ethiopian Battalion under Maj Ringrose. Closer to Gondar there was another bunch of Patriots commanded by *El Bimbashi* (Major) Sheppard. There was another party of Patriots operating around Debra Tabor, as we have seen.

By 28 May *El Bimbashi* Sheppard and his men had occupied the road from Debarech to Amba Giyorgis. There was stiff fighting in the area, which culminated in the capture of Debarech on 31 May. Also overrun were three small forts to the west.

On 17 June Maj Ringrose made an attack on one of the forts at Wolchefit. The Italians had been caught napping, but on 23 June they counter-attacked Ringrose and scattered his troops. Several were captured, including the Patriot commander, Ras Ayalu, and his son. The Italians then managed to recapture Debarech and begin moving west towards Bosa.

The force watching Wolchefit Pass was reinforced by a battery of

28 Field Regiment on 27 June. The force now consisted of No. 2 Motor Machine-gun Group of the Sudan Defence Force (less a company), 51 Commando and 20 Field Company of Sappers and Miners. They were ordered to take the pass and clear an advance on Gondar. The attack was due to go in on 6 July. It would be a complicated procedure. The 3rd Battalion of the 14th Punjabi Regiment had begun advancing from Zarema towards Bosa, and it would join in with the attack.

The force arrived at Bosa on 13 July and began to probe forward the following day. The Italians immediately launched a counterattack. In the confusion Patriot forces joined in the defence against the Italians, and it was difficult to tell friend from foe. The commander of the Punjabi Regiment was killed, and with the element of surprise lost they withdrew. Time was pressing because the 28th Field Regiment was due to sail for the Middle East and could only be used in the region until 19 July.

Meanwhile, around Gondar, some newly arrived CR.42s attacked British positions around Debra Tabor on 11 June. Eight days later *Tenente* Case attacked the same positions in his Ca 133, but his aircraft was hit by anti-aircraft fire. On 27 June a pair of CR.42s attacked five Wellesleys of 47 Squadron; there were no casualties. On 2 July Sgt A.G. Brown of 47 Squadron was shot down over Gondar and all the crew were lost. The victim was claimed by a CR.42.

In fact there were only two CR.42s at Gondar. They were kept serviceable by cannibalising other aircraft. The small aerial contingent was commanded by *Colonnello* Dario Busoni. The few remaining Ca 133s were hidden for most of the day, and were used to drop supplies to the Italian garrison at Wolchefit Pass.

Wellesleys struck at Gondar on 9 July, with a single CR.42 being scrambled to intercept. Soon there would be overwhelming numbers of British aircraft in the area that not even the miracle worker, Busoni, would be able to cope with and respond to. In fact on 11 July three Ju86s moved down to Alomata, just 120 miles from Gondar. At Combolcia the Gladiators of B Flight, 3 SAAF Squadron, had taken up residence. A Flight joined them on 19 July, with three Gladiators and two Hurricanes.

The last Italian aircraft had to be swept from the skies, and the major offensive began on 14 July. Capt C.M. Smuts led three Ju86s against Gondar, with 3 SAAF Squadron's Gladiators turning over on the runway in readiness to intercept, should the CR.42s be lured into chasing the Ju86s back to base. Over Gondar Lt G.E. Abbott was hit by anti-aircraft fire. He began to fall behind and swooped down over Azozo, and then spotted a Ca 133. He immediately noticed that the Ca 133 had no propellers, so instead he attacked a hangar. He then came under machine-gun fire from the ground. The Ju86 sprang an oil leak and his speed reduced dramatically. Abbott force-landed in a field near Bandia and he and his crew managed to escape and join up with Patriot forces.

The CR.42s were in evidence on 17 July when a pair of Ju86s attacked. Over Gondar both of the Ju86s' bomb-release mechanisms failed to operate, but they managed to make it back to base. On 17 July A Flight of 3 SAAF Squadron moved to Addis Ababa, and 2/Lt Lilienfeld nearly wrecked a Hurricane when the wheels sank into muddy ground. From now on any bombing raid against Italian targets would have Hurricane support.

A Ju86 had been flown in to bring up the number of JU86s at Alomata to three. A pair of Hurricanes were due to cover them in their raid over Gondar, but due to technical difficulties the fighters were late getting off, and they only met up with the Ju86s on their return trip. By this time a pair of CR.42s were harassing them. They managed to shoot up all three of the bombers. The Hurricanes strafed Azozo and claimed to have shot up a CR.42 on the ground. By the end of July 41 SAAF Squadron was moving into Alomata.

A solitary CR.42 covered the arrival of an S.75 that had flown from Italy on 30 July; it arrived unmolested.

On 1 August the two CR.42s made an attack on a French-flown Blenheim, but made little impact on the aircraft. On the following day a captured CR.32 and CR.42 were flown down by Maj Biden and Maj Klotze (41 SAAF Squadron) to Nairobi. They would be used for training purposes, but they had both been destroyed before the war ended.

Meanwhile, in Gondar, *Generale* Nasi sat determined to retain what he could of Italian East Africa. He knew that most of the country was now under British control, but he still had a strong force and considerable stores, and he had received additional help from the columns of Italian troops that had flooded towards Gondar. There were natural defences around the city. The ancient capital itself was 7,500 ft above sea level. The mountains to the south were as much as 5,000 ft higher. He had nine Blackshirt battalions, the 4th Colonial Brigade, part of the 22nd Colonial Brigade and a number of other native troops – in all 25,000 men. His army had been placed in various detachments and outposts among the peaks around Gondar.

As the rains came it meant that even the South African Air Force could not mount operations against the Italian ground troops. An increasing number of British ground forces were being withdrawn either to Egypt or to Libya. Many others were tied up in garrison duties, from the Red Sea coast to Addis Ababa and beyond.

Maj Gen C.C. Fowkes still had around 8,000 British troops, comprising Indian units, Sudanese, men from the Gold Coast, West Africa, the King's African Rifles, some Free French and some Highland units. He also had the valuable aid of the Abyssinian Patriots, who were superb scouts and invaluable for observing Italian movement.

No. 41 SAAF Squadron now had all of its three flights at Alomata, some eighteen Hartebeests. Other units were not so fortunate, and well below strength: 3 SAAF Squadron had just a pair of Hurricanes and three Gladiators capable of mounting operations; 15 SAAF Squadron was down to two Fairey Battles; and 16 SAAF had just three serviceable Ju86s.

Despite the lack of aircraft, the attacks on Gondar were resumed. On 2 August Capt P. Hayden-Thomas was shot down by anti-aircraft fire over Gondar. He crash-landed and was picked up by friendly locals and taken on a mule to Debra Tabor. He was then flown back to base at Alomata. On the same day a Gladiator was badly damaged by anti-aircraft fire and a Hartebeest was wrecked when it ran out of fuel and crashed.

The following day Gondar was attacked again, this time by a mixed bag, including three Ju86s, nine Hartebeests, a pair of Fairey Battles and a Hurricane. Lt Anderson's Hartebeest was hit by anti-aircraft fire and he had to crash-land. Another attack came in on 8 August, but a much diminished one, with three Hartebeests and two Gladiators attacking Gondar. The two remaining Fairey Battles shot up a Ca 133 at Azozo. A precious Ju86 was lost on 9 August when its undercarriage gave way while it was taking off, and a Hurricane was wrecked on 12 August when Lt Cobbledick had an accident while taxiing.

Debarech was attacked by three Hartebeests on 14 August. Two of them were badly hit. Lt G.R. Andrews crash-landed and Capt Chapman was captured by some local robbers and then handed over to the Patriots. On 17 August, with a major ground attack expected against Wolchefit and Debarech, a flight of 41 SAAF Squadron moved to Aksum.

On 18 August a Hartebeest was lost when it developed serious engine problems. No. 35 SAAF Squadron was created, receiving the Ju86s of 16 SAAF Squadron. The following day the last remaining operational Fairey Battle flew its last mission, and with that 15 SAAF Squadron withdrew to Kenya for a major refit.

The Italians at Wolchefit Pass still refused to surrender. Pressure was beginning to ease on the movement of ground and air assets to Egypt. Conditions were not ideal for either ground or air offences due to the weather. Air support had certainly dwindled, but so had the threat from the Italian Air Force. As far as the Italians were concerned, after the fall of Addis Ababa the only imperative was to try to hold down as many British units in East Africa as possible, for as long as possible. This would prevent them from being transferred to the Western Desert. Eventually, however, it was dawning on the Italians who remained active in East Africa that the situation had reached the stage where further resistance was becoming pointless.

There was an attack made by Patriot forces led by Maj B.J. Ringrose on 25 August against the Wolchefit Pass. The South African Air Force threw in all its airworthy Hartebeests, and the RAF contributed by flying countless Wellesley sorties against the trenches and positions still held by the Italians. The attack, however, was not an overwhelming success. Having taken over a hundred prisoners, the Patriot forces were forced to withdraw due to mounting pressure and counter-attacks by the Italians.

A Hartebeest flown by Capt Du Toit was hit by ground fire and began to burn. He wrestled with the controls of his aircraft and landed on a road some fifteen miles to the south-east of Gondar. He was picked up by Patriot troops and brought back to base. On the same day Lt W. Arbuthnot, in a Gladiator, failed to return after a reconnaissance flight over Azozo. It would later transpire that his

aircraft had been hit by ground fire in the oil cooler and he had had
to crash-land. Some time later Allied troops found him and brought
him home. On 26 August Lt Mitchell's Gladiator was shot down
close to Azozo airfield. He managed to crash-land, and was pulled
out of the wreckage unconscious by Patriot forces and taken back to
Alomata.

On 13 July twenty Curtiss Mohawk IVs had arrived at Mombasa
from Great Britain. On 27 August B Flight of 3 SAAF Squadron
withdrew from the theatre in order to be re-equipped with these new
aircraft. The first of these aircraft would make an appearance soon.
Despite the arrival of these new Mohawks, the British air forces in
East Africa were still woefully under strength. They had lost seven
aircraft in the past month to anti-aircraft fire.

On 4 September Lt Harcourt-Baldwin in a Hartebeest was hit by
anti-aircraft fire over Debarech and Wolchefit Pass. He managed to
force-land his aircraft to the west of Alomata.

The Italians managed to repair their sole remaining Ca 133 at
Gondar by 8 September. It could now recommence its flying
missions to drop supplies to Wolchefit. The pair of CR.42s were also
active, conscious of the fact that there was an S.75 inbound from
Italy and due very soon. On 11 September a Hurricane intercepted
one of the CR.42s over Wolchefit while it was protecting the Ca 133.
The CR.42 eluded the Hurricane pilot. Italian motorboats operating
on Lake Tana were attacked on 11 September by a pair of Ju86s. On
16 September one of the few remaining Ju86s was hit by anti-aircraft
fire and crash-landed to the north-east of Debra Tabor.

The garrison at Gondar was still determined and holding out,
and it became increasingly apparent that the S.75s that were flying
into Gondar were actually routeing through Djibouti in French
Somaliland. This would be the first chance for the Mohawk aircraft
to show their worth. They were positioned close to the frontier, at
Aiscia, and their role was to interdict any Italian aircraft coming out
of French Somaliland.

On 16 September Capt Parsonson, Capt Snyman and Lt Strong
took off for the first leg of their journey to Yavello in Mohawks.
Strong never made it; he crash-landed near Mega, breaking several
bones. The Mohawk Fighter Flight was in position on 18 September,
and the following day Lt Turner was scrambled in his Mohawk to

intercept two unidentified aircraft. He tried to find them, but the aircraft had eluded him; this was going to be a frustrating business unless the rules of engagement were changed. So far, British aircraft had not invaded French Somaliland air space, but that would now change. From 23 September permission was now given to intercept any S.75s or other Italian aircraft over neutral Vichy French Somaliland.

This move by the Mohawk Fighter Flight was to have enormous and immediately unexpected consequences. On 21 September the last Ca 133 in Gondar burst into flames, probably due to sabotage. Gondar could no longer expect to receive resupply by air.

In order to apply additional pressure, British ground forces again advanced on Wolchefit Pass. They were covered by British aircraft and artillery fire, which claimed almost 1,000 Italians killed and wounded. In any case, the garrison had had enough. Many had deserted and others had slipped through the lines and surrendered to British forces. The British had been planning to attack with two brigades from Debra Tabor, but the plans had been changed, and a single battalion would advance, while the 25th East African Brigade and the 26th East African Brigade attacked from the south. There were also to be diversionary attacks by Sudanese and Patriot troops. This now left *Generale* Nasi in Gondar utterly isolated.

In order to ensure that the air border with Vichy French Somaliland was airtight, three Ju86s of 35 SAAF Flight were moved up close to the border. Out of Aden, 8 Squadron of the RAF flew in four Vincents to assist.

On 4 October it was reported that an Italian S.75 was on the ground at Djibouti. Capt Parsonson flew over Djibouti and failed to spot the aircraft. He tried again on 5 October, and on his second attempt he spotted it sitting on the airfield. Without hesitation he dived and opened fire on the aircraft, setting it on fire and gutting it. The French immediately lodged a complaint. They claimed that it was a Red Cross aircraft. Their accusations and complaints were brushed aside, and Italian aircraft continued to enter French Somaliland.

More Mohawks moved up to Aiscia, and on 14 October the Mohawk Fighter Flight officially became B Flight, 3 SAAF Squadron.

The CR.42s were active around Gondar on 8 October. They had flown several reconnaissance sorties and were now shooting up British vehicles that were moving up for the final assault on Gondar. In the past two months Gondar had been hit by nearly 100,000 lb of bombs.

The British and Commonwealth squadrons were determined to get the last two CR.42s. On 10 October three Gladiators belonging to A Flight of 3 SAAF Squadron landed at Dabat, along with C Flight 41, SAAF Squadron. They immediately drew the attention of the CR.42s, who strafed the airfield but caused no damage.

It was now abundantly clear to *Colonnello* Busoni, the commander of the remaining Italian air forces in Gondar, that the unequal fight was nearly over. He had contacted Italian Air Force headquarters in Rome that if it appeared that Gondar would fall he would order his two remaining pilots, *Sottotenente* Ildebrando Malavolti and *Maresciallo* Giuseppe Mottet, to attack Asmara and Alomata airfields respectively. Malavolti would then bale out and Mottet would try to fly to Djibouti.

There was a close-run thing on 16 October when a Hurricane and three Gladiators nearly caught one of the CR.42s over Azozo, but it escaped.

On 24 October *Colonnello* Busoni was ordered by *Generale* Nasi to mount a reconnaissance patrol over Kulkaber to see whether the British had repaired a bridge. Only one of the CR.42s was serviceable. Busoni wanted to wait until they were both available and could cover one another. *Generale* Nasi gave him an explicit order to mount the operation. Busoni ordered Malavolti to carry out the reconnaissance mission, but Malavolti also wanted to postpone the mission until the other CR.42 was operational. He knew as much as Busoni did that flying alone was to court death, and that undoubtedly he would be intercepted by British and Commonwealth aircraft. Malavolti was certain that it was a one-way trip.

Sure enough, at around 1735 South African pilots at Dabat heard a CR.42 overhead. They then spotted it and scrambled Lt L.C.H. Hope. He headed straight for Gondar, hoping to intercept the CR.42, and finally he spotted it about 1,000 ft below him. He opened fire and Malavolti tried to evade him. Hope continued to chase, and Malavolti lost control as the aircraft began to burst into flames. It spun and landed near Ambazzo. The wreckage was found the following day. Malavolti was dead. Hope flew over the Italian positions the next day and dropped a message: 'Tribute to the pilot of the Fiat. He was a brave man. South African Air Force.'

This was to be the last Italian aircraft shot down over East Africa in the Second World War.

Hope was not to have a particularly pleasant remainder of his tour in East Africa. On 31 October, acting on his own initiative, he attacked some Italian motorboats on Lake Tana and then shot up some Italian vehicles near the lake. His aircraft was hit by anti-aircraft fire and he was shot down and crashed into a tree. He managed to climb out of the wreckage with burns, and then Italian Colonial troops shot him. They then beat him nearly to death before an Italian officer interceded. Hope was blind for two days. He was eventually released after the fall of Gondar, and a court of enquiry was held at the end of November to consider his actions. The court of enquiry found that his actions were prompted by 'excessive zeal and over-keenness'.

By the beginning of November 1941 the South African Air Force had amassed forty-five aircraft ready for the final assault on Gondar. No. 47 Squadron's Wellesleys had also moved up to join in the attack. A Gladiator and a Hartebeest attacked Italian shipping on Lake Tana on 1 November. On 2 November, while carrying out an attack on Gondar, a Hartebeest was hit by anti-aircraft fire. It was damaged, but managed to get back to base.

Capt Du Toit had a close shave on 6 November when his Hartebeest was hit by anti-aircraft fire. His cockpit caught fire and he had to dive in order to put the flames out.

On 9 November Mohawk aircraft had arrived at Alomata and were now fitted out to carry bombs. B Flight, 3 SAAF Squadron, had ten Mohawks, A Flight was equipped with five Mohawks to accompany the single Hurricane and the four Gladiators, and 41 SAAF Squadron retained its twenty five Hartebeests.

Gianda was under attack by the 2nd Ethiopian Battalion on 11 November. Overhead, spotting for the artillery, was a Hartebeest covered by Mohawks. The full weight of the Allied aircraft was thrown against Fercaber on 12 November. There were two aircraft casualties: Lt A.W. Penver's Hartebeest was struck by anti-aircraft fire and he made a forced landing to the east of Gondar, and 2/Lt G.G.J. Van Dyk shot off the cooling system of his own engines with his guns and made a crash-landing close to Dabat. Penver was stuck until 25 November, when he was flown out.

On 11 November an S.75 had been flown from Italy to Djibouti and was due to fly into Gondar on 12 November. It took off and as it approached Gondar at night it hit a mountain close to Debra Marcos and was destroyed.

To the south-east of the city of Gondar there was a strong Italian position on the Kulkeber–Fercaber line. The Italians had dug in along steep slopes and had built fortifications and planted mines and numerous booby traps. South Force, consisting of two battalions with some medium guns, along with a large group of Patriots led by Maj Douglas, launched an assault on 13 November. The Patriots alone numbered up to 5,000 men. The British forces took Kulkeber but were then driven out.

Throughout November there had been persistent rumours that the Germans had managed to fly as many as fifteen aircraft into the theatre. In response to this, on 14 November, Sqn Ldr D.M. Illsley DFC led four Wellesleys of 47 Squadron to hunt for the German aircraft. It was, of course, a rumour and nothing more. But Illsley's aircraft unexpectedly crashed, and he and his crew were killed.

On 17 November Gondar, Azozo, Ambazzo and Defeccia were attacked by an enormous Allied air strike. No fewer than nine Wellesleys, twenty-four Hartebeests and twelve Mohawks dropped nearly 11,000 lb of bombs on their targets. Capt Du Toit had another close encounter with death when his aircraft was hit in the engine by anti-aircraft fire. He just about managed to nurse the aircraft back to Dabat.

There needed to be another way to deal with the determined Italian resistance around Kulkeber. An old track had been discovered, which offered a short-cut between Amba Giyorgis and Kulkeber. On 19 November every available resource was thrown into improving the track so that lorries and other vehicles could move up the steep gradients. In fact in some places tractors had to be used to pull trucks along. Luckily the track was screened from Italian observation, except for one tiny stretch. The Italians spotted the lorries of 25th Brigade, but *Generale* Nasi could not give the isolated garrison at Kulkeber any help. He knew that an assault would soon be on.

On 20 November fourteen waves of Wellesleys, Hartebeests and Mohawks struck Italian positions at Kulkeber and Fercaber. Lt G.R. Jacobs was killed when his Mohawk stalled and then crashed on take-off.

The following day more aircraft attacks were made in support of the 25th East African Brigade, which was attacking Kulkeber from the north. South Force and Douglas's Patriots attacked from the south-east. The 2nd Battalion of the 3rd King's African Rifles finally managed to reach the ridge, but the Italians shelled them and drove them 600 yards downhill. Maj Trimmer rallied the battalion, and along with two companies of the 2nd Battalion of the 4th King's African Rifles, they recaptured the hilltop. The Italians launched three heavy counter-attacks, but by 1500 they had had enough and white flags began to appear. South Force and the Patriots had also made their objectives. The final battle to reach the gates of Gondar had been won. In all, 107 Patriots had been killed and ninety-nine British and Commonwealth troops had been killed or wounded.

The last sortie of the Italian Air Force was flown by *Maresciallo* Giuseppe Mottet on 22 November. His CR.42 attacked British artillery positions at Kulkeber. In the attack he killed Lt Col Ormsby. On the following day the road at Gorgora was attacked by Hartebeests and then by Mohawks. Sadly, the last operational CR.42 was burned on 26 November, to prevent it from falling into enemy hands.

The final attack on Gondar would come from the south-east, largely on account of the poor condition of the Debra Tabor road. A containing force was left at Amba Giyorgis, and the bulk of the 26th Brigade was moved up to Aiva. The brigade had to cross dreadful countryside; there were no roads and transport was at best improvised. They could only use donkeys, mules and horses, so the men had to carry everything they needed for three days of operations. The brigade had to make its final approach down a slope in full view of the enemy.

At dawn on 27 November an enormous artillery barrage opened up on Gondar. All through the day sixteen Hartebeests, eight Mohawks and six Wellesleys dropped 12,500 lb of bombs on Italian targets. The 26th Brigade crossed the River Megech and began to attack the ridge at Defeccia. To the south, the 25th Brigade was pushing up the road towards Azozo. Douglas's Patriots mounted a series of diversionary attacks on Italian positions, known as the Fanta Posts.

The Patriots were making good progress, but the 25th Brigade was making the most ground. They took positions to the south and south-east of Azozo. Luckily for 2/Lt Robinson, whose Hartebeest had been hit in the engine by anti-aircraft fire, British armoured cars and light tanks had just reached Azozo when he crash-landed. The armoured cars and light tanks pushed across the bridge.

Generale Nasi realised that the game was over. He had virtually no reserves, and he sent out envoys to request an armistice, but by now it was nearly too late. *Generale* Nasi surrendered by the end of the day.

Aircraft dropped leaflets telling isolated Italian outposts that the battle was over. The Allies captured 11,500 Italians, 12,000 Africans, 400 machine-guns, twenty-four mortars and forty-eight field guns. British and Commonwealth casualties, excluding the Patriots, amounted to 116 killed and 386 wounded.

The last major stronghold of Italian East Africa had been overrun. All that remained was the mopping-up exercise – a far tougher prospect than could have been reasonably expected.

CHAPTER TEN

Aftermath

Even though *Generale* Guglielmo Nasi had surrendered at Gondar in November 1941, many Italian troops decided to continue the struggle with a guerrilla war in the mountains and deserts of Abyssinia, Eritrea and Somaliland. According to Alberto Rosselli, the Italian historian, some 7,000 Italian soldiers would take part in the continued struggle against the British and Commonwealth troops in the former Italian East Africa. They laboured under the misapprehension that Rommel would finally emerge victorious in North Africa and that he would be in a position to retake the colonies and hand them back to Italy.

There were two main Italian guerrilla organisations: the *Fronte di Resistenza* (Resistance Front) and the *Figlii d'Italia* (Sons of Italy). The *Fronte di Resistenza* was led by *Colonnello* Lucchetti. Its strength was in the main towns of Italian East Africa, and it mainly indulged in sabotage and intelligence gathering. The *Figlii d'Italia* organisation had been formed in September 1941 by Blackshirts of the *Milizia Volontaria per la Sicurezza Nazionale*, a pro-Fascist group of volunteer soldiers. This organisation was directly involved in the guerrilla war against the British and Commonwealth troops, and also mounted reprisal attacks on Italians who they felt were collaborating with the British.

There were also the Amhara fighters led by *Tenente* Amedeo Guillet in Eritrea. A similar group was based at Dessie and led by *Maggiore* Gobbi. *Capitano* Aloisi also led a group in Eritrea, which was largely involved in helping escaped Italian prisoners of war. After the major German and Italian defeat at El Alamein in 1942, the numbers of Eritreans, Somalis and Abyssinians content to remain with the Italians dwindled.

Amedeo Guillet, commander of the *Cavalleggeri del Monferrato*

(Monferrato Cavalry) was the leader of the mounted Amhara warriors band. He is portrayed as being fearless, romantic and loved by his men. At Agordat, he managed to extricate his men along the railway line, at Keren he saved them and brought them safely to Teclasan. At Teclasan, he led a charge which destroyed three British tanks and five trucks. Even the commander of Gazelle Force admitted that he was 'courageous, highly independent, resistant, resourceful ...'.

He freed his men from their oath of allegiance at the end of October 1941. By that stage his group had suffered 826 dead and 600 wounded. Remarkably, despite the reversals, none of his men had deserted. He disguised himself at Massawa as a water carrier, and crossed the Red Sea into neutral Yemen. He was picked up as a suspected British agent, but when his true identity was discovered he was sent back to Massawa.

Those who continued to operate adopted the title *banda* (or group), and were active in northern Eritrea and Somaliland. Although they were well armed, they tended to lack ammunition, which restricted their ability to mount operations. In January 1942, many of the *bande* began to work under the co-ordinated control of *Generale* Muratori. Muratori was instrumental in organising the Azebo Oromo tribe to rise up against the British in northern Abyssinia. It was to take almost a year before the revolt was crushed.

By the spring of 1942, it was rumoured that the Abyssinian Emperor Haile Selassie had decided to open diplomatic dialogue with the Italian *bande*. It appeared that in the event of the resurgence of German and Italian fortunes in Africa, he would be prepared to accept Protectorate terms under the Italians. However, in the summer of 1942, *Colonnello* Calderari in Somaliland, *Colonnello* Di Marco in the Ogaden, *Colonnello* Ruglio among the Danakil and 'Blackshirt centurion' De Varda in Abyssinia were striking out at a number of British targets, and the British responded by shifting troops, aircraft and tanks from the Sudan and from Kenya to suppress them.

Part of the policy in the suppression was the rounding-up of Italian civilians who had been giving support to the guerrilla groups. Many were deported to the coastal areas of Somaliland. Following Montgomery's crushing victory over Rommel's German and Italian forces in North Africa in October 1942, the taste for guerrilla warfare diminished. A contributory factor was the capture of *Maggiore* Lucchetti (the head of the *Fronte di Resistenza*). Some guerrillas remained operational until the summer of 1943, but at this point, with Italy having left her former allies, many tried to escape back to Italy. *Tenente* Amedeo Guillet, for example, reached Taranto on 3 September 1943. He immediately requested that the Italian War Ministry provide an 'aircraft loaded with equipment to be used for guerrilla attacks in Eritrea'. The Italian armistice a few days later ended his plans.

One of the final die-hards was Corrado Turchett. He was involved in ambushes against British troops as late as October 1943. The last Italian officer to still be operating in Eritrea was believed to be *Colonnello* Nino Tramonti.

The Duke of Aosta had been aware of the impossibility of receiving any significant aid from Italy from the outset of the war. He had done his best and split the enormous Italian East Africa into five sectors. Each of the commanders had been given instructions to resist to the last. He also allowed them all the necessary operational and decision-making independence they needed. Aosta managed to succeed in part by attracting significant British attention away from Greece and Tripoli. The Duke managed to protect the Italian civilians by insisting on their protection by the British from the potentially vengeful Abyssinians. He avoided all unnecessary bloodshed and abandoned centres of population. The Duke died in captivity in 1942.

Throughout the campaign in East Africa, the Italian troops fought with resolution and courage. When the war began, the Italian forces were composed of 91,000 Italian nationals (of whom 7,000 were officers) belonging to the Army, Air Force and Revenue Guards. The colonial soldiers numbered around 200,000. They were equipped with 3,300 machine-guns; sixty-four medium tanks; thirty-nine light tanks; 126 armoured cars and trucks; 813 guns of different calibres but all dated; 325 aircraft of which only 244 were combat ready. In comparison, the British were outnumbered, but better armed and more mobile as they were mechanised. As we have seen, this was not a detail, but a major factor in the vast territories over which the conflict was fought.

It had been an air war that had been dominated by the biplane fighter, the CR.32 and CR.42 and the Gloster Gladiator, but what of the aces, the men who had flown them? Some had seen combat in Spain and others were fresh to aerial dogfights. Undoubtedly, not only the Italian pilots, but the British and Commonwealth ones too, were supremely brave men, fighting over inhospitable terrain, often against hopeless odds. The following few paragraphs examine the careers and sometimes the deaths of some of the more successful Italian pilots. Omissions are purely incidental.

Luigi Baron was born in 1918 at Castelfranco Veneto; he was to serve with 412a *Squadriglia*, equipped with Fiat CR.42s. He ended the campaign as the second most successful of the Italian fighter pilots in the East Africa. A Gladiator of 237 Squadron was operating over Keren on 25 March 1941 and spotted a pair of CR.42s, but it was then attacked by a Hurricane of 1 SAAF Squadron. This squadron engaged CR.42s twice during the day, once in the morning when one was hit by Lt Irvine (possibly the 237 Squadron Gladiator and not a CR.42). In the afternoon Lt Robin Pare and Lt White encountered two CR.42s from 412 *Squadriglia*. They were at 15,000 ft. Pare shot one of them down, but the other escaped. The Italians admitted that one of the CR.42s was shot down; the one flown by *Sergente* Pietro Morlotti was killed. A second was later written off. Two other CR.42s were damaged that day, with both of the pilots being wounded. Two Hurricanes were also claimed by the CR.42s. Baron claimed one of the Hurricanes, but he was wounded in the leg and baled out. Baron remained in hospital for two years and was then repatriated to Italy. He arrived safely in Italy after a two-month voyage, and was given the *Medaglia d'Argento al Valor Militare* and the *Medaglia di Bronzo al Valor Militare*. He was also decorated with the German Iron Cross 2nd Class. He ended his war with twelve kills.

Carlo Canella was born on 22 June 1914 and was commissioned (in the *Servizio Permanente Effettivo*) on 28 October 1938. He too served with 412a *Squadriglia*. On 12 June 1940, he shot down a British Wellesley bomber over the Keren area. In the early hours of 16 October Flt Lt Mitchell (430 Flight), in a Vincent, attacked Tessenei airfield. He was followed back to Gedaref by a Ca 133, and so the Italians now knew where the aircraft were based. The Italians attacked the airfield at 0525, with an S.79 flown by *Generale*

Piacentini leading in six CR.42s of the 412 *Squadriglia*; the pilots were *Capitano* Antonio Raffi, *Tenente* Visintini, *Tenente* Carlo Canella, *Sergente Maggiore* Lugi Baron, Scarselli and *Tenente* De Pauli. The fighters destroyed all eight Wellesleys of 47 Squadron's detachment and two of 430 Flight's Vincents. Canella ended the war with seven biplane victories. For his actions he was awarded two *Medaglie d'Argento al Valor Militare* and one *Medaglia di Bronzo al Valor Militare*.

Antonio Giardinà served with the 410a *Squadriglia*, and flew a Fiat CR.32. At noon on 24 June 1940, four Blenheims of 39 Squadron and two of 11 Squadron hit Diredawa in flights of three. Giardinà was up on a standing patrol. He dived out of the sun on the leading flight and attacked them, damaging all three of the aircraft. On 11 July 1940 a Blenheim of 8 Squadron, flown by Flg Off P.A. Nicholas (Aden), made a reconnaissance over Jijiga. The aircraft was intercepted by *Sottotenente* Veronese and *Sergente Maggiore* Giardinà, who attacked the bomber, claiming to have probably hit it.

On 15 March 1941 Hurricanes of 3 SAAF Squadron attacked Diredawa. The Hurricane pilots found three Fiat CR.32s of the 410 *Squadriglia* in the air. One of the CR.32 pilots, *Sergente Maggiore* Giardinà, had just begun an attack on a Ju86 also attacking the airfield, when he suddenly spotted a Hurricane approaching to attack him. *Sottotenente* Osvaldo Bartolozzi rushed to Giardinà's aid without checking his own tail, the next moment hearing an explosion and being hit in the face and neck by splinters. He immediately broke away and began turning with his attacker, avoiding two more bursts of fire. He landed with 188 holes in his aircraft, but no serious damage. Giardinà fought on for several minutes, returning fire, and at last the Hurricane left. He was then able to land.

At 0700 on 28 March 1941, five CR.42s and two CR.32s from Gauani under the command of *Tenente* Franco De Micheli of the 413a *Squadriglia* made an attack on Jijiga airfield. In the first pass a Ju52/3m (No. 660), a Valentia (No. 264) and a Hartebeest were set on fire; two of the Ju52/3ms that were damaged in an attack on the 26th were also shot up again, as was a Leopard Moth of the Communication Squadron. The Italians had not found the fighter satellite strip, and two Hurricanes of 3 SAAF Squadron flown by Capt S. van Breda Theron and Lt Venter scrambled. Theron was no sooner in the air than his aircraft received a bullet in the cooling system (from an airfield defence Lewis gun, it was suspected); he went in to land again, but as he did so he was attacked by *Sergente Maggiore* Giardinà in a CR.32. The Hurricane was set on fire and Theron was wounded in the leg. As soon as Giardinà saw Theron leap out onto the wing, which he did the moment his Hurricane touched the ground, Giardinà ceased firing. Venter was attacked by three Fiats and his aircraft was riddled with bullets, but he managed to shoot down one Fiat, which fell in flames and crashed. The pilot was *Sottotenente* Silvano.

Giardinà was shifted to 412a *Squadriglia* and began flying CR.42s. On 2 July 1941 *Sergente Maggiore* Giuseppe Mottet and Giardinà claimed one shared Vickers Wellesley of 47 Squadron, which was shot down over Gondar, the aircraft falling in flames. The pilot, Sgt Alexander George Brown, and his crew were all killed. Later in the war Giardinà served with 300a *Squadriglia* in the night defence of Rome. He was to end the war with five biplane victories. Giardinà was decorated with two *Medaglie d'Argento al Valor Militare* and one *Medaglia di Bronzo al Valor Militare.*

Giuseppe Mottet was born in Fontanemore (Aosta) on 12 September 1912. In 1937, he volunteered for the Spanish Civil War and was assigned to 20a *Squadriglia*, XXIII *Gruppo* 'Asso Di Bastoni', flying Fiat CR.32s. Mottet flew about ninety missions during his tour in Spain, primarily on escort flights to bombers and field protection sorties. In 1939 he received an order to transfer to the 411a *Squadriglia* in *Africa Orientale Italiana* (AOI, or Italian East Africa). He arrived at Addis Ababa on 30 August.

From 10 June 1940 to 27 November 1941 he flew many reconnaissance flights and strafing attacks, and was involved in dogfights. On 14 November 1940 he flew as Number Two in a section of two aircraft when they were involved in combat with four unknown enemy aircraft over Jimma airfield. Three of the aircraft were claimed shot down, and this was later confirmed.

On 9 April 1941, Giuseppe Mottet was engaged by Hurricanes over Gimma while defending the base flying a Fiat CR.32, together with another fighter. Capt Frost and Lt Hewitson of 3 SAAF Squadron shot him down. The aircraft was a write-off but Mottet was unhurt.

On 2 July 1941 Mottet and *Sergente Maggiore* Antonio Giardinà claimed one shared Vickers Wellesley. This was a Wellesley of 47 Squadron, which was shot down over Gondar, the aircraft falling in flames. In a report from 411a *Squadriglia* on 11 August it was reported that he had flown 160 hours of combat missions from 22 August 1939 to date. On 15 October he was promoted to *Maresciallo* at Gondar. From 31 October, after the death of his CO, *Tenente* Malavolti, he was the only Italian fighter pilot in Italian East Africa. On 22 November 1941 the last CR.42 flown by Mottet was sent out and attacked British artillery at Kulkaber. Upon landing, he destroyed the CR.42 and joined the Italian troops, fighting until the surrender five days later. Giuseppe Mottet was decorated with the *Medaglia d'Argento al Valor Militare.*

Enzo Omiccioli was born in Fano on 1 June 1915. In the beginning of the East African campaign he was serving with 410a *Squadriglia*, equipped with Fiat CR.32s. On 15 June Omiccioli intercepted a Blenheim (39 Squadron) over Diredawa, but no result was claimed. In July Omiccioli was on a brief attachment to the 411a *Squadriglia*. On 11 July four Hawker Hartebeests of 40 SAAF Squadron made an attack around Moyale. There they encountered three Ca 133s, escorted by three CR.32s of the *Squadriglia*. The fighters attacked the South African aircraft, and Lt Neville Keith Rankin was last seen in a spin with one Fiat on the tail of his aircraft; he and his gunner, Air Sgt Dennis Haig Hughes, were both killed. Lt L.H.G. Shuttleworth's aircraft was hit, but he made good his escape. The Italians reported meeting five aircraft, and claimed to have probably shot down two of them, one of these being claimed by *Sergente Maggiore* Omiccioli.

Omiccioli was loaned to the 412a *Squadriglia*, equipped with CR.42s. On 3 February six Gladiators from 1 SAAF Squadron flew into a new landing-strip called 'Pretoria', where they refuelled. They took off again at 1145 to strafe airfields in the Gondar area. A landing-site was spotted to the south of Azozo on which five Ca 133s were sitting. Another airfield was nearby, from which CR.42s were taking off. The Gladiators were attacked by the Fiats. In the combat Capt Brian Boyle and Capt Gerald Le Mesurier each claimed a Fiat shot down. The only loss sustained by the Italians in this combat was *Sergente Maggiore* Omiccioli, who was shot down and killed. He was posthumously awarded Italy's highest decoration for valour, the *Medaglia D'Oro al Valor Militare* (Gold Medal). At the time of his death, he had a total of five victories, all of them claimed while flying biplanes.

Corrado Ricci was born in 1912, and he joined the *Regia Aeronautica* in 1931. After serving in Spain he served with the 410a *Squadriglia*, equipped with Fiat CR.32s. At 0800 on 1 August 1940, the two secret Italian landing-grounds at Chinele, near Diredawa, were discovered and strafed by two Blenheims. Six Blenheims each from 8 and 39 Squadrons, escorted by two Blenheim IVFs of 203 Squadron, were sent off to attack the fields in the afternoon. At 1500 the bombers approached at 16,000 ft and dived to 10,000 ft to bomb.

Capitano Ricci, commanding officer of the 410a *Squadriglia*, had taken off in his CR.32 as the second wave of bombers approached, and he chased these. He later wrote:

> I look around; nothing to see. But ... something is coming from the sunshine ... Here they are, six diving bombers. It seems to me they are heading towards our secret airfields. I hope they had been alerted! They are flying over Diredawa; I'll chase them out of the town border. They hadn't bombed the town, so they're really heading to the airfields. They are going to pass at my side, at my same level, fast as a bolide [meteorite]! I attack the front section of three from the side, the other section still being to the rear. While I'm firing, I find myself in their trail; I shoot at the leader, then at the right wingman; the two aircraft seem to leave tiny trails of smoke, but I'm not sure of it. One of my machine-guns jams, but I don't recharge it because I don't want to lose aim. Tracer shells passed nearby my side, I hear shots behind me; I am attacked too. I evade with a large, barrel-shaped tonneau; while I'm upside down I can see the second section passing at my right side, slightly lower than me. At the end of the manoeuvre I'm at six of the left wingman, but in the meanwhile I recharged the jammed gun, so I shoot again, sharing my rounds to all three, while bombs are falling. First section is far ahead, the two aircraft I fired at are still smoking. ... I concentrate on the aiming: it's the turn of the right wingman now. The gun jams again! I

recharge it. All three aircraft leave a light trail of smoke, like the two of the first section. I shoot again ... the aircraft I'm shooting at seems to slow down ... is it an illusion? No, it is really slowing down: while the other two are going, it extracts the gun turret and begins to shoot at me. I fire again; the British pilot manoeuvres to prevent me to hide behind his tail. I discharge brief bursts ... I must slow down to not collide with him. We are at ten metres from ground; the British extracts the flaps and lands on the sand in a cloud of dust.

He had, in fact, shot down a Blenheim of 8 Squadron. At 0600 on 8 August Berbera airfield was attacked by two CR.32s and one CR.42 from 410a *Squadriglia*, based at Hargeisa, led by *Capitano* Ricci flying in one of the CR.32s. The Italian aircraft had taken off from Diredawa at 0500. Ricci later wrote:

I was the first to take off, with Tellurio at my wing; soon after started Cacciavillani and Komienz, but the first skipped on ground, and then stood with tail up: what could have happened to him? Komienz joined us. I checked my compass with a pocket light to keep the course. After half an hour of flight the light is coming, but we could not yet see Berbera; five minutes more: nothing again ... I again checked the chart; the course is right, but I have no reference point on the ground because it is so flat; I know that the wind is strong, and its direction change as the sun rise, but I can't evaluate it. I continue a little bit on chance. At the end I decide to turn 90-degrees left; after a few minutes a sparkling ahead makes me happy: it's the sea! I start a light dive, and I increase it as we are approaching, so we find us to fly grazing to the yellowish sand: it's the only way to come unseen! I can see the town, it's small, whitish; there's a ship in the harbour. Here is the airfield: two dark aircraft, side by side, stand out. They are Gladiators. My wingmen close at me, and this bothers me; slowly, I gain speed and I put them away from me. We are skimming the ground and some small hills cover us to enemy's sight; just a little bit ... Here we are! With a steep climb I gain 500 m height, then I dive on the fighter at left; while I'm aiming a man leaves it and falls headlong ... what a long-legged he is! I shoot: a strong wind disturbs my shoot, my rounds are on ground, but some hit the target. I pull hard, quite skimming the wing of the enemy aircraft; I hear behind my shoulders that Tellurio and Komienz are firing too. The anti-aircraft weapons awake; bluish tracer shells, shrapnel explosions; the ships fires like a volcano, the machine-guns in their nest at the airfield's edge are shooting: the air is hot! A big turn: the other Gloster is burning, mine is not, but with a second burst I get it burning too. We can go! I take a snapshot with my old camera that I bring with me at every flight: I have to prove the results of the action. We go away, with a grazing flight. A sand column rise just in front of me; here another and other around: they are the British grenades. I climb to 200 m altitude: black burst around us, some other sand gush here and there, then all is over.

At the beginning of December he made an emergency crash-landing after the engine on his CR.32 had failed. After this incident *Capitano* Ricci was sent for a period of convalescence. Six Blenheims of 8 Squadron from Aden bombed Diredawa early on 9 March 1941, six CR.42s and a single monoplane being reported as seen on the ground, although only two or three fighters were actually present; the monoplane was a S.81, already damaged beyond repair, but retained as a decoy.

Three CR.32s of the 410a *Squadriglia* approached the bombers head on, and the leader, *Capitano* Ricci, turned sharply to attack the right-hand Blenheim. This manoeuvred to evade him, and Ricci found himself right next to another Blenheim, piloted by Sqn Ldr Hanlon. Ricci opened fire as it began to pull away from him, and saw his bullets exploding on the rear of the right-hand engine nacelle. Sqn Ldr Hanlon had to force-land on Perim Island during the homeward flight as a result of the damage sustained.

Capitano Ricci had been able to intercept the bombers and attack them before they had dropped their bombs. He recalled:

A morning I scramble with Puliti and I'm radio-guided to intercept two sections of three Blenheims each, which were going to bomb Diredawa. I think I could made only a single front attack, because, since they are faster than me, I could never reach them for a second pass; so, I decide to attack them from the rear to increase my possibilities. With a big turn I dive on the formation, which at a certain point is hidden from my sight by my wing; I fear to collide with them, but meanwhile I think that however they should take care to avoid me! Indeed I came very close to the right wingman, which suddenly veered away from the patrol and was soon attacked by Puliti, while I find myself right on the side of the leader, after having risked to hit its wing with my plane. I immediately start to fire, aiming at the right engine, but the slipstream shatters my aim, while the rudder dangerously pass me by; but a long, black smoke trail came from the engine, just while a piece tears off from the fuselage. I think to have got it, and I go to attack another alone one, that escapes me by diving. Here is a third one, it's alone too: I attack it. He's a courageous pilot: instead to evade, he challenges to me with beautiful turns; I'm surprised to see little smoke trails from its fuselage, but perhaps it's the gunner that's shooting at me. During the manoeuvres my weapons continue to jam while I'm shooting in tight turns, but at the end I find myself in a good advantage; the foe realises it and, with a good overturn, go in a vertical dive, then heads towards Dankalia while I'm pursue him, shooting, while it leaves me behind, more and more. He disappears, apparently undamaged. The ground observers, however, don't see it pass: they spot only five while heading home. Sometime after, we knew that a Blenheim force-landed in the Tajura area, in the French Somaliland, but the crew should have been able to return to Arabia: perhaps they are those!

Ricci was allowed to return to Italy in April 1941 because he was suffering from appendicitis. He ended the war with five victories, all of them claimed while flying biplanes during the Spanish Civil War and the Second World War.

Arnoldo Soffritti was born on 5 April 1913 in Bondeno (Ferrara). He served with the 412a *Squadriglia*, equipped with Fiat CR.42s. On the afternoon of 29 January 1941, in a dogfight between 1 SAAF Squadron and 412a *Squadriglia* over Gura, Soffritti's CR.42 was damaged. On the morning of 2 February 1941 a Lysander of 237 Squadron, flown by Flg Off M.A. Johnson, was on tactical reconnaissance, and the aircraft was claimed shot down by Soffritti. On 7 February, two Wellesleys from 47 Squadron made a reconnaissance from Barentu to Adi Ugri. They were intercepted by the 412a *Squadriglia* and both were shot down, one being claimed by Soffritti. On 19 March 1941, two Hurricanes of 1 SAAF Squadron were patrolling over the Keren area when they were attacked by three CR.42s, *Maresciallo* Soffritti claiming to have shot down one. Between 0710 and 0830 on 28 March 1941, Soffritti claimed to have shot down a Hurricane in the Ad Teclesan area, and in Eritrea on 4 April 1941, he claimed to have shot down a British bomber between 0730 and 0805. Soffritti was captured at Dessie on 26 April 1941, by which time he was credited with eight biplane victories, five probable, eleven destroyed on the ground. Soffritti won two *Medaglie d'Argento al Valor Militare*.

Alberto Veronese was a veteran from the Spanish Civil War, and in East Africa he served with 410a *Squadriglia*, equipped with Fiat CR.32s. On 11 July 1940 a Blenheim of 8 Squadron, flown by Flg Off P.A. Nicholas, was intercepted and attacked by *Sottotenente* Veronese and *Sergente Maggiore* Giardinà, who claimed to have probably hit it.

Veronese made a head-on attack against one of three Blenheims of 39 Squadron on 12 August 1940. He shot the aircraft down, but was wounded in the encounter. Six days later, *Sottotenente* Veronese and *Sergente Maggiore* Volpe of 410a *Squadriglia* shot down a Blenheim from 8 Squadron flown by Sgt Gay to the north-west of Laferug. Veronese and *Sergente Maggiore* Athos Tieghi shared a kill on 12 September when they tackled Lt Edward George Armstrong DFC of 11 SAAF Squadron in his Fairey Battle over Shashamanna

The last French Martin 167F in Aden was on a reconnaissance mission over Diredawa on 16 December when it was attacked by a pair of CR.32s of 410a *Squadriglia*. Veronese closed on the tail of the Martin and opened fire, but the speed of the French aircraft was too much for the slower biplane. Veronese had climbed too high and was hit by anoxia, and he had to land and be taken to the sick bay.

Soon afterwards, Veronese was promoted to *tenente*, and on 4 February 1941 he and *Tenente* Folcherio attacked a pair of Blenheims from Aden of 203 Squadron flown by Sqn Ldr J.M.N. Pike and Flt Lt Gethin. Both of the Blenheims were hit and had to crash-land.

Makale was attacked again on the morning of 18 February by another pair of Blenheims from the same squadron. Veronese shot down Sqn Ldr A.L.H. Solano and then chased Sqn Ldr Scott, damaging his aircraft so badly that it had to crash-land when it got back to Aden.

Seven Hurricanes of 1 SAAF Squadron strafed Makale on 23 February. Maj L.A. Wilmot, leading the lower section of three Hurricanes, was shot down by Veronese, but then Lt Andrew Duncan shot him down. He parachuted to safety, slightly wounded. Effectively, his wounds put him out of the combat for good in East Africa. He had become the most successful pilot of 410a *Squadriglia*, with six kills and two shared kills. He was evacuated to Italy, and after the surrender in 1943 he joined up with the Italian Co-Belligerent Air Force and served in 356a *Squadriglia*. Veronese was killed on 4 September 1944 by German anti-aircraft fire in Greece. During the war he was decorated with two *Medaglie d'Argento al Valor Militare*.

Mario Visintini was born in Parenzo d'Istria on 26 April 1913. He was to become the top Italian biplane fighter ace. In January 1940 he was promoted to *tenente* for war merits. After serving in Spain he was transferred to East Africa on 5 April 1940. Initially he was posted to 413a *Squadriglia*. Before the start of the war in June 1940 he was transferred to the 412a *Squadriglia* in Eritrea. His first kill of the war took place on 14 June 1940, when he shot down a Wellesley of 14 Squadron flown by Plt Off Reginald Patrick Blenner Plunkett. He claimed a second Wellesley on 3 July over Decamere, when Flg Off Samuel Gustav Soderholm was killed. On 12 July he shot down another Wellesley, this time flown by Sgt Frederick (Freddy) Nelson of 47 Squadron. On 29 July he was decorated with the *Medaglia d'Argento al Valor Militare*.

On 1 September Visintini shared a claim with another pilot when they shot down a Wellesley of 14 Squadron flown by Sgt Norris. On 30 September, Sqn Ldr George Justin Bush in a Blenheim of 45 Squadron was victim to Visintini. During the morning of 9 February Visintini took part, together with four other pilots from 412a *Squadriglia*, in an attack on Agordat and its satellite airfield. Sixteen aircraft were claimed shared destroyed on the ground, including five Hurricanes, five Hawker biplanes, two Gladiators, two Wellesleys, one Valentia and one Westland Lysander.

On 11 February Visintini shot down a Hurricane over Keren. This claim was probably made in combat with Hurricanes from 1 SAAF Squadron, which had eleven aircraft on patrols over the area during the day. Later in the day Visintini took off to fly back to guide other pilots home. It seems, however, that during the flight he was blown off course by high winds, and while descending through clouds he crashed into the side of Mount Nefasit and was instantly killed. He was posthumously awarded the *Medaglia D'Oro al Valor Militare* for his outstanding combat record. According to Italian War Bulletin No. 252 of 14 February 1941, he was credited with seventeen confirmed victories in Italian East Africa. The document attached to his *Medaglia D'Oro* states fifty combats, sixteen destroyed and thirty-two shared destroyed. At the time of his death, Visintini had seventeen victories, all of them claimed while flying biplane fighters.

What of French Somaliland? After the fall of France in 1940, as we have seen, French Somaliland declared its loyalty to Vichy France. The colony remained loyal to the Vichy regime throughout the East African campaign, but tried to stay out of the conflict. By December 1942, with the Italians defeated and the colony isolated, it was alone. Free French and Allied forces recaptured the colony, and ultimately a battalion from Djibouti was involved in the liberation of France in 1944.

B Flight had returned to Aiscia after the fall of Gondar to patrol the border with French Somaliland. On 11 December 1941, Lt Gazzard took off in a Mohawk to chase a French Potez 631 that had just buzzed the runway. Gazzard shot at the Potez and saw it billowing smoke, but it escaped him. Perhaps this was the last aerial combat of the war over the former Italian East Africa.

It had been a campaign that had stretched the resources, the minds and the bodies of British and Commonwealth troops; it had also seen a more than creditable display by the Italians, particularly in the air. No. 47 Squadron was dispatched to Egypt to become a reconnaissance squadron, while 3 SAAF headed back to South Africa, where its Mohawks would be used to trained pilots for the desert war. As for the Ansons and Ju86s, they would struggle on for a time until they were finally too worn out and were replaced with Marylands and Bristol Beauforts.

APPENDIX 1

Claims of Aircraft Shot Down

6 Squadron Gladiator claims
26/9/41 Sgt Ron Walker, N5851: Savoia-Marchetti SM81 shot down over Kufra Oasis, North Africa.

33 Squadron claims
14/6/40 Plt Off V.C. Woodward, N5783: Caproni Ca310 shared shot down with Sgt Craig over Fort Capuzzo.
14/6/40 Sgt Craig, N5768: Caproni Ca310 shared shot down with Plt Off Woodward over Fort Capuzzo.
14/6/40 Flg Off E.H. Dean, L9046: Fiat CR.32 shot down over Fort Capuzzo.
14/6/40 Plt Off V.C. Woodward: Fiat CR.32 shot down over Fort Capuzzo.
19/6/40 Unknown: Fiat CR.42 shot down over Sollum.
19/6/40 Unknown: Fiat CR.42 shot down over Sollum.
29/6/40 Plt Off V.C. Woodward: Fiat CR.32 shot down over Fort Capuzzo.
29/6/40 Plt Off V.C. Woodward: Fiat CR.42 shot down over Fort Capuzzo.
29/6/40 Flg Off P.R.W. Wickham*: Meridionali Ro.37 shot down 3 miles west of Sidi Aziez.
29/6/40 Flg Off P.R.W. Wickham*: Fiat CR.32 shot down 3 miles west of Sidi Aziez.
30/6/40 Flg Off P.R.W. Wickham*: Fiat CR.42 shot down 3 miles west of Sidi Aziez.
30/6/40 Unknown: Fiat CR.42 shot down over Bardia.
30/6/40 Unknown: Fiat CR.42 shot down over Bardia.
1/7/40 Sgt W. Vale: Fiat CR.32 shot down over Fort Capuzzo.
4/7/40 Unknown N5779: Fiat CR.42 shot down near Sollum.
4/7/40 Flg Off E.H. Dean N5782: Fiat CR.42 shot down near Sollum.
4/7/40 Flg Off Worcester*: Fiat CR.42 shot down over Monastir Airfield.
4/7/40 Flg Off Worcester*: Fiat CR.42 shot down over Monastir Airfield.
4/7/40 Flg Off Worcester*: Fiat CR.42 shot down over Monastir Airfield.
4/7/40 Flg Off Worcester*: Fiat CR.42 shot down over Monastir Airfield.
4/7/40 Flg Off Bennet*: Fiat CR.42 shot down over Monastir Airfield.
4/7/40 Flg Off R.H. Smith*: Fiat CR.42 shot down over Monastir Airfield.
4/7/40 Unknown*: Fiat CR.42 shot down over Monastir Airfield.
4/7/40 Unknown*: Fiat CR.42 shot down over Monastir Airfield.
4/7/40 Unknown*: Fiat CR.42 shot down over Monastir Airfield.
4/7/40 Flt Sgt Cottingham, N5765: Fiat CR.42 shot down over Monastir Airfield.

4/7/40 Flt Sgt Cottingham, N5765: Fiat CR.42 shot down over Monastir Airfield.

4/7/40 Plt Off E.J. Woods, N5781: Fiat CR.42 shot down over Monastir Airfield.

4/7/40 Flt Sgt Cottingham: SIAI-Marchetti SM79 shot down over Monastir Airfield.

15/7/40 Sgt W. Vale: SIAI-Maerchetti SM79 shared shot down over Mersa Matruh.

24/7/40 Unknown: Fiat CR.42 shot down

24/7/40 Plt Off V.C. Woodward: Fiat CR.42 shot down.

24/7/40 Plt Off V.C. Woodward: Fiat CR.42 probably shot down.

24/7/40 Flt Lt M.T. St J. Pattle: Fiat CR.42 shot down over Sollum.

25/7/40 Flt Lt M.T. St J. Pattle: Fiat CR.42 shot down over Bardia.

25/7/40 Flt Lt M.T. St J. Pattle: Fiat CR.42 shot down over Bardia.

25/7/40 Flt Lt M.T. St J. Pattle: Fiat CR.42 shot down over Bardia.

25/7/40 Sgt Slater: Fiat CR.42 shot down over Bardia.

25/7/40 Sgt Slater: Fiat CR.42 shared shot down with Flg Off V C Woodward over Bardia.

25/7/40 Flg Off V.C. Woodward: Fiat CR.42 shared shot down with Sgt Slater over Bardia.

25/7/40 Flg Off V.C. Woodward: Fiat CR.42 shot down over Bardia. Pilots served with 112 Squadron and were attached to 33 Squadron at the time the claims were made.

237 Squadron Gladiator claims

16/3/41 Plt Off P.H.S. Simmonds: Fiat CR.42 shot down over Mount Sanchil.

14/4/41 Unknown: Caproni Ca133 destroyed on ground at Alomata airfield.

14/4/41 Unknown: Caproni Ca133 destroyed on ground at Alomata airfield.

14/4/41 Unknown: Caproni Ca133 destroyed on ground at Alomata airfield.

14/4/41 Unknown: SIAI-Maerchetti SM79 destroyed on ground at Alomata airfield.

14/4/41 Unknown: Caproni Ca148 destroyed on ground at Alomata airfield.

15/4/41 Plt Off P.H.S. Simmonds: SIAI-Marchetti SM79 damaged near Deberach.

21/4/41 Unknown: Caproni Ca133 destroyed on ground at Alomata airfield.

21/4/41 Unknown: Caproni Ca133 destroyed on ground at Alomata airfield.

21/4/41 Unknown: SIAI-Marchetti SM79 destroyed on ground at Alomata airfield.

29/4/41 Flg Off P.H.S. Simmonds: Caproni Ca133 shared destroyed on ground with Flg Offs Spencer and Robinson at Alomata airfield.

29/4/41 Flg Off Spencer: Caproni Ca133 shared destroyed on ground with Flg Offs Simmonds and Robinson at Alomata airfield.

29/4/41 Flg Off Robinson: Caproni Ca133 shared destroyed on ground with Flg Offs Simmonds and Spencer at Alomata airfield.

29/4/41 Flg Off P.H.S. Simmonds: Caproni Ca133 destroyed on the ground at Cer-Cer airfield.

29/4/41 Flg Off Spencer: SIAI-Marchetti SM79 destroyed on the ground at Cer-Cer airfield.

29/4/41 Flg Off Spencer: Fiat CR.42 shared destroyed on the ground with Flg Off Kleynhams on Cer-Cer airfield.

29/4/41 Flg Off Kleynhams: Fiat CR.42 shared destroyed on the ground with Flg Off Spencer at Cer-Cer airfield.

29/4/41 Flg Off Robinson: Fiat CR.32 destroyed on the ground at Cer-Cer airfield.

15/5/41 Unknown: Caproni Ca133 destroyed on the ground at Azozo airfield.

15/5/41 Unknown: SIAI-Machete SM79 destroyed on the ground at Azozo airfield.

K Flight claims

29/6/40 Plt Off Hamlyn, L7619: Savoia-Marchetti SM81 shot down over Aden.

1/8/40 Plt Off P.O.V. Green, K7974: Caproni Ca133 shot down over Gederef area.

15/11/40 Plt Off Wolsey: Savoia-Marchetti SM79 Damaged over Port Sudan.

15/11/40 Plt Off Wolsey: Savoia-Marchetti SM79 Damaged over Port Sudan.

21/11/40 Plt Off P.O.V. Green: Savoia-Marchetti SM79 Damaged over Port Sudan.

21/11/40 Plt Off Smither: Savoia-Marchetti SM79 Damaged over Port Sudan.

22/2/41 Plt Off Wells, N5815: Fiat CR.42 shot down over KUB-KUB.

24/2/41 Flt Lt J.E. Scouler, N5878: Savoia-Marchetti SM79 Shot down over Mersa Taklai.

APPENDIX 2

Portrait of an Italian Airman

Maresciallo (WO) Alberto Gobbo

lberto Gobbo was born in Bressa, near Udine, Italy, in 1911. He had a
passion for flying and when he was just 18 he attended a glider course
at Pavullo nel Frignano. A year later, he was on a flying course in an
Aviatik at Udine Airfield (Campoformido). He soon gained his pilot's licence.

Gobbo joined the *Regia Aeronautica* (Italian Royal Air Force) and started
his career as a sergeant student pilot at Grottaglie Flight School (Taranto).
Initially he flew in Caproni Ca 100s (called Caproncino). He was then posted
to *72a Squadriglia Caccia* (No. 72 Fighter Squadron), *17deg Gruppo Caccia* (No.
17 Fighter Group), *1deg Stormo Caccia* (No. 1 Fighter Wing) at Campoformido
Airfield, Udine.

No. 1 Fighter Wing was considered to be the best in the *Regia Aeronautica*,
and it was equipped with the best Italian fighter, the Fiat CR20 ASSO.
Campoformido was also the home base of the Italian national aerobatic team,
known as 'The Crazy Team' (*La Pattuglia Folle*). Gobbo learned close-
formation flying with the team.

At the outbreak of the war in Abyssinia in 1936, Gobbo was transferred to
No. 1 Fighter Wing in Catania (Sicily). Gobbo also volunteered to fly in the
Spanish Civil War in 1938. In the war, he flew the new Fiat CR.32. He claimed
seven kills and won two silver medals for gallantry, and was promoted to the
rank of warrant officer. When he came home from Spain he was posted to No.
35 Fighter Wing in Caselle Torinese (Turin).

In the war in East Africa, Gobbo was attached to 411a *Squadriglia* Caccia
(No. 411 Fighter Squadron) with four CR.32s based at Shashamanna (near
Jimma). He explained the realities of war as an Italian pilot:

Four Fairey Battles of No. 11 Squadron, South African Air Force,
based at Archer's Post in Kenya, flew over our field and started their
attack with a steep dive against ground targets. Their targets were the
Italian bombers parked just under the trees at the edge of the airfield,
as well as the four CR.32 fighters parked without camouflage in the
middle of the field, and the adjacent airfield buildings. There were no
alarm mechanisms nor any ground defences – this was a luxury reserved
only for the HQ and the major commands. The 'party' started at exactly

1030 local time, with the deafening music made by the Fairey Battles' Rolls-Royce engines, the exploding bombs, and by the gun and machine-gun fire that opened up. Fortunately, only two of the four CR.32s were damaged by a few machine-gun rounds – due, very likely, to poor SAAF gunnery. (I must point out that the four CR.32 fighters, wonderfully placed in the middle of the field, were a gift to the base commander, Lt Col Pilot G. Dal Monte. I was the operational pilot responsible for the fighters and had asked the base commander, many a time, to move the aircraft under cover. His decision and position had remained an unshakable 'No!' This decision would later have dire implications for him with General Command (HQ) 'Superaereo', Addis Ababa.)

Not one of our four fighters took off immediately, because the pilots were hiding in the air raid shelters. At that moment, while the 'Fifometro' (fright meter – similar to the aircraft's water temperature gauge) showed 90°, we heard the engine of a CR.32 running. The aircraft had been started and left running by a brave ground technician in the desperate hope that some pilot would attempt to save Italian honour.

With bombs bursting, I ran to the Fiat and jumped into the cockpit, immediately moving the throttle back to have the maximum r.p.m. With no time in which to heat the engine or to find a usable ground strip from which to take off, I was in need of a miracle. Taxiing frantically, I was horrified to see a Fairey Battle begin to strafe the runway, aiming at my aircraft. But luck smiled on this desperate man that day. Amazingly, the Battle missed me, and my landing-gear cleared the ground, collecting some twigs and leaves as I narrowly scraped over the trees. With a screaming engine, my Fiat went like a bat out of hell. I managed to gain enough altitude to reach some cloud, and after making the first 360° turn I saw two huge black smoke columns rise up from the airfield. Two Savoia Marchetti S.81 bombers were burning. I reached an altitude of 600 metres and headed towards the camp, noticing one enemy Fairey Battle. The SAAF pilot continued his attack with a slight dive and reduced speed, so it was easy for me to cut into his path at an angle of 10° and fire my weapons from a short distance. Hit in several vital places by my fire, the Fairey Battle, piloted by Flt Lt F.C. Armstrong SAAF, went down in a vertical dive, crashing near the camp command offices without releasing his bombs. Looking down, I saw an enormous column of black smoke rising rapidly. The impact explosion of this plane caused a great crater. Many Italians came out from their shelters and jubilantly raised their arms to the sky, celebrating my victory.

I had just had time to do a short turn when I found another Fairey Battle, heading straight towards me at great velocity, apparently intent on attacking me. I was aware of my low speed (about 220 kph), but we were at the same altitude and so I decided to attack him head on. Kicking my rudder to the side, I managed to obtain a 40° angle between myself and the Fairey Battle's course. I started to fire for a few seconds, rolled over his nose and regained his tail in my sight. This manoeuvre was sufficient, and an accurate burst hit the Battle. With increasing speed, the South African raider, trailing white smoke, left me alone.

Taking advantage of a by then clear sky (no other enemy planes were visible), I gained more altitude. At 1,500m I could see the field and surrounding area. I changed my bearing away from the base, but had to descend to 1,000m as rapidly growing cumulus clouds reduced my visibility. Glancing at the nearby village straddling an important road crossing, I noticed a column of about ten Italian trucks driving in a westerly direction. The weather conditions in that area were not good and the visibility was deteriorating rapidly. Again, luck was on my side. To my right, 400 m below and at an 80° angle to me, the beautiful shape of the Fairey Battle appeared, flying very determinedly but with reduced speed towards the truck column. I prepared my guns and sights for an attack, and with a slight dive I headed over to surprise my opponent. The Battle was still oblivious to my presence. My altitude advantage, angle of attack and the prevailing light conditions gave me complete advantage and allowed me to make the most of a rapid attack. I opened with a burst of four 7.65mm rounds. Because my Fiat CR.32 had gained too much speed, I reduced it markedly so that it was possible for me to keep the Battle under fire for a longer time. The final approach to the Battle enabled me to start firing from a distance of 150 m, behind and slightly above his left side. My tracers, viewed in the sunlight, and the explosive 12.7mm bullets penetrated the adversary's fuselage in a few places. The two aircraft were so close to each other that it became very easy to aim without looking through the sight. The Battle's pilot pulled the stick up, directing the aircraft into a steep, violent climb, followed by a left turn, to avoid my fire. Again I was able to fire at him with good results, and the Battle headed into a thunderstorm cloud. I followed him at full throttle into the cloud. Some days later, we received news that this Fairey Battle had been able to reach and cross the boundary between Abyssinia and Kenya, making a forced landing. Only the gunner had been seriously injured; the pilot and the bomb aimer had escaped unharmed from the aircraft.

After chasing the Fairey Battle into the cloud, it was 1115, and I had a moment to relax my nerves, to reorganise my mind and to check the state of my aircraft, which I considered an integral part of me. I decided to make my way back to my airfield, and, to do this slowly, climbed to 2,000m. By then, I was 20km away from my base. Masses of dark cloud, which forced me to circle around them in order to avoid them, interfered with my navigation. When I was about 10 km from my base, I noticed a lonely Fairey Battle through the clouds, probably heading back to Kenya across Margherita Lake after his attack. An examination of my ammunition showed that I had about a third remaining. I immediately armed my guns and, on full throttle, began a vertical dive, aiming at about 300m in front of my enemy. My approach was perfect and everything was in my favour – I had altitude advantage, high speed, great timing and, above all, he was not expecting me.

As I got within range, I aimed carefully and fired, hitting the enemy aircraft from nose to tail. In a few seconds, I was so close that I risked a mid-air collision. I continued to fire my accurate bursts from a short distance of about 20m, hitting my enemy's fuselage on the left side, then the right side, and finally on the tail surfaces. The effect of this fire soon became visible; a big wake of white smoke appeared that rapidly became grey and then black. I throttled back to a safer position. The Battle's speed remained the same and the pilot made no attempt to escape by accelerating to full throttle. I gave chase with my CR.32 until we reached the village of Dalle, about 35km from Shashamanna. The Battle's altitude and speed continued to decrease, but the weather pattern in front of us took the form of a low-lying thunderstorm. After a few seconds of the Fairey Battle reaching the turbulence, I decided to turn back, sure that the Battle was not going to reach his base. I checked my aircraft for ammunition and fuel levels. They were low, so I headed home at an altitude of 500 m. The weather on the way home was good and I could navigate visually. Flying over my airfield, I noted with much surprise that the whole base had returned to normal and that all base personnel had gathered in the main square, celebrating their escape from danger. All normal activity was forgotten. With a half roll and a high 'G' turn over the end of the airfield, I descended and, after a few seconds, touched down on the runway. Taxiing like a dancer over the wavy terrain, I reached the parking area, where a crowd awaited me with a warm welcome. As I climbed out of the cockpit, I felt the stress of the dogfights on body and mind, but I was happy with my performance, and the crowd's excitement invigorated me. I walked over to the wheels of my CR.32 and, with a lot of emotion, touched the dry twigs gathered during the take-off.

By 1120, the raid was over. Two small grey columns of smoke came from the two Savoya Marchetti S.81s which had been destroyed by the Fairey Battles. The Battles had also caused minor damage to the ground installations. About forty litres of fuel remained in my Fiat CR.32, and the left-over ammunition amounted to a mere twelve bullets of type SIT 127 mm (markers, explosive, incendiary), twenty-one bullets of type PIT 7.65 mm (markers, incendiary), armour-piercing drillers, and the machine-gun was jammed.

At about 1700, a 'Macna' arrived at our airfield. This was a Trimotor Caproni, Ca133, also nicknamed 'The Empire's Cow'. On board were three enemy aviators, the crew of the last Fairey Battle which I had shot down over Dalle Village. They were identified as the pilot, Flt Lt J.E. Lindsay, the gunner, Flt Sgt V.P. McVicar, and the photographer, Flt Sgt L.A. Feinberg, all of No. 11 Squadron, South African Air Force.

The meeting between victor and victim was really emotional, and all the airfield's personnel took part in this affair. On landing, the South African pilot asked to meet the pilot of the Fiat CR.32 that had downed him. In a spirit of aviation chivalry, not seen much today, Flt Lt Lindsay wanted to embrace me. He told us his version of events. With his windshield full of engine oil, low air speed and an injured leg – he had been hit by a 12.7 mm round – he had been able to maintain the Battle in a glide. Unable to find a ground strip, he had been forced to land his aircraft in the middle of a village. The crash-landing caused the aircraft to plough into the locals, two of whom were killed during the ensuing crash. Once the Battle had come to a stop, the injured Lt Lindsay had helped his collapsed crew members out of their seats and pulled them clear of the burning aircraft. Soon afterwards, angry villagers, armed with spears and knives, gathered around the Battle to plunder it. Exploding fuel and ammunition soon stopped that, and they kept their distance. The crew managed to prime the aircraft's explosive charge and destroy the wreck before the Italian troops reached them. Months later, another captured SAAF pilot, Cmdr J.R. Wikers, told us that all four Fairey Battles which had taken part in the 12 September raid on Shashamanna had been downed and that none of them had returned home.

After these events over Shashamanna, Italian East Africa, on 12 September 1940, WO Gobbo was awarded the 3rd class silver medal for gallantry (in the field). The citation read: 'A fighter pilot with exceptional skill, with many actions in the Spanish skies, took off under an enemy bombardment and was able to attack, with daring, four enemy aircraft, downing two and damaging the others.'

Gobbo remained with No 411 Squadron in Addis Ababa until March 1941. When the capital was surrounded and captured by the British, Gobbo and his wife were taken prisoner. He escaped and worked in Asmara under an assumed name as a waiter in a hotel. He was discovered by British Intelligence, arrested and interrogated. They found out about his Fascist tendencies, his service in Spain and East Africa, and he was then sent to South Africa, where he remained a prisoner of war until 1946.

Appendix Three

The Italian Air Force on
10 June 1940

1st Air Region (Milano)

4th Bomber Division 'DRAGO' (Dragon) (Novara)

43rd Bomber Wing, with:
98th Bomber Squadron (BR.20 – Cameri)
99th Bomber Squadron (BR.20 – Cameri)

7th Bomber Wing, with:
4th Bomber Squadron (BR.20 – Lonate Pozzolo)
25th Bomber Squadron (BR.20 – Lonate Pozzolo)

13th Bomber Wing, with:
11th Bomber Squadron (BR.20 – Piacenza)
43rd Bomber Squadron (BR.20 – Piacenza)

2nd Fighter Division 'BOREA' (Boreas, poetic name of the North Wind) (Torino-Caselle)

3rd Fighter Wing, with:
18th Fighter Squadron (CR.42 – Novi Ligure)
23rd Fighter Squadron (CR.42 – Novi Ligure)

53rd Fighter Wing, with:
150th Fighter Squadron (CR.42 – Torino-Caselle)
151st Fighter Squadron (CR.42 – Torino-Caselle)

6th Bomber Division 'FALCO' (Hawk) (Padova)

9th (independent) Fighter Squadron (CR.42 – Gorizia)

16th Bomber Wing, with:
50th Bomber Squadron (Cant Z.1007bis – Vicenza)
50th Bomber Squadron (Cant Z.1007bis – Vicenza)

18th Bomber Wing, with:
31st Bomber Squadron (BR.20 – Aviano)
37th Bomber Squadron (BR.20 – Aviano)

47th Bomber Wing, with:
106th Bomber Squadron (Cant Z.1007bis – Ghedi)
107th Bomber Squadron (Cant Z.1007bis – Ghedi)

2nd Air Region (Palermo)

3rd Bomber Division 'CENTAURO' (Centaur) (Catania)

11th Bomber Wing, with:
33rd Bomber Squadron (SM.79 – Comiso)
34th Bomber Squadron (SM.79 – Comiso)

41st Bomber Wing, with:
59th Bomber Squadron (SM.79 – Gela)
60th Bomber Squadron (SM.79 – Gela)

24th Bomber Wing, with:
52nd Bomber Squadron (SM.79 – Catania)
53rd Bomber Squadron (SM.79 – Catania)

11th Bomber Brigade 'NIBBIO' (Kite) (Castelvetrano)

96th Independent Bomber Squadron (SM.95c – Reggio Calabria)

30th Bomber Wing, with:
87th Bomber Squadron (SM.79 – Sciacca)
90th Bomber Squadron (SM.79 – Sciacca)

36th Bomber Wing, with:
108th Bomber Squadron (SM.79 – Castelvetrano)
109th Bomber Squadron (SM.79 – Castelvetrano)

1st Fighter Division 'AQUILA' (Eagle) (Palermo)

6th Independent Fighter Squadron (MC.200 – Comiso)

30th Recon Flight (Ro.37bis – Palermo)
1st Fighter Wing, with:
17th Fighter Squadron (CR.42 – Palermo)
157th Fighter Squadron (CR.42 – Palermo)

3rd Air Region (Roma)

5th Bomber Division 'EOLO' (Aeolus – Latin God of the Winds) (Viterbo)

46th Bomber Wing, with:
104th Bomber Squadron (SM.79 – Pisa)
105th Bomber Squadron (SM.79 – Pisa)

9th Bomber Wing, with:
26th Bomber Squadron (SM.79 – Viterbo)

29th Bomber Squadron (SM.79 – Viterbo)

8th Fighter Brigade 'ASTORE' (Goshawk) (Roma-Ciampino)

7th Independent Fighter Squadron (Ba.88 – Campiglia)

51st Fighter Wing, with:
20th Fighter Squadron (G.50 – Roma-Ciampino)
21st Fighter Squadron (G.50 – Roma-Ciampino)

52nd Fighter Wing, with:
22nd Fighter Squadron (G.50 – Pontedera)
24th Fighter Squadron (G.50 – Pontedera)

4th Territorial Air Zone (Bari)

116th Independent Bomber Squadron (BR.20 – Grottaglie)

2nd Independent Fighter Squadron (CR.32 – Grottaglie)

35th Bomber Wing, with:
86th Bomber Squadron (Cant Z.501 – Brindisi)
96th Bomber Squadron (Cant Z.506bis – Brindisi)

37th Bomber Wing, with:
54th Bomber Squadron (SM.81 – Lecce)
29th Bomber Squadron (SM.81 – Lecce)

Sardinia Air Command (Cagliari)

10th Bomber Brigade 'MARTE' (Mars – Latin God of War) (Cagliari)

3rd Independent Fighter Squadron (CR.32 – Monserrato)

19th Independent Ground Attack Squadron (Ba.88 – Alghero)

124th Recon Flight (Ro.37 – Cagliari-Elmas)

8th Bomber Wing, with:
27th Bomber Squadron (SM.79 – Villacidro)
28th Bomber Squadron (SM.79 – Villacidro)

31st Bomber Wing, with:
93rd Bomber Squadron (Cant Z.506bis – Cagliari-Elmas)
94th Bomber Squadron (Cant Z.506bis – Cagliari-Elmas)

32nd Bomber Wing, with:
88th Bomber Squadron (SM.79 – Decimomannu)
89th Bomber Squadron (SM.79 – Decimomannu)

Albania Air Command (Tirana)

38th Independent Bomber Squadron (SM.81 – Tirana)

160th Independent Fighter Squadron (CR.32 – Tirana)

120th Recon Flight (Ro.37bis – Tirana)
Aegean Air Command (Rhodes)

161st Independent Fighter Squadron (Ro.44 – Leros)

163rd Independent Fighter Squadron (CR.32 – Maritza)
39th Bomber Wing, with:
56th Bomber Squadron (SM.81 – Gadurra)
92nd Bomber Squadron (SM.81 – Maritza)

Libya Air Command – West (Tripoli)

1st Sahara Recon Squadron (Ca 309 – Mellaha)

26th Independent Recon Squadron (Ca 309 – Hon)

122nd Recon Flight (Ro.37bis – Mellaha)

136th Recon Flight (Ro.37bis – Tripoli)

15th Bomber Wing, with:
46th Bomber Squadron (SM.79 – Tarhuna)
47th Bomber Squadron (SM.79 – Tarhuna)

33rd Bomber Wing, with:
35th Bomber Squadron (SM.79 – Bir Bhera)
37th Bomber Squadron (SM.79 – Bir Bhera)

50th Ground Attack Wing, with:
12th Ground Attack Squadron (Ba.65 – Sorman)
16th Ground Attack Squadron (Ca 310bis – Sorman)

2nd Fighter Wing, with:
13th Fighter Squadron (CR.42 – Castel Benito)
1st Recon Squadron (Ca 309 – Mellaha)

Libya Air Command – East (Bengasi)

2nd Sahara Recon Squadron (Ca 309 – El Adem)

127th Recon Flight (Ro.37bis – El Adem)

137th Recon Flight (Ro.37bis – El Adem)

13th Bomber Division 'PEGASO' (Bengasi)

14th Bomber Wing, with:
44th Bomber Squadron (SM.81 – El Adem)
45th Bomber Squadron (SM.81 – El Adem)

10th Bomber Wing, with:

30th Bomber Squadron (SM.79 – Benina)
32nd Bomber Squadron (SM.79 – Benina)

14th Fighter Brigade 'REX' (King, in Latin) (Tobruk)

8th Fighter Squadron (CR.32 – Tobruk)
10th Fighter Squadron (CR.42 – Tobruk)

Italian East Africa Air Command – North (Assab)

25th Bomber Squadron (Ca 133 – Bahar Dar)
26th Bomber Squadron (Ca 133 – Gondar)
27th Bomber Squadron (Ca 133 – Assab)
28th Bomber Squadron (SM.81 – Zula)
118th Bomber Flight (Ca 133 – Assab)
Recon Flight 'North' (Ca 133 – Agordat)
409th Fighter Flight (CR.42 – Massaua)
413th Fighter Flight (CR.42 – Assab)

Italian East Africa Air Command – Central (Addis Ababa)

4th Bomber Squadron (SM.81 – Scenele)
29th Bomber Squadron (SM.81 – Assab)
44th Bomber Squadron (SM.79 – Ghiniele)
49th Bomber Squadron (Ca 133 – Gimma)
41st Recon Flight (Ca 133 – Addis Ababa)
110th Recon Flight (Ro.37 – Dire Daua)
410th Fighter Flight (CR.32 – Dire Daua)
411th Fighter Flight (CR.32 – Dire Daua)

Italian East Africa Air Command – South (Mogadishu)

31st Bomber Squadron (Ca 133 – Neghelli)
Recon Flight "South" (Ca 133 – Mogadishu)

Special Air Services Command (Militarised airlines long-range aeroplanes)

147th Squadron (SM.75)
148th Squadron (SM.73)
149th Squadron (SM.82)
604th Flight (SM.75)
608th Flight (SM.82)
610th Flight (SM.75)
615th Flight (SM.83)
616th Flight (SM.74)
604th Flight (SM.75)
Italian East Africa Detachment (SM.73/Ca 148c/Ca 133T/Fokker F.)

Libya Parachutist School Detachment (SM.81)

Air Force Command for the Army

Under Army GHQ control:

27th Recon Flight (Ro.37bis – Casabianca)
42nd Recon Flight (Ro.37bis – Bari)
121st Recon Flight (Ro.37bis – Airasca)
131st Recon Flight (Ro.37bis – Napoli-Capodichino)

Under Army Group West control:

31st Recon Flight (Ro.37 – Venaria Reale)
33rd Recon Flight (Ro.37bis – Bresso)
34th Recon Flight (Ca 311 – Cervere)
39th Recon Flight (Ro.37 – Venaria Reale)
40th Recon Flight (Ro.37 – Venaria Reale)
114th Recon Flight (Ro.37 – Tornino-Mirafiori)
118th Recon Flight (Ro.37bis – Levaldigi)
119th Recon Flight (Ca 311 – Bologna)
123rd Recon Flight (Ro.37bis – Levaldigi)
129th Recon Flight (Ro.37bis/Ca 311 – Mondovi)
132nd Recon Flight (Ro.37bis – Levaldigi)

Under Army Group East control:

24th Recon Flight (Ro.37 – Verona-Boscomantico)
25th Recon Flight (Ro.37 – Jesi)
28th Recon Flight (Ro.37 – Lucca-Tassignano)
29th Recon Flight (Ro.37 – Arezzo)
32nd Recon Flight (Ro.37bis – Udine-Campoformido)
34th Recon Flight (Ro.37 – Parma)
35th Recon Flight (Ro.37 – Verona-Boscomantico)
36th Recon Flight (Ro.37 – Padova)
38th Recon Flight (Ro.37bis – Gorizia-Merna)
87th Recon Flight (Ro.37 – Padova)
113th Recon Flight (Ro.37bis – Bologna-Borgo Panigale)
115th Recon Flight (Ro.37 – Verona-Boscomantico)
116th Recon Flight (Ro.37bis – Gorizia-Merna)
125th Recon Flight (Ro.37bis – Udine-Campoformido)
128th Recon Flight (Ro.37 – Parma)

Air Force Command for the Navy

Under Upper Adriatic Sea Department control:
4th Recon Section (Cant Z.501 – Pola)

Under Ionian and Lower Adriatic Sea Department control:

142nd Recon Flight (Cant Z.501 – Taranto)
145th Recon Flight (Cant Z.501 – Brindisi)
171st Recon Flight (Cant Z.501 – Brindisi)
3rd Recon Section (Cant Z.501 – Taranto)

Under Upper Tyrrhenian Sea Department control:

141st Recon Flight (Cant Z.501 – La Spezia-Cadimare)
187th Recon Flight (Cant Z.501 – La Spezia -Cadimare)
1st Recon Section (Cant Z.501 – La Spezia-Cadimare)

Under Lower Tyrrhenian Sea Department control:

182nd Recon Flight (Cant Z.501 – Nisida)

Under Sardinia Naval Command control:

146th Recon Flight (Cant Z.501 – Cagliari-Elmas)
148th Recon Flight (Cant Z.501 – Vigna)
183rd Recon Flight (Cant Z.501 – Cagliari-Elmas)
188th Recon Flight (Cant Z.501 – Cagliari-Elmas)
199th Recon Flight (Cant Z.506 – Santa Giusta)
5th Recon Section (Cant Z.501 – Olbia)

The Sardinia flights were grouped under the 85th Recon Squadron

Under Sicily Navy Command control:

144th Recon Flight (Cant Z.501 – Stagnone)
170th Recon Flight (Cant Z.506bis – Augusta)
184th Recon Flight (Cant Z.501 – Augusta)
186th Recon Flight (Cant Z.501 – Augusta)
189th Recon Flight (Cant Z.501 – Siracusa)

The Sicily flights were grouped under the 83rd Recon Squadron

Under Albania Naval Command control:

288th Recon Flight (Cant Z.506bis – Brindisi)

Under Libya Naval Command control:

143rd Recon Flight (Cant Z.501 – Menelao)

Under Aegean Sea Naval Command control (84th Recon Squadron):

147th Recon Flight (Cant Z.501 – Leros)
185th Recon Flight (Cant Z.501 – Leros)

APPENDIX FOUR

Italian Aircraft Production Figures
1939-45

Fighters and fighter-bombers

Fiat CR.32	1180	Designed by Rosatelli and the prototype first flown in 1933. Despite the fact that it appeared antiquated, this fighter biplane was produced in substantial quantities right up until the outbreak of World War II. Powered by a 600 hp Fiat A.30 R.A. engine, it had a maximum speed of 248 mph.
Fiat CR.42	1780	Powered by an 840 hp Fiat A.74 R.C.38 radial engine. In its original production format carried an armament of one 12.7 mm and one 7.7 mm gun.
Fiat G.50	785	The production model of the Freccia, the G.50bis, flew for the first time on 13 September 1940.
Fiat G.55	185	A single-engined, single-seat fighter aircraft used in 1943–45. It was designed and built in Turin by FIAT-Aeritalia.
Macchi MC.200	1500	Entered service in October 1939. Single-seat interceptor fighter, fighter-bomber aircraft.
Macchi MC.202	1100	The C.202 was a development of the earlier C.200 Saetta, with a more powerful German Daimler-Benz DB 601 engine.
Macchi MC.205	312	Entered production only five months after its maiden flight, and began reaching front-line units in February 1943.
Reggiane Re.2000	28	Interceptor/fighter.
Reggiane Re.2001	243	Falco II was considered by most experts equal to the Macchi MC.202, although the Macchi fighter was still produced in greater numbers.
Reggiane Re.2002	249	Prototype flew in October 1940, approximately three months after the Re.2001. Re.2002s saw action with the Allied landings in Sicily.
Reggiane Re.2005	36	A fighter/fighter-bomber produced during the later years of World War II. Along with the

Macchi C.202/C.205 and Fiat G.55, the Re.2005 was one of the three 'Serie 5' Italian fighters built around the Daimler-Benz DB 605 engine.

Heavy fighters and fighter-bombers

Breda Ba.65	220	Initially intended as an interceptor and attack-reconnaissance aeroplane, the Ba.65 carried wing-mounted armament of two 12.7 mm and two 7.7 mm Breda-SAFAT machine-guns, and provided internal stowage for a 440 lb bomb-load in addition to external ordnance of 2,200 lb.
Breda Ba.88	148	The first unit to receive the Ba.88 was the 7th *Gruppo*, arriving in North Africa in September 1940. The relatively poor performance and inadequate defensive armament resulted in the Ba.88 being taken out of production.
Savoia-Marchetti SM.85	34	Powered by two 460 hp Piaggio P.VII R.C.35 radials. A small production batch was built. The type was unsuccessful and never used operationally.
Fiat CR.25	11	Designed as a long-range escort fighter. It was powered by two 840 hp Fiat A.74 R.C.38 radial engines which provided a top speed of 273 mph.
CANSA FC.20	12	Powered by two 840 hp Fiat A.74 R.C.38 radials, and the F.C.20bis, which was intended for ground attack.
IMAM Ro.57	53	Powered by two 840 hp Fiat A.74 R.C.38 radials, the Ro.57 carried two 12.7 mm and two 20 mm guns in the nose, and had a maximum speed of 304 mph.

Bombers

Savoia-Marchetti SM.81	535	Powered by three 700 hp radials, and with its fixed undercarriage had a maximum speed of only 217 mph. Delivered to the bomber squadrons in 1934.
Savoia-Marchetti SM.79	1370	Appeared in 1935 as an eight-passenger commercial monoplane powered by three 650 hp Alfa Romeo 125 R.C.35 radials. The initial bomber production version was powered by three 850 hp Alfa Romeo 126 R.C.34 radials.
Savoia-Marchetti SM.82	411	Appeared in 1938, entered service in 1941 and was employed as a long-range heavy bomber.

Savoia-Marchetti SM.84	309	Powered by three 1,000 hp Piaggio P.XI R.C.40 radials, was first reported in action against British shipping in the Mediterranean in November 1941.
Fiat BR.20	534	Modern twin-engined low-wing monoplane, the initial production model was powered by two 1,030 hp Fiat A.80 R.C.41 radials. 350 machines of this type were built between 1937 and 1940.
Cant Z.1007	562	The production model, the Z.1007bis *Alcione*, differed from the prototype in having three 1,0000 hp Piaggio P.XIbis R.C.40 radials.
Cant Z.1018	18	Powered by 1,400 hp Alfa Romeo 135 R.C.32 radials, began to appear in service in 1943.
Caproni Ca 135	73	A medium bomber designed by Cesare Pallavicino. It flew for the first time in 1935, and entered service in 1937.
Piaggio P.32	28	A medium bomber designed by Giovanni Pegna.
Piaggio P.108	25	A four-engined heavy bomber. First flew in 1939 and entered service in 1942.

Recon, Transport and Bombers

Caproni Ca 111	152	Long-range reconnaissance aircraft and light bomber.
Caproni Ca 133/148	432	It had two small bomb-bays in its structure and was armed with four 7.7 mm (0.303 in.) Breda-SAFAT machine-guns.
Caproni 309/310/ 311/313/314	1349	Light twin-engined aircraft.
IMAM Ro.37	620	Two-seat reconnaissance biplanes.
IMAM Ro.43/44	229	Ro.43 two-seat fighter-reconnaissance floatplane, and the single-seat Ro.44 float-plane fighter biplane.
Cant Z.501	465	A single-engined flying-boat.
Cant Z.506	378	Airone (Heron) was a triple-engined floatplane.
Fiat RS.14	187	A long-range maritime strategic reconnaissance floatplane.
Savoia-Marchetti SM.73/74/75/83	130	The military SM.81 variant served as a bomber, transport, and reconnaissance aeroplane.
Fiat G.12	103	Long-range cargo transport aircraft.

BIBLIOGRAPHY

Barker, A.J., *Eritrea 1941*, Faber and Faber, 1966

Birkby, Carel, *It's A Long Way to Addis*, Frederick Muller, 1942

Brown, James Ambrose, *The War of A Hundred Days: Springboks in Somalia and Abyssinia 1940–1941*, Ashanti Publishing, 1990

Churchill, Winston S., *The Second World War* (Vols I and III), Cassell, 1950

Crosskill, W.E., *The Two Thousand Mile War, Robert Hale*, 1980

Del Boca, Angelo, *The Ethiopian War 1939–1941*, University of Chicago Press, 1965

Durand, Mortimer, *Crazy Campaign: A Personal Narrative of the Italo-Abyssinian War*, Routledge, 1936

Glover, Michael, *An Improvised War: The Ethiopian Campaign 1940–1941*, Leo Cooper, 1987

Harmsworth, Geoffrey, *Abyssinian Adventure*, Hutchinson, 1935

Mosley, Leonard, *Haile Selassie, The Conquering Lion*, Weidenfeld and Nicholson, 1964

Orpen, Neil, *East African and Abyssinian Campaigns*, Purnell, 1968

Rosenthal, Eric, *The Fall of Italian East Africa*, National Book Association/Hutchinson, 1941

Shores, Christopher, *Dust Clouds in the Middle East: The Air War For East Africa, Iraq, Syria, Iran and Madagascar 1940–1942*, Grub Street, 1996

War Office, *The Abyssinian Campaigns: The Official Story of the Conquest of Italian East Africa*, HM Stationery Office, 1942

War Office, 'Operations in East Africa, November 1940 to July 1941', *London Gazette*, July 1946

INDEX